T0210781

The Future of Human-Computer Integration

The Future of Human-Computer Integration: Industry 5.0 Technology, Tools, and Algorithms provides a valuable insight into how Industry 5.0 technologies, tools, and algorithms can revolutionise industries and drive innovation.

By emphasising the convergence of computer technology and human interaction, readers will learn the concepts of Industry 5.0, from the fundamentals to advanced techniques, with real-world examples and case studies in different industry sectors. The authors equip readers with the knowledge to mitigate risks to ensure success in this complex human and computer synchronisation in the era of Industry 5.0. This collection of writings by experts in their respective fields invites readers to journey through the transition from Industry 4.0 to Industry 5.0. Practical insights are offered alongside cutting-edge applications, such as blockchain, the Internet of Things (IoT), QR code, and augmented reality (AR), as well as the consideration of privacy, trust, and authentication through digital signatures. Such technologies and applications hold much promise to revolutionise industries and drive innovation.

Topics in this book include the role of AI in human-computer interaction, efficient asset management using blockchain, computational thinking in program development, synergy of 5G and IoT in healthcare services, advances in increasing data capacity of QR codes, and personalised user experience with augmented reality. The authors also consider the challenges, risks, and concerns of such technologies and their applications in Industry 5.0. This book comprehensively explores Industry 5.0 from a computer science perspective as it delves into the technology aspects and tools for Industry 5.0. It offers readers a detailed understanding of how computer science intersects with Industry 5.0, how to humanise it, and its application to industry.

This book has been written for technology professionals and practitioners, especially ones in healthcare, smart systems, and the oil and gas sectors. It will serve as a useful reference for students studying such advanced courses as digital technology, digital transformation, emergent technologies, and innovation through new technologies.

Norliza Katuk is an Associate Professor at the School of Computing, Universiti Utara Malaysia (UUM). She has served as an editor-in-chief for the *Journal of*

Information and Communication Technology since 2022 and an editorial board member since 2002.

Roberto Vergallo is a Researcher at the University of Salento, Lecce, Italy. His main research topics include the application of IoT, AI, and DLT to enhance and develop new customer experiences in digital payments and digital banking.

Tito Sugiharto is the Dean of the Faculty of Computer Science at the Universitas Kuningan, West Java, Indonesia. He researches mainly in the area of interactive multimedia such as augmented reality and its applications.

The Future of Human-Computer Integration

Industry 5.0 Technology, Tools, and Algorithms

Edited by Norliza Katuk
with Roberto Vergallo and Tito Sugiharto

CRC Press
Taylor & Francis Group
Boca Raton London New York

CRC Press is an imprint of the
Taylor & Francis Group, an **informa** business

Designed cover image: Shutterstock

First edition published 2024
by CRC Press
2385 NW Executive Center Drive, Suite 320, Boca Raton FL 33431

and by CRC Press
4 Park Square, Milton Park, Abingdon, Oxon, OX14 4RN

CRC Press is an imprint of Taylor & Francis Group, LLC

ISBN: 9781032765822 (hbk)
ISBN: 9781032765785 (pbk)
ISBN: 9781003479727 (ebk)

DOI: 10.1201/9781003479727

Typeset in Times New Roman
by KnowledgeWorks Global Ltd.

Contents

Preface

This book exposes readers to a profound exploration of Industry 5.0. In this preface, we extend a sincere welcome to embark on a comprehensive journey through the forthcoming chapters. The preface acts as a guide, unveiling distinct facets of technological evolution that will reshape industries and redefine the dynamics of human-computer collaboration.

Beyond the individual aims of each chapter, the overarching objective of *The Future of Human-Computer Integration* is to serve as a comprehensive guide for professionals across diverse disciplines. This book strives to foster a holistic understanding of how computer science and Information and Communication Technology (ICT) intricately relate to and shape the landscape of Industry 5.0.

In a world where interdisciplinary collaboration is increasingly pivotal, this book acts as a bridge, connecting professionals from various fields to the central tenets of computer science and ICT within the context of Industry 5.0. The chapters collectively aim to demystify complex technological concepts, making them accessible to professionals outside the traditional realms of computer science.

Professionals in engineering, business, healthcare, and beyond will find insights tailored to their specific domains, offering a nuanced perspective on how computer science and ICT advancements are influencing and transforming their respective industries—this book endeavours to break down silos and promote a shared understanding, encouraging cross-disciplinary dialogue and collaboration.

By exposing professionals to the intricate interplay between human intelligence and computational capabilities, this book aims to empower individuals to leverage the potential of Industry 5.0 in their respective fields. Whether the readers are an engineer seeking to optimise processes, a healthcare professional exploring IoT applications, or a business leader navigating the impact of AI, this book endeavours to provide knowledge and insights necessary to navigate the complex intersection of computer science, ICT, and Industry 5.0.

As the digital landscape continues to evolve, this book's collaborative and inclusive ethos seeks to equip professionals with the tools and understanding needed to thrive in an era where the fusion of human and computational capabilities redefines the future of industries. *The Future of Human-Computer Integration* is not just a book about technology; it is a roadmap for professionals from diverse disciplines to embark on a collective journey towards a technologically-driven future. Specifically, readers will understand various aspects of Industry 5.0 through the following chapters.

Chapter 1, "Introduction to Industry 5.0: Technology and Tools for Harmonising Humans and Computer," establishes a foundational understanding of Industry 5.0, tracing its evolution and elucidating the critical role of technology, tools, and algorithms in fostering seamless interactions between humans and computers.

Moving to Chapter 2, "Artificial Intelligence in Industry 5.0: Revolutionising Human-Computer Synchronisation," our objective is to uncover the transformative impact of Artificial Intelligence in Industry 5.0. We delve into machine learning, natural language processing, and ethical considerations to elucidate how AI revolutionises human-computer collaboration.

In Chapter 3, "Blockchain for Oil and Gas Industry Asset Management: Pioneering Industry 5.0 Solutions," our focus is to illuminate the application of blockchain technology in the oil and gas industry. We provide insights into efficient asset management practices within Industry 5.0.

Chapter 4, "Blockchain Consensus Mechanism in Named Data Networking: Enabling Trust in Industry 5.0," aims to explore integrating blockchain consensus mechanisms in Named Data Networking. Our goal is to establish trust and enhance data security within Industry 5.0.

Transitioning to Chapter 5, "Computational Thinking Technique for Programmers: Empowering Industry 5.0 Innovators," our goal is to empower innovators with the fundamentals of computational thinking. We offer practical insights and applications to foster creative problem-solving within the Industry 5.0 landscape.

In Chapter 6, "Agile Software Test: Optimising Quality Assurance in Industry 5.0 Projects," our comprehensive overview of agile software testing methodologies addresses challenges and aims to maximise efficiency in quality assurance processes within Industry 5.0 projects.

Chapter 7, "Smartphone Penetration Test: Securing Industry 5.0 Mobile Applications," delves into the importance of penetration testing for smartphone applications in Industry 5.0. We outline comprehensive testing strategies and risk mitigation approaches.

In Chapter 8, "Digital Signature: Enabling Trust and Security in Industry 5.0 Transactions," our exploration focuses on the significance of digital signatures in Industry 5.0 transactions. We provide insights into implementation technologies, algorithms, and practical applications.

Chapter 9, "Revolutionising Industry 5.0 with the Internet of Things," uncovers the transformation brought about by the Internet of Things in Industry 5.0. We provide insights into real-world applications, harnessing IoT technologies, and addressing challenges.

Chapter 10, "5G-enabled IoT Applications in Healthcare: Transforming the Industry 5.0 Healthcare Landscape," explores the synergy of 5G and IoT in healthcare. Our goal is to detail innovative applications, address challenges, and envision future developments in remote patient monitoring.

In Chapter 11, "Enhancing Data Capacity of a QR Code: Empowering Industry 5.0 Applications," our investigation centres on advancements in QR code technology. We explore their increased data capacity and security considerations for integration within Industry 5.0 applications.

Chapter 12, "Augmented Reality Meets Artificial Intelligence towards Personalised User Experience in Cultural Heritage Sites," examines the intersection of augmented reality and artificial intelligence for personalised user experiences in cultural heritage sites. We aim to provide insights into implementation, challenges, and future directions.

With each chapter, we aim to provide a nuanced understanding, foster knowledge, and provide practical applications in the dynamic landscape of Industry 5.0. As the readers embark on this journey, may these insights help everyone shape the future of industries in the digital era.

Acknowledgements

We extend our heartfelt gratitude to all the contributors to the chapters featured in this book, each of whom played a pivotal role in shaping the discourse on *The Future of Human-Computer Integration*. We appreciate the contributors' dedication to advancing knowledge in computing and informatics, which has significantly enriched the content of this publication.

We also sincerely thank the contributors who submitted their work to the 9th International Conference on Computing and Informatics (ICOCI 2023). Furthermore, our gratitude extends to the School of Computing, Universiti Utara Malaysia, for their generous financial support towards realising ICOCI 2023. This support has not only facilitated the conference but has also been instrumental in fostering a collaborative environment for exchanging ideas and advancing research in computing and informatics.

Thank you to all participants in this project for their efforts and commitment to excellence. This collaborative endeavour would not have been possible without each contributor's dedication and our esteemed institution's support. All contributions are acknowledged with deep appreciation.

Contributors

Azizi Abas
School of Computing, Universiti Utara
  Malaysia
Kedah, Malaysia

Rimaniza Zainal Abidin
Extended Reality & Human Interaction
  Centre of Excellence, Faculty of
  Information Science & Technology,
  Universiti Kebangsaan Malaysia
Selangor, Malaysia

Eka Wahyu Aditya
School of Computing and Informatics,
  Albukhary International University
Kedah, Malaysia

Asmalinda Adnan
Data Management & Software Solution
  Research Lab, School of Computing,
  Universiti Utara Malaysia
Kedah, Malaysia

Ijaz Ahmad
Faculty of Information Technology and
  Electrical Engineering, University
  of Oulu
Oulu, Finland

Rahayu Ahmad
School of Computing, Universiti Utara
  Malaysia
Kedah, Malaysia

Mahdi Nafea Khalid Al-Ajwad
School of Computing, Universiti Utara
  Malaysia
Kedah, Malaysia
and
Basrah Oil Company
Basrah, Iraq

Haslina Arshad
Extended Reality & Human Interaction
  Centre of Excellence, Faculty of
  Information Science & Technology,
  Universiti Kebangsaan Malaysia
Selangor Malaysia

Fazli Azzali
School of Computing, Universiti Utara
  Malaysia
Kedah, Malaysia

Fauziah Baharom
Data Management & Software Solution
  Research Lab, School of Computing,
  Universiti Utara Malaysia
Kedah, Malaysia

Juliana Aida Abu Bakar
Extended Reality & Human Interaction
  Centre of Excellence, School of
  Creative Industry Management &
  Performing Arts, Universiti Utara
  Malaysia
Kedah, Malaysia

Samera Obaid Barraood
Department of Computer Science,
College of Computers and Infor-
mation Technology, Hadhramout
University
Hadhramout, Yemen

Ekaterina Chzhan
School of Information and Space
Technology, Siberian Federal
University
Krasnoyarsk, Russia

Derar Eleyan
Applied Computing Department,
Palestine Technical University
Kadoorie, Palestine

Mohd Zul Haziq Mohd Fadzli
Faculty of Computer Science and
Information Technology, Universiti
Malaysia Sarawak
Sarawak, Malaysia

Abdul Rehman Gilal
Knight Foundation School of
Computing and Information
Sciences, Florida International
University
Florida, United States

Adib Habbal
Computer Engineering Department,
Faculty of Engineering, Karabuk
University
Karabuk, Türkiye

Eidlan Hadi Mazlan Hanafi
Extended Reality & Human Interaction
Centre of Excellence, School of
Creative Industry Management &
Performing Arts, Universiti Utara
Malaysia
Kedah, Malaysia

Suhaidi Hassan
InterNetWorks Research Laboratory,
School of Computing, Universiti
Utara Malaysia
Kedah, Malaysia

Nur Hafiza Jamaludin
Data Management & Software
Solution Research Lab, School
of Computing, Universiti Utara
Malaysia
Kedah, Malaysia

Mohamad Nazim Jambli
Faculty of Computer Science
and Information Technology,
Universiti Malaysia
Sarawak
Sarawak, Malaysia

Norliza Katuk
School of Computing, Universiti Utara
Malaysia
Kedah, Malaysia

Shafinah Farvin Packeer Mohamed
Data Management & Software
Solution Research Lab, School
of Computing, Universiti Utara
Malaysia
Kedah, Malaysia

Fathey Mohammed
Department of Business Analytics,
Sunway Business School, Sunway
University
Selangor, Malaysia

Haslina Mohd
Data Management & Software
Solution Research Lab, School
of Computing, Universiti Utara
Malaysia
Kedah, Malaysia

Noradila Nordin
School of Games & Creative Technology, University for the Creative Arts
Farnham, United Kingdom

Mohd Hasbullah Omar
InterNetWorks Research Laboratory, School of Computing, Universiti Utara Malaysia
Kedah, Malaysia

Ulka Chandini Pendit
Sheffield Hallam University
Sheffield, United Kingdom

Rohaida Romli
Data Management & Software Solution Research Lab, School of Computing, Universiti Utara Malaysia
Kedah, Malaysia

Athirah Rosli
Faculty of Ocean Engineering Technology and Informatics, Universiti Malaysia Terengganu
Terengganu, Malaysia
and
InterNetWorks Research Laboratory, School of Computing, Universiti Utara Malaysia
Kedah, Malaysia

Puteri Nurul'Ain Adil Md Sabri
School of Computing, Universiti Utara Malaysia
Kedah, Malaysia

Sohail Safdar
Faculty of Technology, School of Computing, University of Portsmouth
Portsmouth, United Kingdom

Tito Sugiharto
Faculty of Computer Science, Universitas Kuningan
West Java, Indonesia

Sinarwati Mohamad Suhaili
Pre-University, Universiti Malaysia Sarawak
Sarawak, Malaysia

Roberto Vergallo
Department of Innovation Engineering University of Salento
Lecce, Italy

Nur Haryani Zakaria
Data Management & Software Solution Research Lab, School of Computing, Universiti Utara Malaysia
Kedah, Malaysia

1 Introduction to Industry 5.0: Technology and tools for harmonising human and computer

Norliza Katuk[1], Roberto Vergallo[2], and Tito Sugiharto[3]

[1] *School of Computing, Universiti Utara Malaysia, Kedah, Malaysia*

[2] *Department of Innovation Engineering, University of Salento, Lecce, Italy*

[3] *Faculty of Computer Science, Universitas Kuningan, Jawa Barat, Indonesia*

1.1 Exploring the evolution of Industry 5.0

Industry 4.0, synonymously known as the fourth industrial revolution, signifies the current automation and data exchange trend in manufacturing technologies (Nosalska et al., 2020). Klaus Schwab, founder of the World Economic Forum, introduced this term and highlighted it as the fusion of digital, biological, and physical worlds (Lee et al., 2018). A key characteristic of Industry 4.0 is the integration of the Internet of Things (IoT), which refers to the interconnection of physical devices embedded with sensors and software to collect and exchange data (Pivoto et al., 2021). It enables machines to communicate with each other, creating a network of intelligent systems that can operate autonomously. Alongside IoT, the introduction of cloud computing, fog computing, and big data has significantly shifted in Industry 4.0 (Aceto et al., 2020). It allows companies to store and manage vast amounts of data, enabling real-time analysis and decision-making (Marinelli et al., 2021). Accessing these resources remotely offers flexibility and scalability, essential elements in today's fast-paced industrial environment. Another crucial element is the emergence of cyber-physical systems (CPS) (Salih Ahmed et al., 2021). These are systems where a mechanism is controlled or monitored by computer-based algorithms. CPS plays a vital role in creating smart factories, where machinery and equipment can improve processes through self-optimisation and automation. Despite the revolutionary advancements, the progression of Industry 4.0 is not without challenges. Data security and privacy, the need for a skilled workforce capable of managing these advanced systems, and the fear of job displacement due to automation require attention and solutions (Tseng et al., 2021).

The primary issue lies in the reliance on voluminous data, which brings forth challenges related to data security and privacy (Xu et al., 2018). As more devices interconnect, the potential for cyberattacks increases, posing a significant risk to the integrity of the systems and the sensitive information they hold. Another

DOI: 10.1201/9781003479727-1

concern is the skill gap. The advanced technologies of Industry 4.0 require a workforce equipped with new skills (Li, 2022). As traditional roles become automated, there is an increasing need for professionals who can manage, analyse, and secure digital systems. The transition may also lead to job displacement, raising social and economic concerns (Kovacs, 2018). Industry 4.0 also challenges human-machine interaction (Laudante, 2017). While machines can automate tasks, they lack the human touch, the ability to understand and respond to emotions, or the ability to think creatively and critically (Raja Santhi & Muthuswamy, 2023). This limitation is where Industry 5.0 comes into play. Industry 5.0, the next phase, aims to bridge the gap between man and machine (Pereira & dos Santos, 2023). It focuses on collaboration rather than replacement, envisioning a workspace where humans and robots work side by side. Robots will handle routine tasks, while humans focus on tasks that require creativity and critical thinking (Coronado et al., 2022). This collaborative approach ensures that the human touch is preserved, addressing the fear of complete automation and potential job losses. It also paves the way for an era in which technology enhances human capabilities rather than replaces them, leading to an improved and sustainable industrial future (Narkhede et al., 2023).

Industry 5.0 is regarded as the forthcoming phase in the evolution of industrial revolutions. It underscores the vital role of human-machine collaboration. While Industry 4.0 was marked by the advent of the IoT and big data, Industry 5.0 brings back the human, environmental, and socio-economic elements into the industrial framework. This new era is characterised by the collaboration between robots and humans, enhancing the resilience of industrial systems and facilitating the achievement of sustainability objectives. The European Commission has outlined the key aspects of Industry 5.0, which include human-centric operations, resilience, and sustainability (Grosse et al., 2023). In the context of the industrial revolution, Industry 4.0 centred on digitalisation and artificial intelligence (AI) technologies to enhance production efficiency, sometimes overlooking essential aspects like social fairness and sustainability. However, Industry 5.0 takes a different path. It shifts the focus towards research and innovation, recognising their pivotal role in maintaining the industry's service to humanity over the long term while staying within the ecological boundaries of our planet. This new perspective emphasises a more balanced and sustainable approach to industrial progress (Xu et al., 2021).

Industry 5.0 represents the next phase of industrial development, focusing on the collaboration between humans and machines (Pizoń & Gola, 2023). It envisions a workspace where humans and robots co-exist, with robots handling routine tasks and humans focusing on tasks requiring creativity, critical thinking, and emotional intelligence. The essence of Industry 5.0 lies in its human-centric approach, ensuring that the human touch is retained in the era of automation. It is viewed as a means to enhance human capabilities rather than replace them, leading to an improved and sustainable industrial future. Moreover, Industry 5.0 is also about customisation and personalisation at scale, a shift from the mass production model of Industry 4.0 (Pizoń & Gola, 2023). It aims to meet individual customer needs and preferences, providing an enhanced customer experience.

1.2 Understanding the role of technology, tools, and algorithms in human-computer synchronisation

Technology, in its various forms, has drastically transformed human-computer interaction (HCI) over the past few decades. HCI, which refers to computer technology design and use, encompasses the interfaces between people and computers (Bannon, 2011). The evolution of this interaction, fuelled by technological advances, has changed how we work, communicate, learn, and entertain ourselves, making computers more accessible and integrated into our daily lives. In the early days of computing, interaction was limited and often cumbersome. Early computers used command-line interfaces, where users had to type specific commands to complete tasks. This interaction required a steep learning curve and was not user-friendly, especially for non-technical people. However, the advent of graphical user interfaces (GUIs) in the 1980s marked a significant shift in HCI. With their windows, icons, menus, and pointers, GUIs allowed users to interact with computers using a mouse rather than typing commands (Jansen, 1998). This development made computers more accessible to the general public, paving the way for personal computing.

The rise of the internet in the 1990s further revolutionised HCI. It introduced a new level of interactivity, allowing users to connect and share information globally. With their hyperlinks and multimedia capabilities, web browsers provided a new, more interactive way to access and share information. The development of Web 2.0 technologies in the early 2000s, which included social networking sites, blogs, and wikis, further enhanced this interactivity, allowing users to create and share their content. The advent of smartphones and tablet devices marked another significant milestone in HCI (Yong, 2014). These devices introduced touch interfaces, which made interaction even more intuitive. Users could now tap, swipe, and pinch to navigate and control their devices. With their apps and connectivity, mobile devices have made computers portable and ever-present, further integrating them into our daily lives. In the past decade, HCI has moved beyond the screen by developing natural user interfaces (NUIs). NUIs aim to make the interaction more intuitive and natural by using gestures, voice, and even thought (Szabó, 2019). Technologies like voice assistants, gesture recognition, and augmented reality (AR) are examples of NUIs. These technologies aim to make the interaction seamless, blending the digital and physical worlds.

Furthermore, the rise of AI and machine learning (ML) technologies is set to take HCI to a new level. AI allows computers to learn from interactions, providing personalised experiences and anticipating user needs (Bharadiya, 2023). For example, AI-powered chatbots and personal assistants can interact with users conversationally, providing a more human-like interaction. Despite the vast strides made in HCI, it continues to evolve. With emerging technologies like brain-computer interfaces, which aim to allow direct communication between the human brain and computers, the future of HCI promises to be even more intertwined with our lives (Müller-Putz et al., 2015). In the landscape of Industry 5.0, where human-machine collaboration is paramount, various tools and platforms have emerged to facilitate seamless synchronisation and collaboration (Maddikunta et al., 2022). These tools enhance productivity, streamline workflows, and foster innovation in a hybrid workforce. One of the essential tools in this regard is the IoT. It enables connected, intelligent systems to communicate, making real-time data available for decision-making (Tien, 2017). For instance, IoT devices can monitor machine performance or track inventory in real-time, providing valuable insights to humans and machines. This real-time data accessibility aids in proactive decision-making, increasing efficiency and productivity. AI and ML are other critical tools that drive synchronisation in Industry 5.0. AI-powered platforms can analyse vast volumes of data, identify patterns, and make predictions, thereby assisting humans in decision-making (Ahmad et al., 2021). ML algorithms can learn from these data patterns, progressively improving their predictions and recommendations. These features help automate routine tasks, freeing human workers to focus on more complex, creative tasks.

Collaborative robots, or cobots, also play an increasingly important role in Industry 5.0 (Doyle-Kent & Kopacek, 2021). Unlike traditional robots, cobots are designed to work alongside humans, assisting them in their tasks. They can be easily programmed and reprogrammed by human workers, allowing for greater flexibility and adaptability in production processes. Digital twin technology is another innovative tool facilitating synchronisation. A digital twin is a virtual replica of a physical system, process, or product (Mincă et al., 2022). It allows for simulations and scenario testing without disrupting the actual operations. This technology enables human workers and machines to experiment, innovate, and solve problems in a risk-free virtual environment. Cloud-based platforms and services have also become essential for collaboration in Industry 5.0. Cloud platforms allow for data and application accessibility from anywhere, at any time. They provide a unified platform where human workers and machines can access the same information, fostering collaboration and ensuring everyone is on the same page (Sindhwani et al., 2022). Project management tools and collaborative platforms like Slack, Asana, and Microsoft Teams have also gained prominence (Marion & Fixson, 2021). These tools enable real-time communication, task management, and file sharing, facilitating team coordination, including human and machine elements. Furthermore, AR and virtual reality (VR) technologies are being used for training, simulations, and remote collaboration. AR can overlay digital information onto the physical world, assisting workers in complex tasks, while VR can create immersive virtual environments for training or collaborative problem-solving.

In Industry 5.0, where humans and machines collaborate in unprecedented ways, algorithms and AI are paramount. These technologies are the backbone of the new industrial revolution, driving synchronisation, enhancing productivity, and enabling innovation. Algorithms, in essence, are sets of rules or procedures for solving problems. In the context of Industry 5.0, they are instrumental in managing complex tasks and operations. Algorithms regulate the interaction between humans and machines, ensuring smooth operation and effective collaboration. They can optimise workflows, automate routine tasks, and predict future trends based on past data, enhancing efficiency and reducing errors. AI takes this a step further. AI algorithms, or ML models, can learn from data (Collins & Moons, 2019). They can identify patterns, predict, and adapt their behaviour based on new information. This capability allows AI to assist humans in decision-making, providing insights and recommendations based on data analysis.

One of the critical applications of AI in Industry 5.0 is predictive maintenance (Maddikunta et al., 2022). Analysing data from IoT devices and sensors, AI algorithms can predict when a machine will likely fail or require maintenance. It allows for proactive maintenance, reducing downtime and increasing productivity. AI can also enhance quality control processes. ML models can analyse images or sensor data to identify product defects, often more accurately and quickly than human inspectors. It improves product quality and frees human workers for more complex, creative tasks. Furthermore, AI is pivotal in managing supply chains in Industry 5.0. AI algorithms can analyse data from various sources, including production, inventory, and market trends, to optimise supply chain operations (Riahi et al., 2021). They can predict demand, manage inventory, and even plan optimal delivery routes, ensuring efficient and timely delivery of products (Tirkolaee et al., 2021). AI is also being used to drive innovation in product design and development. Generative design algorithms can generate multiple design options based on specified parameters, allowing engineers to explore various possibilities.

AI can also simulate how a product will perform under various conditions, helping to optimise the design before production. Another key area where AI is making a significant impact is workforce management. AI algorithms can analyse worker performance, skills, and availability data to optimise workforce scheduling and task allocation (Vrontis et al., 2022). It enhances productivity and improves worker satisfaction by ensuring a fair distribution of tasks. Algorithms and AI are pivotal in driving synchronisation within Industry 5.0. They are enhancing productivity and efficiency and enabling innovation and growth (Mhlanga, 2021). As these technologies continue to evolve, they will further transform how humans and machines collaborate, indicating a new era of industrial production. Therefore, the future of Industry 5.0 lies in the intelligent application of algorithms and AI, bringing about a seamless integration of human intellect and machine efficiency.

1.3   Overview of technology for Industry 5.0

Industry 5.0, the fifth industrial revolution, is set to change how we work and live dramatically. This new era is characterised by the harmonisation of human and machine labour powered by emerging technologies. Apart from AI, other technologies, including IoT, blockchain, 3D printing, and others, are driving unprecedented efficiency and productivity while opening up new opportunities for innovation. The IoT is a critical technology shaping Industry 5.0 (Aslam et al., 2020). IoT devices, which range from sensors and wearables to smart appliances, collect vast amounts of data from their environments. This data is then analysed to derive insights, drive automation, and enable predictive capabilities. For instance, IoT sensors on a manufacturing line can monitor equipment performance in real-time, enabling predictive maintenance and reducing downtime. While traditionally associated with cryptocurrencies, blockchain technology has promising applications in Industry 5.0. Blockchain's decentralised and tamper-proof nature makes it ideal for tracking and validating transactions across the supply chain, ensuring transparency and traceability (Katuk, 2019). It can also facilitate secure, peer-to-peer transactions between machines in an IoT network, paving the way for autonomous machine-to-machine interactions.

3D printing, or additive manufacturing, is revolutionising production in Industry 5.0 (George & George, 2023). It allows for rapid prototyping and production of customised parts, reducing waste and speeding up the design-to-production process. 3D printing, combined with AI and generative design, enables the creation of complex geometries and structures previously impossible to manufacture. AR and VR are also making their mark in Industry 5.0. These technologies can enhance worker training, provide real-time information overlays to assist in complex tasks, and enable remote collaboration (Chander et al., 2022). For instance, a technician could use AR glasses to visualise instructions overlaid on their real-world view while repairing a machine, reducing error and improving efficiency. Big data and analytics are the final pieces of the Industry 5.0 puzzle. The vast amounts of data generated by IoT devices and other technologies must be analysed to derive actionable insights. Big data tools can handle these large data sets, and analytics algorithms can sift through the data to identify trends, make predictions, and inform decision-making (Song, 2023).

Quick response (QR) codes are gaining traction in the industrial sector due to their ability to store large amounts of data in a small, scannable format. These two-dimensional barcodes can hold information ranging from website uniform resource locators (URLs) to part specifications, making them ideal for tracking and identifying components in a manufacturing process. Moreover, when combined with IoT and AI technologies, QR codes can monitor the real-time status of goods, track inventory, and even aid in quality control processes (Varriale et al., 2023). 5G, the fifth generation of wireless technology, is a critical enabler of Industry 5.0. With its ultra-high speeds, near-zero latency, and ability to connect many devices simultaneously, 5G is set to supercharge the IoT and enable real-time data analysis. It will pave the way for more responsive, efficient, and connected industrial processes. For instance, 5G could allow for real-time remote control of heavy machinery or seamless coordination between factory parts.

Security in Industry 5.0 is a concern (Shruti et al., 2024) and appears to be a multifaceted issue, encompassing data security, network security, and the physical security of IoT devices. As more devices get connected and more data gets generated, the potential attack surface for cyberthreats expands. Therefore, robust security measures are crucial. These could include advanced encryption methods, secure identity and access management, regular security audits, and the use of blockchain for secure, traceable transactions. Moreover, AI can detect unusual patterns and potential threats in real-time, enhancing cybersecurity efforts.

1.4   Innovations for smooth interaction

The era of Industry 5.0 is characterised by the harmonious collaboration between humans and machines, fostering an environment where technology complements human capabilities rather than replacing them (Leng et al., 2022). The technologies and applications created innovations that provide creative ways or solutions and enhance processes and works. Consequently, the innovation facilitates smooth, intuitive, and productive HCIs central to this symbiotic relationship. An example of innovation is AR applications that overlay digital information onto the physical world in real-time. It creates an immersive experience that blurs the boundaries between the virtual and real worlds. Through AR, workers can access real-time data, instructions, and visual aids right in sight. It enhances their understanding of complex tasks, reduces errors, and improves safety. For instance, AR can guide a factory worker through a machine repair with step-by-step instructions projected onto their view, making the task more manageable and efficient.

Natural language processing (NLP) is another groundbreaking technology driving smooth human-machine interactions. NLP, a subset of AI, allows machines to understand, interpret, and generate human language. An example of innovation achieved through ML allows workers to communicate with machines in their natural, everyday language, eliminating the need for specialised programming skills. Whether voice assistants on the factory floor respond to verbal commands or chatbots provide immediate answers to employee queries, NLP is making HCI more intuitive and accessible. Innovation could also be achieved through ML, which enables machines to learn from experience and improve performance over time without being explicitly programmed. In the context of HCI, ML can help machines understand individual user preferences and behaviours, enabling a personalised and adaptive user experience. For instance, ML algorithms can analyse a worker's past actions to predict their future needs, proactively providing relevant information or adjusting the interface accordingly.

We must mention haptic technology (Mourtzis et al., 2023), which enables tactile interaction between humans and machines. Haptic interfaces provide physical feedback in response to user actions, creating an immersive and realistic experience. In an industrial setting, haptic gloves can simulate the sensation of touching a physical object, providing workers with a more intuitive and accurate way to interact with digital models or remote machinery. It reduces the risk of errors and enhances the user experience. These technologies can create a more inclusive, adaptable, and efficient industrial environment. They can foster a culture of continuous learning and improvement, where machines and humans learn from each other and evolve together.

However, the path to realising these benefits is not without its challenges. One of the foremost obstacles is the high initial investment required to adopt these technologies. Small- and medium-sized enterprises may find it particularly challenging to afford these cutting-edge solutions. The second challenge is the lack of a skilled workforce. A workforce that is comfortable using them and can troubleshoot issues, interpret data, and train others is needed to fully leverage these technologies' potential. It calls for significant investment in training and education. The third challenge lies in data security and privacy. As we integrate more technology into our industrial processes, the volume of data generated and shared increases, creating potential vulnerabilities. Organisations must prioritise data security and privacy to protect sensitive information and maintain user trust. Lastly, there is the challenge of managing change. Introducing new technologies can disrupt existing workflows and require significant organisational structure and culture changes. It can meet resistance from employees accustomed to specific working methods. Therefore, effective change management strategies are crucial to ensure a smooth transition.

Soon, we can expect the lines between the physical and digital worlds to blur even further as more immersive technologies like extended reality (XR), which includes VR, AR, and mixed reality (MR), take centre stage. These will allow for more seamless interaction between humans and machines, promoting a better understanding of complex data and fostering a more intuitive user experience. AI will continue to evolve, becoming more sophisticated and autonomous. We might witness the emergence of self-learning systems that enhance their performances without human intervention. It does not mean machines will replace humans. Instead, they will become more capable collaborators, extending human capabilities and freeing us from mundane tasks.

The IoT will continue to expand, connecting an even more significant number of devices and systems. It will result in unprecedented data, leading to big data analysis and predictive maintenance breakthroughs. We could see the rise of more advanced predictive models capable of identifying potential issues before they occur, thereby minimising downtime and enhancing productivity. Robotics will also make significant strides, with more collaborative robots, or "cobots", working alongside humans. These cobots will have advanced sensors and AI to understand and respond to human actions in real-time. They will become an integral part of the workforce, taking on dangerous, monotonous, or physically demanding tasks for humans.

In terms of potential breakthroughs, quantum computing might revolutionise the industry. Although still nascent, quantum computing promises to solve complex problems much faster than traditional computers. If realised, it could drastically reduce the time taken for data processing and optimisation tasks, providing a significant competitive advantage. One more breakthrough to take note of is the advancement of green technologies. As sustainability becomes a more pressing concern, we might see more innovations aimed at reducing the environmental impact of industries. It could include everything from energy-efficient machinery to processes that minimise waste and promote circular economy principles.

Overall, the future of Industry 5.0 is set to be exciting and transformative. The trajectory of innovation will continue to move towards a more connected, autonomous, and sustainable future where humans and machines work hand in hand to achieve common goals. It is a future where technology enhances productivity and fosters a more inclusive and sustainable industrial environment.

References

Aceto, G., Persico, V., & Pescapé, A. (2020). Industry 4.0 and health: Internet of things, big data, and cloud computing for healthcare 4.0. *Journal of Industrial Information Integration, 18*, 100129. https://doi.org/10.1016/j.jii.2020.100129

Ahmad, T., Zhang, D., Huang, C., Zhang, H., Dai, N., Song, Y., & Chen, H. (2021). Artificial intelligence in sustainable energy industry: Status quo, challenges and opportunities. *Journal of Cleaner Production, 289*, 125834. https://doi.org/10.1016/j.jclepro.2021.125834

Aslam, F., Aimin, W., Li, M., & Ur Rehman, K. (2020). Innovation in the era of IoT and industry 5.0: Absolute innovation management (AIM) framework. *Information, 11*(2), 124. https://doi.org/10.3390/info11020124

Bannon, L. (2011). Reimagining HCI: Toward a more human-centered perspective. *Interactions, 18*(4), 50–57. https://doi.org/10.1145/1978822.1978833

Bharadiya, J. P. (2023). Machine learning and AI in business intelligence: Trends and opportunities. *International Journal of Computer (IJC), 48*(1), 123–134.

Chander, B., Pal, S., De, D., & Buyya, R. (2022). Artificial intelligence-based internet of things for industry 5.0. In S. Pal, D. De, & R. Buyya (Eds.), *Artificial intelligence-based internet of things systems* (pp. 3–45). Springer International Publishing. https://doi.org/10.1007/978-3-030-87059-1_1

Collins, G. S., & Moons, K. G. M. (2019). Reporting of artificial intelligence prediction models. *The Lancet, 393*(10181), 1577–1579. https://doi.org/10.1016/S0140-6736(19)30037-6

Coronado, E., Kiyokawa, T., Ricardez, G. A. G., Ramirez-Alpizar, I. G., Venture, G., & Yamanobe, N. (2022). Evaluating quality in human-robot interaction: A systematic search and classification of performance and human-centered factors, measures and metrics towards an industry 5.0. *Journal of Manufacturing Systems, 63*, 392–410. https://doi.org/10.1016/j.jmsy.2022.04.007

Doyle-Kent, M., & Kopacek, P. (2021). Adoption of collaborative robotics in industry 5.0. An Irish industry case study. *IFAC-PapersOnLine, 54*(13), 413–418. https://doi.org/10.1016/j.ifacol.2021.10.483

George, A. S., & George, A. H. (2023). Revolutionizing manufacturing: Exploring the promises and challenges of industry 5.0. *Partners Universal International Innovation Journal, 1*(2), 22–38. https://doi.org/10.5281/zenodo.7852124

Grosse, E. H., Sgarbossa, F., Berlin, C., & Neumann, W. P. (2023). Human-centric production and logistics system design and management: Transitioning from industry 4.0 to industry 5.0. *International Journal of Production Research, 61*(22), 7749–7759. https://doi.org/10.1080/00207543.2023.2246783

Jansen, B. J. (1998). The graphical user interface. *ACM SIGCHI Bulletin, 30*(2), 22–26.

Katuk, N. (2019). The application of blockchain for halal product assurance: A systematic review of the current developments and future directions. *International Journal of Advanced Trends in Computer Science and Engineering, 8*(5), 1893–1902.

Kovacs, O. (2018). The dark corners of industry 4.0—Grounding economic governance 2.0. *Technology in Society, 55*, 140–145. https://doi.org/10.1016/j.techsoc.2018.07.009

Laudante, E. (2017). Industry 4.0, innovation and design. A new approach for ergonomic analysis in manufacturing system. *The Design Journal, 20*(sup1), S2724–S2734. https://doi.org/10.1080/14606925.2017.1352784

Lee, M., Yun, J. J., Pyka, A., Won, D., Kodama, F., Schiuma, G., & Zhao, X. (2018). How to respond to the fourth industrial revolution, or the second information technology revolution? Dynamic new combinations between technology, market, and society through open innovation. *Journal of Open Innovation: Technology, Market, and Complexity, 4*(3), 21. https://doi.org/10.3390/joitmc4030021

Leng, J., Sha, W., Wang, B., Zheng, P., Zhuang, C., Liu, Q., & Wang, L. (2022). Industry 5.0: Prospect and retrospect. *Journal of Manufacturing Systems, 65*, 279–295. https://doi.org/10.1016/j.jmsy.2022.09.017

Li, L. (2022). Reskilling and upskilling the future-ready workforce for industry 4.0 and beyond. *Information Systems Frontiers*. https://doi.org/10.1007/s10796-022-10308-y

Maddikunta, P. K. R., Pham, Q.-V., Prabadevi, B., Deepa, N., Dev, K., Gadekallu, T. R., & Liyanage, M. (2022). Industry 5.0: A survey on enabling technologies and potential applications. *Journal of Industrial Information Integration, 26*, 100257. https://doi.org/10.1016/j.jiii.2021.100257

Marinelli, M., Deshmukh, A. A., Janardhanan, M., & Nielsen, I. (2021). Lean manufacturing and industry 4.0 combinative application: Practices and perceived benefits. *IFAC-Papers OnLine, 54*(1), 288–293. https://doi.org/10.1016/j.ifacol.2021.08.034

Marion, T. J., & Fixson, S. K. (2021). The transformation of the innovation process: How digital tools are changing work, collaboration, and organizations in new product development. *Journal of Product Innovation Management, 38*(1), 192–215. https://doi.org/10.1111/jpim.12547

Mhlanga, D. (2021). Artificial intelligence in the industry 4.0, and its impact on poverty, innovation, infrastructure development, and the sustainable development goals: Lessons from emerging economies? *Sustainability, 13*(11), 5788. https://doi.org/10.3390/su13115788

Mincă, E., Filipescu, A., Cernega, D., Şolea, R., Filipescu, A., Ionescu, D., & Simion, G. (2022). Digital twin for a multifunctional technology of flexible assembly on a mechatronics line with integrated robotic systems and mobile visual sensor—Challenges towards industry 5.0. *Sensors, 22*(21), 8153. https://doi.org/10.3390/s22218153

Mourtzis, D., Angelopoulos, J., & Panopoulos, N. (2023). The future of the human-machine interface (HMI) in society 5.0. *Future Internet, 15*(5), 162. https://doi.org/10.3390/fi15050162

Müller-Putz, G., Leeb, R., Tangermann, M., Höhne, J., Kübler, A., Cincotti, F., & Millán, J. R. (2015). Towards noninvasive hybrid brain-computer interfaces: Framework, practice, clinical application, and beyond. *Proceedings of the IEEE, 103*(6), 926–943. https://doi.org/10.1109/JPROC.2015.2411333

Narkhede, G., Pasi, B., Rajhans, N., & Kulkarni, A. (2023). Industry 5.0 and the future of sustainable manufacturing: A systematic literature review. *Business Strategy & Development, 6*(4), 704–723. https://doi.org/10.1002/bsd2.272

Nosalska, K., Piątek, Z. M., Mazurek, G., & Rządca, R. (2020). Industry 4.0: Coherent definition framework with technological and organizational interdependencies. *Journal of Manufacturing Technology Management, 31*(5), 837–862. https://doi.org/10.1108/JMTM-08-2018-0238

Pereira, R., & dos Santos, N. (2023). Neoindustrialization—Reflections on a new paradigmatic approach for the industry: A scoping review on industry 5.0. *Logistics, 7*(3), 43. https://doi.org/10.3390/logistics7030043

Pivoto, D. G. S., de Almeida, L. F. F., da Rosa Righi, R., Rodrigues, J. J. P. C., Lugli, A. B., & Alberti, A. M. (2021). Cyber-physical systems architectures for industrial internet of things applications in industry 4.0: A literature review. *Journal of Manufacturing Systems, 58*, 176–192. https://doi.org/10.1016/j.jmsy.2020.11.017

Pizoń, J., & Gola, A. (2023). Human–machine relationship—Perspective and future roadmap for industry 5.0 solutions. *Machines, 11*(2), 203. https://doi.org/10.3390/machines11020203

Raja Santhi, A., & Muthuswamy, P. (2023). Industry 5.0 or industry 4.0S? Introduction to industry 4.0 and a peek into the prospective industry 5.0 technologies. *International Journal on Interactive Design and Manufacturing (IJIDeM), 17*(2), 947–979. https://doi.org/10.1007/s12008-023-01217-8

Riahi, Y., Saikouk, T., Gunasekaran, A., & Badraoui, I. (2021). Artificial intelligence applications in supply chain: A descriptive bibliometric analysis and future research directions. *Expert Systems with Applications, 173*, 114702. https://doi.org/10.1016/j.eswa.2021.114702

Salih Ahmed, R., Sayed Ali Ahmed, E., & Saeed, R. A. (2021). Machine learning in cyber-physical systems in industry 4.0. In A. K. Luhach & A. Elçi (Eds.), *Artificial intelligence paradigms for smart cyber-physical systems* (pp. 20–41). IGI Global. https://doi.org/10.4018/978-1-7998-5101-1.ch002

Shruti, Rani, S., & Srivastava, G. (2024). Secure hierarchical fog computing-based architecture for industry 5.0 using an attribute-based encryption scheme. *Expert Systems with Applications*, *235*, 121180. https://doi.org/10.1016/j.eswa.2023.121180

Sindhwani, R., Afridi, S., Kumar, A., Banaitis, A., Luthra, S., & Singh, P. L. (2022). Can industry 5.0 revolutionize the wave of resilience and social value creation? A multi-criteria framework to analyze enablers. *Technology in Society*, *68*, 101887. https://doi.org/10.1115/DETC2022-89711

Song, L. (2023). Business intelligence (BI) and big data analytics (BDA) in industry 5.0: Application of adaptive optimization algorithms (AOA) to improve firm performance. *Transformations in Business & Economics*, *22*(2), 45–63.

Szabó, B. K. (2019, October 23–25). Interaction in an immersive virtual reality application. In 2019 10th IEEE International Conference on Cognitive Infocommunications (CogInfoCom). https://doi.org/10.1109/CogInfoCom47531.2019.9089957

Tien, J. M. (2017). Internet of things, real-time decision making, and artificial intelligence. *Annals of Data Science*, *4*(2), 149–178. https://doi.org/10.1007/s40745-017-0112-5

Tirkolaee, E. B., Sadeghi, S., Mooseloo, F. M., Vandchali, H. R., & Aeini, S. (2021). Application of machine learning in supply chain management: A comprehensive overview of the main areas. *Mathematical Problems in Engineering*, *2021*, 1476043. https://doi.org/10.1155/2021/1476043

Tseng, M.-L., Tran, T. P. T., Ha, H. M., Bui, T.-D., & Lim, M. K. (2021). Sustainable industrial and operation engineering trends and challenges toward industry 4.0: A data driven analysis. *Journal of Industrial and Production Engineering*, *38*(8), 581–598. https://doi.org/10.1080/21681015.2021.1950227

Varriale, V., Cammarano, A., Michelino, F., & Caputo, M. (2023). Industry 5.0 and triple bottom line approach in supply chain management: The state-of-the-art. *Sustainability*, *15*(7), 5712. https://doi.org/10.3390/su15075712

Vrontis, D., Christofi, M., Pereira, V., Tarba, S., Makrides, A., & Trichina, E. (2022). Artificial intelligence, robotics, advanced technologies and human resource management: A systematic review. *The International Journal of Human Resource Management*, *33*(6), 1237–1266. https://doi.org/10.1080/09585192.2020.1871398

Xu, L. D., Xu, E. L., & Li, L. (2018). Industry 4.0: State of the art and future trends. *International Journal of Production Research*, *56*(8), 2941–2962. https://doi.org/10.1080/00207543.2018.1444806

Xu, X., Lu, Y., Vogel-Heuser, B., & Wang, L. (2021). Industry 4.0 and industry 5.0—Inception, conception and perception. *Journal of Manufacturing Systems*, *61*, 530–535. https://doi.org/10.1016/j.jmsy.2021.10.006

Yong, K. F. (2014). *Emerging human-computer interaction interfaces: A categorizing framework for general computing*. Massachusetts Institute of Technology.

2 Artificial intelligence in Industry 5.0

Revolutionising human-computer synchronisation

Norliza Katuk[1], Abdul Rehman Gilal[2], and Sohail Safdar[3]

[1] *School of Computing, Universiti Utara Malaysia, Kedah, Malaysia*

[2] *Knight Foundation School of Computing and Information Sciences, Florida International University, Miami, United States*

[3] *Faculty of Technology, School of Computing, University of Portsmouth, Hampshire, United Kingdom*

2.1 The role of AI in Industry 5.0

As we delve into the grand narrative of technological advancement, it becomes clear that artificial intelligence (AI) is no longer a mere concept of tomorrow but an active agent of change in today's world. This chapter seeks to unravel the intricate role of AI in shaping Industry 5.0, a revolutionary phase in industrial evolution where the integration of AI and human intellect is redefining operational paradigms. AI, once a concept predominantly featured in science fiction, now finds itself at the core of the industrial sector, facilitating the transition from Industry 4.0 to Industry 5.0 (Golovianko et al., 2023). This transition is characterised by a harmonious symbiosis between humans and machines, fostering co-creation and collaboration (Noble et al., 2022). The influence of AI in this transformative journey is far-reaching and profound, optimising product designs, enhancing workforce management, and driving innovation. Integrating AI into the industrial sector is pivotal and transformative, laying the groundwork for a future where humans and machines work in unison. From streamlining operations to catalysing innovation, AI is the driving force behind the evolution of industrial processes. It is not just about automation but about enhancing human capabilities and augmenting our capacity for innovation and creativity.

AI in Industry 5.0 is paving the way for a more productive, efficient, and creative future (Joshi & Masih, 2023). It is a future where human ingenuity is amplified by machine intelligence, where the boundaries between the physical and digital worlds blur, and where industries transform in once unimaginable ways. To truly understand the impact of AI, we need to look beyond the technology itself and consider how it is reshaping industries and society. AI is more than a tool; it is a transformative force redefining how we work, live, and interact with the world around us. As we move forward into the era of Industry 5.0, understanding the role of AI is not just important but essential. Therefore, exploring the world of AI and

DOI: 10.1201/9781003479727-2

its role in Industry 5.0 will provide us with a comprehensive understanding of this transformative technology. From its application in optimising product designs to its role in workforce management and innovation, AI is not just shaping our industries but also our future. Nevertheless, before delving into that, we need to grasp the historical context of AI.

The concept of AI was first introduced in the mid-20th century during a conference at Dartmouth College in 1956 (Groumpos, 2022), where the term *Artificial Intelligence* was coined. The idea was to explore whether machines could simulate every aspect of human intelligence (Entezari et al., 2023). In simple words, AI is a field of computer science that enables machines to mimic human intelligence (Sadiku et al., 2022). It involves creating algorithms that allow computers to learn from data, make decisions, and improve over time. The concept of "intelligent applications and algorithms" essentially refers to using AI and algorithms to seamlessly integrate human intellect and machine efficiency. In the context of Industry 5.0, algorithms are sets of rules or procedures that solve complex tasks and manage operations. They regulate the interaction between humans and machines, ensuring smooth operation and effective collaboration. AI takes this a step further. AI algorithms can learn from data, identify patterns, predict, and adapt their behaviour based on new information (Bharadiya, 2023). This capability allows AI to assist humans in decision-making, providing insights and recommendations based on data analysis.

In essence, the intelligent applications and AI algorithms in Industry 5.0 are about leveraging technology to augment human capabilities. It is about using AI to automate routine tasks, optimise workflows, and predict future trends, enhancing efficiency and reducing errors (Boute et al., 2022). However, it is also about using AI to assist humans in complex and creative tasks, to make informed decisions, and to drive innovation (Truong & Papagiannidis, 2022). Thus, intelligent applications and AI lie at the heart of Industry 5.0, defining its character and shaping its future. An example of a significant change is remarkable product design and optimisation advancements, including in pharmaceuticals (Vora et al., 2023), waste-water treatment (Safeer et al., 2022), furniture (Tsang et al., 2022), fashion (Guo et al., 2023), printing and packaging (Sukdeo & Mothilall, 2023), and construction (Oluleye et al., 2023), to name a few. It is reshaping how products are conceived, designed, tested, and brought to market, significantly reducing time and cost while improving quality and performance. One of the significant AI capabilities in product design is its ability to simulate product performance under various conditions. It is particularly crucial in industries where products are subjected to extreme environments or rigorous usage. This simulation can predict how a product will react to different stressors, such as temperature changes, pressure, impact, or even time. This predictive analysis enables designers to optimise their products to withstand these conditions, enhancing durability and reliability.

For example, in the automotive industry, AI can simulate crash scenarios (Candela et al., 2023) and predict the impact on different vehicle parts. These insights allow designers to modify the design to improve safety features. Similarly, AI can simulate flight conditions in the aerospace industry to optimise aircraft design for fuel efficiency and performance (Le Clainche et al., 2023). Moreover, AI can generate several design options based on specified parameters in a process known as generative design (Jang et al., 2022). It enables engineers to explore various possibilities, select the most promising designs, and optimise them. It accelerates the design process and results in innovative and optimised product designs that might not have been conceivable using traditional methods. In essence, AI in product design and optimisation is about leveraging the power of data and algorithms to simulate scenarios, predict outcomes, and generate innovative solutions. It is about harnessing AI's power to create better-performing, more reliable, sustainable, and efficient products. This intelligent application of AI in product design is revolutionising industries and paving the way for a future where products are designed with precision, efficiency, and a deep understanding of their intended use and environment.

AI also significantly impacts workforce management, primarily through its ability to analyse and optimise worker data (Chowdhury et al., 2023). This intelligent management of workforce resources boosts productivity and improves worker satisfaction. AI algorithms can analyse various data points related to worker performance, including productivity levels, skill sets, and availability. These insights comprehensively understand each worker's strengths, weaknesses, and work patterns. However, the real game-changer comes when AI uses this data to optimise workforce scheduling and task allocation (Pereira et al., 2023). AI can intelligently allocate tasks to the most suitable workers by considering worker skills, availability, and past performance. It not only ensures that tasks are completed efficiently and effectively, but it also ensures a fair distribution of tasks. When workers are assigned tasks that align with their skills and availability, they are more likely to feel valued and satisfied, leading to improved morale and reduced turnover. AI can also optimise workforce scheduling by considering worker availability, shift preferences, and business needs. This intelligent scheduling can help avoid understaffing or over-staffing, thereby reducing costs and ensuring optimal productivity. On the other hand, AI's predictive capabilities can forecast workforce needs based on historical trends, seasonal variations, and market fluctuations. It can help businesses proactively hire, train, or reassign workers as needed, ensuring that workforce needs are always met.

Let us explore the use of AI in supply chain management. In the context of Industry 5.0, AI emerges as a transformative tool, reshaping all stages of supply chain management. It started from the early phase of the supply chain with raw material selection; AI algorithms can assess the quality, availability, and cost of different materials, assisting in making informed decisions. It ensures the use of optimal resources, thereby enhancing product quality and reducing waste (Helo & Hao, 2022). Next, AI can streamline processes in the production phase by predicting potential issues and suggesting countermeasures. It can also forecast the most efficient production schedules, considering factors like machine availability, maintenance schedules, and energy consumption. This results in improved productivity and shorter production times. AI's role in inventory management is also significant. By analysing historical data and current market trends, AI can accurately predict demand, allowing for better inventory planning and minimising storage costs (Deng & Liu, 2021). When it comes to packaging, AI can suggest the best packaging materials and designs based on the product and transportation requirements, contributing to cost savings and sustainability efforts (Dai, 2023). In the delivery phase, AI shines by optimising logistics. It can plan the most efficient delivery routes, considering factors like traffic, weather, and delivery schedules, ensuring timely and cost-effective delivery of products (Guerrero-Ibañez et al., 2021). Finally, AI can effectively manage returns and after-sales service by predicting common issues, planning reverse logistics, and providing automated customer service. Figure 2.1 illustrates the roles of AI in the supply chain. AI's application in supply chain management for Industry 5.0 is all-encompassing, providing benefits at every stage, from raw material selection to after-sales service. By leveraging AI, businesses can enhance efficiency, reduce costs, and improve customer satisfaction, propelling them towards success in the era of Industry 5.0.

AI's role in Industry 5.0 is not just about improving current processes. It is also about driving innovation and growth. Through techniques like machine learning (ML) and generative design, AI can create new solutions that humans could not have conceived alone. It leads to innovative products and services that give businesses a competitive edge. In essence, AI in Industry 5.0 is about harnessing the power of data and leveraging it to improve productivity and efficiency. As AI technologies continue to evolve, their impact on Industry 5.0 is set to grow, paving the way for a future where humans and machines work together seamlessly to achieve common goals.

Figure 2.1 The role of AI in the supply chain.

2.2   Machine learning and human-computer interaction

ML, a subset of AI, has revolutionised the human-computer interaction (HCI) field. Its ability to learn from data and improve over time has made it indispensable in creating intuitive and personalised user experiences. Let us delve deeper into the mechanics of how ML enhances HCI and the myriad ways in which it does so. ML can learn from data without explicit programming. It uses statistical techniques to discover patterns in data and uses these patterns to make predictions or decisions. Let us consider the example of predictive maintenance in industries. ML algorithms can analyse data from interconnected devices and sensors to predict when a machine will likely need maintenance (Ayvaz & Alpay, 2021). This proactive approach helps reduce downtime and boost productivity. Similarly, ML plays a significant role in improving quality control processes. These algorithms can quickly and accurately analyse images or sensor data to identify product defects (Benbarrad et al., 2021), often surpassing the capability of human inspectors. It increases product quality and frees human workers to perform more complex and creative tasks.

The advent of ML has paved the way for significant advancements in the field of HCI, particularly with its application in augmented reality (AR). HCI is a field that focuses on how humans interact with computers, and AR presents a new and immersive medium for this interaction. Applying ML to AR has the potential to revolutionise HCI by creating more intuitive, interactive, and contextual experiences. For example, in industrial settings, AR can overlay digital information onto the physical world, providing workers with real-time, step-by-step instructions (Apostolopoulos et al., 2022). It could be for repairing machinery, where an AR interface could present a visual guide overlaid directly onto the machine parts. Not only does this enhance understanding and efficiency, but it also reduces errors, thereby promoting safer work environments. The application of AR, powered by ML, is a perfect example of an advanced HCI, where the computer interaction is designed to intuitively fit within the human's task rather than the human needing to adapt to a computer interface.

Additionally, the ML algorithms underlying these AR applications can learn from past interactions, improving their ability to assist users over time. This learning aspect further strengthens the human-computer relationship, as the computer can adapt and personalise its interactions based on the user's needs and behaviour. ML applications in AR are pushing the boundaries of HCI, making computer interactions more human-like, intuitive, and contextually aware. As these technologies continue to evolve, we can expect them to redefine the landscape of HCI, making our interaction with digital devices even more seamless and integrated into our everyday tasks. In the context of HCI, the learning ability of ML algorithms can be leveraged to understand and adapt to human behaviour. An ML algorithm can glean insights about the user's behaviour, preferences, and needs by analysing data about a user's previous interactions. Consequently, it can predict the user's future actions and provide responses or actions tailored to the user's preferences. Let us consider a real-world scenario. Suppose a worker in a factory is operating a complex piece of machinery. An ML-enabled system can track and analyse the worker's past actions to understand their work patterns. Based on this understanding, the system can predict what the worker will likely do next, proactively provide relevant information, or adjust the interface to suit the worker's needs. It streamlines the worker's interaction with the machine, enhances productivity, and reduces the likelihood of errors.

Personalised recommendation systems, as seen in platforms like Amazon and Netflix, are another excellent example of ML in HCI. These systems use ML algorithms to analyse a user's past behaviour and preferences to recommend products or content that the user might like. It makes the user's interaction with the platform more engaging and satisfying, leading to higher user retention. ML can also be instrumental in enhancing accessibility in HCI. For instance, ML algorithms can be trained to recognise and interpret sign language (Amrutha & Prabu, 2021), enabling people with hearing impairments to interact with computers. Similarly, ML can be used to develop systems that can interpret Braille, thus making computers more accessible to people with vision impairments. In addition to making HCI more intuitive and personalised, ML can also be used to predict and prevent potential problems in HCI. For example, ML algorithms can be trained to analyse user behaviour and detect anomalies that might indicate a problem, such as a user struggling to use a particular feature. Based on this detection, the system can provide timely help or guidance to the user, enhancing the user experience.

As we look towards the future, the convergence of ML and HCI is set to become even more pronounced, fundamentally altering how we interact with digital systems. ML's ability to learn from data and make predictions will continue to enable more personalised and adaptive user experiences. In the future, ML algorithms could analyse a user's past actions to provide relevant information or adjust the interface proactively. It could lead to more intuitive, context-aware systems that anticipate and adapt to user needs, leading to a more natural form of HCI that seamlessly blends the digital and physical worlds. Moreover, the rise of Industry 5.0 emphasises human-machine collaboration, where tools like ML and AI play pivotal roles in driving synchronisation and boosting productivity. For instance, ML can help automate routine tasks, allowing humans to focus on more complex, creative endeavours, thereby redefining the boundaries of HCI. Emerging technologies like brain-computer interfaces, which aim to establish direct communication between the human brain and computers, hint at an even more integrated future for HCI. In this scenario, ML could be leveraged to interpret neural signals, further blurring the line between human thought and computer response. The future of HCI, powered by advancements in ML, promises a more interconnected, intuitive, and personalised digital experience. As ML algorithms become more sophisticated, our interaction with digital systems will grow more seamless, fundamentally reshaping our relationship with technology.

2.3   Natural language processing for Industry 5.0 communication

Natural language processing (NLP) is a branch of AI focusing on the interaction between humans and computers using natural language. Its primary aim is to enable machines to understand, interpret, and generate human language in a valuable and meaningful way (Meera & Geerthik, 2022). NLP encompasses several technologies and approaches. For instance, machine translation, often seen in apps like Google Translate, uses NLP to convert text or speech from one language to another. Sentiment analysis is another approach, often used in social media monitoring tools, to identify and categorise opinions expressed in a text, primarily to determine whether the writer's attitude towards a particular topic is positive, negative, or neutral. Chatbots and virtual assistants like Siri and Alexa are perhaps NLP's most commonly recognised applications. They use NLP to understand user commands and respond in a human-like manner. Moreover, NLP is used in text-to-speech and speech-to-text applications, enabling systems to read out text in a human-like voice or transcribe spoken words into written text.

In the era of Industry 5.0, the integration of humans and machines is more important than ever. NLP is one of the key technologies driving this harmonious collaboration, which allows machines to understand, interpret, and generate human language. It revolutionises our communication with machines; traditionally, interacting with machines requires specialised programming skills. Workers had to learn and implement complex command structures to operate machines or extract data. NLP, however, has completely transformed this landscape. It allows workers to communicate with machines in their natural, everyday language, eliminating the need for specialised programming skills. It makes interactions more intuitive and significantly reduces the time and effort required to train workers. Take the example of voice assistants on the factory floor. These AI-powered systems leverage NLP to understand verbal commands from workers. Whether asking for real-time updates on production statistics or instructing machines to perform specific tasks, voice assistants can interpret and respond to these commands, making HCI more efficient and accessible.

Similarly, chatbots facilitate immediate and effective communication in the workplace (Majumder & Mondal, 2021). Using NLP, chatbots can understand and respond to employee queries, providing instant support. They can answer common questions about work procedures, provide updates on project status, or even assist with complex tasks like data analysis. This instant support improves productivity and frees human resources for more creative and complex tasks. Moreover, NLP can facilitate personalised and adaptive user experiences. By analysing past interactions and learning from them, NLP can help machines understand individual user preferences and behaviours. For instance, if a worker frequently asks for a particular type of data, the system can learn to proactively provide this information, thereby saving time and enhancing efficiency. NLP also has the potential to improve safety in the workplace. In high-risk environments, workers can use voice commands to operate machinery, keeping their hands free and reducing the risk of accidents.

Moreover, workers can use voice commands to quickly alert the system and initiate safety protocols in an emergency (Do et al., 2022). Furthermore, NLP can enhance collaborative efforts in Industry 5.0. It can facilitate effective communication between different machines and between humans and machines by enabling machines to understand and respond to human language. In addition, it can optimise workflow, improve efficiency, and foster a collaborative environment. NLP is a groundbreaking technology driving smooth human-machine interactions in Industry 5.0. It makes communication more intuitive, efficient, and accessible by enabling machines to understand and respond to human language. Its applications make it an indispensable tool for effective communication in Industry 5.0. Continuing with the discussion, NLP also plays a pivotal role in enhancing the decision-making process in Industry 5.0. The ability of NLP to analyse vast amounts of unstructured data, such as customer reviews or social media posts, empowers organisations to gather valuable insights (Vuong & Mai, 2023). These insights could be about customer preferences, market trends, or potential risks, which can inform strategic decisions and provide a competitive edge.

In addition, NLP can significantly improve customer service in Industry 5.0. For instance, customer support bots can handle routine inquiries, freeing human agents to handle more complex issues (Olujimi & Ade-Ibijola, 2023). These bots can understand queries using NLP, provide accurate responses, and learn from each interaction to improve future responses. It leads to faster resolution times, increased customer satisfaction, and enhanced brand loyalty. Moreover, with the rise of remote work and global collaborations, NLP can break down language barriers. Real-time translation and transcription services powered by NLP can help teams from different linguistic backgrounds to communicate effectively, fostering a diverse and inclusive work environment. NLP's capabilities are not limited to text- and voice-based communication. It also extends to understanding sentiments and emotions, an Emotion AI or Affective Computing subfield. NLP systems can gauge the users' emotional state by analysing textual cues and vocal tones. It can be constructive in customer service scenarios where understanding the customer's sentiment can guide the conversation towards a more satisfactory resolution.

Furthermore, NLP can be leveraged for workforce training and knowledge management in Industry 5.0. AI-powered training programmes can use NLP to provide personalised learning experiences, adapting to the learner's pace and style. Similarly, knowledge management systems can use NLP to understand and categorise information, making it easier for employees to find and use it. NLP can contribute to the sustainability efforts of Industry 5.0. Automated report generation, efficient data analysis, and reduced need for paper-based communication can all contribute towards a more sustainable industrial environment. Simply said, NLP is a tool for better communication in Industry 5.0 and a catalyst for improved decision-making, enhanced customer service, practical workforce training, and sustainable industrial practices. Its potential applications are vast, and its impact is profound. As Industry 5.0 evolves, NLP will undoubtedly continue to play an instrumental role in shaping the future of human-machine interaction.

2.4   Ethical use of AI

AI usage ethics are paramount to ensuring a fair, equitable, and safe digital world. As AI systems interact with, learn from, and impact humans and societies, their deployment must align with ethical standards. In the context of Industry 5.0, the misuse of AI can have profound implications. Some misuse cases could happen like:

a   Invasive surveillance, such as inappropriate monitoring of workers, infringes on their privacy rights in their workspace using cameras or facial recognition systems.

b Disinformation or deep fakes, like spreading false but realistic images or videos, could disrupt workflows and decision-making processes.
c AI can also be exploited for sophisticated cyberattacks as it relies on interconnected systems for efficient operation, leading to significant data breaches, disrupting industrial processes, and causing financial losses.
d AI can propagate biases, leading to unfair outcomes. It can unintentionally propagate biases embedded in training data, leading to unfair and discriminatory outcomes in essential sectors like hiring or law enforcement, causing significant harm.
e Misuse of AI in autonomous industrial equipment could lead to safety issues, causing harm to human workers and the environment.

Let us delve into issues raised due to the unethical use of AI. Data privacy leakage (Majeed & Hwang, 2023) is one of the crucial issues, as AI systems often require massive amounts of data to function optimally. These data could range from personal details and shopping habits to sensitive health information. The potential risk lies in the misuse or unauthorised access to these data, leading to privacy infringements. Businesses must ensure they have robust data protection measures, following stringent protocols to obtain user consent before collecting and processing their data. It safeguards individuals' privacy and fosters trust in the technology and the organisation deploying it. Another ethical challenge is algorithmic bias. AI systems learn from the data they are trained on. If this data contains biases, the AI algorithms can inadvertently perpetuate and amplify these biases, leading to unfair or discriminatory outcomes. For example, a hiring AI trained on data from a company that has historically favoured a particular gender may develop a bias, disadvantaging potential candidates of the other gender. To combat this, AI models must be trained on diverse and representative data sets. Regular audits should also be conducted to identify and rectify any inherent biases in these systems.

AI also brings with it the potential for job displacement (Stahl, 2021). As AI systems become more efficient at handling routine tasks, there is a risk that individuals employed in these roles may lose their jobs. While automation can lead to greater productivity, this must not come at the cost of widespread unemployment. Businesses and governments should focus on reskilling and upskilling initiatives, equipping the workforce with the skills needed for the jobs of the future. These initiatives should be seen as an investment in human capital and a crucial aspect of ethical AI deployment. Further, transparency, or the "black box" problem of AI, is another significant ethical concern. When AI systems make decisions, it is often hard to understand how they arrived at that conclusion. This lack of transparency can be problematic, primarily when AI is used in high-stakes healthcare or criminal justice, where decisions have profound implications. The development of explainable AI models and transparent AI governance frameworks is crucial. Users should be able to understand how an AI system is making decisions. It will increase trust in the technology and allow for more informed and responsible use.

Based on the above examples, misuse of AI can lead to serious ethical, social, and security issues, underscoring the need for stringent AI governance and ethical guidelines. Therefore, strict governance and ethical guidelines are crucial to prevent these potential misuses of AI in Industry 5.0. In the Industry 5.0 era, the ethical use of AI is integral for ensuring a harmonious, productive, and equitable workspace where humans and robots coexist. AI's ethical use ensures that, as we leverage technology for efficiency and innovation, we also respect and protect human rights, privacy, and fairness. The ethical use of AI is essential for several reasons. First, it promotes fair decision-making. AI systems often make decisions based on algorithms that learn from historical data. If the data contains biased information, AI can inadvertently perpetuate these biases, leading to unfair outcomes. Ethical AI use ensures these systems are designed and used responsibly to avoid such occurrences. Second, AI systems often handle sensitive data, and ethical use ensures this data is handled securely and privately, respecting user autonomy and preventing misuse. Third, the ethical use of AI ensures accountability. AI systems can have significant impacts, and ethical use means those deploying AI can be held accountable for its consequences. Finally, the ethical use of AI aligns with the human-centric approach of Industry 5.0. It ensures that as we leverage AI for efficiency and innovation, we also respect and protect human rights, dignity, and value human input.

We can harness its benefits while minimising potential risks, fostering trust, and promoting its acceptance among users by ensuring ethics in AI. We need transparency in AI systems to achieve this (von Eschenbach, 2021). Understanding how AI makes decisions can help mitigate biases and ensure fair outcomes. It can be achieved through explainable AI models that allow us to interpret and validate their decisions. Next, privacy protection is crucial. AI systems handle vast amounts of data, especially in interconnected Industry 5.0 environments. Ensuring secure data handling practices and robust cybersecurity measures can prevent data breaches and protect user privacy. Other than that, human oversight should be maintained. While AI can automate routine tasks, crucial decisions should still involve human judgement. It not only ensures the human touch in processes but also enhances accountability. Additionally, continuous ethics training for AI developers and users can instil a culture of ethical AI usage. Regular audits and checks can ensure adherence to these practices. Clear guidelines and regulations must be in place at organisational, national, and global levels. These should lay out ethical standards for AI usage, providing a framework for accountability and remediation. Ethical AI usage in Industry 5.0 is a responsibility and a prerequisite for a sustainable, inclusive, and human-centric industrial future.

References

Amrutha, K., & Prabu, P. (2021). ML based sign language recognition system. In 2021 International Conference on Innovative Trends in Information Technology (ICITIIT). https://doi.org/10.1109/ICITIIT51526.2021.9399594

Apostolopoulos, G., Andronas, D., Fourtakas, N., & Makris, S. (2022). Operator training framework for hybrid environments: An augmented reality module using machine learning object recognition. *Procedia CIRP, 106*, 102–107. https://doi.org/10.1016/j.procir.2022.02.162

Ayvaz, S., & Alpay, K. (2021). Predictive maintenance system for production lines in manufacturing: A machine learning approach using IoT data in real-time. *Expert Systems with Applications, 173,* 114598. https://doi.org/10.1016/j.eswa.2021.114598

Benbarrad, T., Salhaoui, M., Kenitar, S. B., & Arioua, M. (2021). Intelligent machine vision model for defective product inspection based on machine learning. *Journal of Sensor and Actuator Networks, 10*(1), 7. https://doi.org/10.3390/jsan10010007

Bharadiya, J. P. (2023). Machine learning and AI in business intelligence: Trends and opportunities. *International Journal of Computer (IJC), 48*(1), 123–134.

Boute, R. N., Gijsbrechts, J., & Van Mieghem, J. A. (2022). Digital lean operations: Smart automation and artificial intelligence in financial services. In V. Babich, J. R. Birge, & G. Hilary (Eds.), *Innovative technology at the interface of finance and operations: Volume I* (pp. 175–188). Springer International Publishing. https://doi.org/10.1007/978-3-030-75729-8_6

Candela, E., Doustaly, O., Parada, L., Feng, F., Demiris, Y., & Angeloudis, P. (2023). Risk-aware controller for autonomous vehicles using model-based collision prediction and reinforcement learning. *Artificial Intelligence, 320,* 103923. https://doi.org/10.1016/j.artint.2023.103923

Chowdhury, S., Dey, P., Joel-Edgar, S., Bhattacharya, S., Rodriguez-Espindola, O., Abadie, A., & Truong, L. (2023). Unlocking the value of artificial intelligence in human resource management through AI capability framework. *Human Resource Management Review, 33*(1), 100899. https://doi.org/10.1016/j.hrmr.2022.100899

Dai, Y. (2023). Research on the design of green and low-carbon food packaging based on artificial intelligence technology. *Global NEST Journal, 25*(5), 90–97. https://doi.org/10.30955/gnj.004705

Deng, C., & Liu, Y. (2021). A deep learning-based inventory management and demand prediction optimization method for anomaly detection. *Wireless Communications and Mobile Computing, 2021,* 9969357. https://doi.org/10.1155/2021/9969357

Do, V., Huyen, A., Joubert, F. J., Gabriel, M., Yun, K., Lu, T., & Chow, E. (2022). A virtual assistant for first responders using natural language understanding and optical character recognition. *Pattern Recognition and Tracking XXXIII.* https://doi.org/10.1117/12.2620729

Entezari, A., Aslani, A., Zahedi, R., & Noorollahi, Y. (2023). Artificial intelligence and machine learning in energy systems: A bibliographic perspective. *Energy Strategy Reviews, 45,* 101017. https://doi.org/10.1016/j.esr.2022.101017

Golovianko, M., Terziyan, V., Branytskyi, V., & Malyk, D. (2023). Industry 4.0 vs. industry 5.0: Co-existence, transition, or a hybrid. *Procedia Computer Science, 217,* 102–113. https://doi.org/10.1016/j.procs.2022.12.206

Groumpos, P. P. (2022). A critical historic overview of artificial intelligence: Issues, challenges, opportunities and threats. *Artificial Intelligence and Applications, 1*(4), 197–213. https://doi.org/10.47852/bonviewAIA3202689

Guerrero-Ibañez, J., Contreras-Castillo, J., & Zeadally, S. (2021). Deep learning support for intelligent transportation systems. *Transactions on Emerging Telecommunications Technologies, 32*(3), e4169. https://doi.org/10.1002/ett.4169

Guo, Z., Zhu, Z., Li, Y., Cao, S., Chen, H., & Wang, G. (2023). AI assisted fashion design: A review. *IEEE Access, 11,* 88403–88415. https://doi.org/10.1109/ACCESS.2023.3306235

Helo, P., & Hao, Y. (2022). Artificial intelligence in operations management and supply chain management: An exploratory case study. *Production Planning & Control, 33*(16), 1573–1590. https://doi.org/10.1080/09537287.2021.1882690

Jang, S., Yoo, S., & Kang, N. (2022). Generative design by reinforcement learning: Enhancing the diversity of topology optimization designs. *Computer-Aided Design, 146*, 103225. https://doi.org/10.1016/j.cad.2022.103225

Joshi, A., & Masih, J. (2023). Enhancing employee efficiency and performance in industry 5.0 organizations through artificial intelligence integration. *European Economic Letters (EEL), 13*(4), 300–315.

Le Clainche, S., Ferrer, E., Gibson, S., Cross, E., Parente, A., & Vinuesa, R. (2023). Improving aircraft performance using machine learning: A review. *Aerospace Science and Technology, 138*, 108354. https://doi.org/10.1016/j.ast.2023.108354

Majeed, A., & Hwang, S. O. (2023). When AI meets information privacy: The adversarial role of AI in data sharing scenario. *IEEE Access, 11*, 76177–76195. https://doi.org/10.1109/ACCESS.2023.3297646

Majumder, S., & Mondal, A. (2021). Are chatbots really useful for human resource management? *International Journal of Speech Technology, 24*(4), 969–977. https://doi.org/10.1007/s10772-021-09834-y

Meera, S., & Geerthik, S. (2022). Natural language processing. In *Artificial intelligent techniques for wireless communication and networking* (pp. 139–153). John Wiley & Sons Inc. https://doi.org/10.1002/9781119821809.ch10

Noble, S. M., Mende, M., Grewal, D., & Parasuraman, A. (2022). The fifth industrial revolution: How harmonious human–machine collaboration is triggering a retail and service [r] evolution. *Journal of Retailing, 98*(2), 199–208. https://doi.org/10.1016/j.jretai.2022.04.003

Olujimi, P. A., & Ade-Ibijola, A. (2023). NLP techniques for automating responses to customer queries: A systematic review. *Discover Artificial Intelligence, 3*(1), 20. https://doi.org/10.1007/s44163-023-00065-5

Oluleye, B. I., Chan, D. W. M., & Antwi-Afari, P. (2023). Adopting artificial intelligence for enhancing the implementation of systemic circularity in the construction industry: A critical review. *Sustainable Production and Consumption, 35*, 509–524. https://doi.org/10.1016/j.spc.2022.12.002

Pereira, V., Hadjielias, E., Christofi, M., & Vrontis, D. (2023). A systematic literature review on the impact of artificial intelligence on workplace outcomes: A multi-process perspective. *Human Resource Management Review, 33*(1), 100857. https://doi.org/10.1016/j.hrmr.2021.100857

Sadiku, M. N., Musa, S. M., & Chukwu, U. C. (2022). *Artificial intelligence in education.* iUniverse.

Safeer, S., Pandey, R. P., Rehman, B., Safdar, T., Ahmad, I., Hasan, S. W., & Ullah, A. (2022). A review of artificial intelligence in water purification and wastewater treatment: Recent advancements. *Journal of Water Process Engineering, 49*, 102974. https://doi.org/10.1016/j.jwpe.2022.102974

Stahl, B. C. (2021). *Artificial intelligence for a better future: An ecosystem perspective on the ethics of AI and emerging digital technologies.* Springer Nature.

Sukdeo, N. I., & Mothilall, D. (2023). The impact of artificial intelligence on the manufacturing sector: A systematic literature review of the printing and packaging industry. In 2023 International Conference on Artificial Intelligence, Big Data, Computing and Data Communication Systems (icABCD). https://doi.org/10.1109/icABCD59051.2023.10220486

Truong, Y., & Papagiannidis, S. (2022). Artificial intelligence as an enabler for innovation: A review and future research agenda. *Technological Forecasting and Social Change, 183*, 121852. https://doi.org/10.1016/j.techfore.2022.121852

Tsang, Y. P., Wu, C. H., Lin, K.-Y., Tse, Y. K., Ho, G. T. S., & Lee, C. K. M. (2022). Unlocking the power of big data analytics in new product development: An intelligent product design framework in the furniture industry. *Journal of Manufacturing Systems*, *62*, 777–791. https://doi.org/10.1016/j.jmsy.2021.02.003

von Eschenbach, W. J. (2021). Transparency and the black box problem: Why we do not trust AI. *Philosophy & Technology*, *34*(4), 1607–1622. https://doi.org/10.1007/s13347-021-00477-0

Vora, L. K., Gholap, A. D., Jetha, K., Thakur, R. R. S., Solanki, H. K., & Chavda, V. P. (2023). Artificial intelligence in pharmaceutical technology and drug delivery design. *Pharmaceutics*, *15*(7), 1916. https://doi.org/10.3390/pharmaceutics15071916

Vuong, N. A., & Mai, T. T. (2023). Unveiling the synergy: Exploring the intersection of AI and NLP in redefining modern marketing for enhanced consumer engagement and strategy optimization. *Quarterly Journal of Emerging Technologies and Innovations*, *8*(3), 103–118.

3 Blockchain for oil and gas industry asset management

Pioneering Industry 5.0 solutions

Mahdi Nafea Khalid Al-Ajwad[1,2], Rahayu Ahmad[1], and Fathey Mohammed[3]

[1]*School of Computing, Universiti Utara Malaysia, Kedah, Malaysia*

[2]*Basrah Oil Company, Basrah, Iraq*

[3]*Department of Business Analytics, Sunway Business School, Sunway University, Selangor, Malaysia*

3.1 Introduction to blockchain technology and its relevance in the oil and gas industry

Much evidence shows that information and communication technology (ICT), such as machine learning, artificial intelligence, and the Internet of Things (IoT), play a significant role in oil and gas operations. Recently, blockchain has been introduced as an enabler for Industry 5.0 ecosystems, which can improve efficiency in the oil and gas sector by facilitating legacy operations and converting it into a digitisation form (Lakhanpal & Samuel, 2018). The blockchain is a data group connected as a chain with many transactions. This chain can be expandable when adding a new block and producing the shared ledger of all historical transactions in the system (Nofer et al., 2017). Lakhanpal and Samuel (2018) defined a shared (distributed) ledger as shared digital data updated synchronously within distributed nodes on different sites. There is no centralised node to manage this ledger or store this data in it. Hence, blockchain is a distributed ledger storing data as an expandable continued record. This chain of blocks can save every transaction between two nodes inside the blockchain network by verifying the procedure and saving permanently (Lakhanpal & Samuel, 2018).

Blockchain works with a decentralised network; other technologies have supported it, such as hash cryptography, digital signature, and consensus algorithms. There is no centralised node like a server in the traditional system to manage the blockchain system. Alternatively, all nodes will share the data (Lu et al., 2019). The most known blockchain system is Bitcoin, a blockchain-based cryptocurrency. However, this technology can be used in different scenarios in many industries (Zheng et al., 2018).

Blockchain has six main characteristics: decentralisation, immutability, transparency, efficiency, security, and anonymity (Lu et al., 2019). In a decentralised blockchain technology network, all data is stored in many nodes within the network instead of one central node in the legacy system. The data in each node is

DOI: 10.1201/9781003479727-3

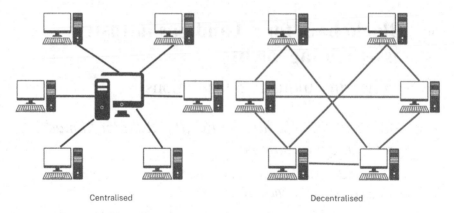

Centralised   Decentralised

Figure 3.1 The centralised and the decentralised network.

Source: Lu et al. (2019). Adapted with permission.

the same and is updated simultaneously. In centralised topology, one central server manages and saves data in which one point of failure exists (see Figure 3.1).

Regarding immutability, the confirmed data in the blockchain system is complex and can change quickly, improving security in a blockchain network. It can make changing data by hacking or manipulation difficult and make this network more trustworthy and reliable. For example, for blockchain data changing, the changing of a block in Bitcoin's chain needs approval from 51% of all nodes. Consensus algorithms inside the network should approve any change that can happen to this data. In addition, the data content inside the blockchain network is protected by encrypted code to prevent any attempt to attack (Fernández-Caramés & Fraga-Lamas, 2018). To ensure the trustworthiness of the blockchain system, it needs to be transparent, which means everyone will track every data update in all nodes in the blockchain network. Consequently, every operation carried out in the transactions inside the blockchain will be followed up by others.

A decentralised network improves the efficiency of data sharing within a decentralised network instead of putting these data in a central database where all data is saved in all nodes. It can reduce risks and diminish costs; this technology can increase system efficiency. In addition, systems depending on centralised topology can face many hacking attacks. The blockchain-based system is more secure as it uses cryptography. All the transactions that are achieved in the blockchain system are nameless identities. The system cares about the validity of the transaction itself instead of the identity of the participants. However, every participant who makes the transaction inside a blockchain-based system has a public key that represents the identity of it instead of a real name (Pal & Kant, 2021). This anonymity gives this network more privacy by hiding the identity to prevent any disclosure of information by attackers.

The peer-to-peer (P2P) network infrastructure is the central topology used in blockchain technology. Each blockchain participant should join this network. Two keys are being used in this network by every node. The first is used to encrypt data when it is sent to a node, which is called a public key. The second key is the private key, which grants the ability to decrypt and read the message received from other nodes (Fernández-Caramés & Fraga-Lamas, 2018). When the message is podcasted inside the P2P network, the node with the specific private key can read this message. Other nodes do not read this message without this private key. This key-access technique, known as asymmetric cryptography, gives a differential of blockchain P2P networks compared to typical P2P networks (Lakhanpal & Samuel, 2018). Any error within this transaction data transmission can prevent its decryption. The nodes can verify the transaction's validity before re-sending it to other nodes. As a result, these nodes help spread this data in a blockchain system. A transaction published within the network and recognised as valid is ordered and arranged into a timestamped block by a node called a minor (Fernández-Caramés & Fraga-Lamas, 2018).

Blockchain requires a protocol to prove the validity of the transactions saved inside it. A new transaction record cannot be added to the blockchain network without this validity. Any added record after verifying will be challenging to update or delete. Algorithms that conduct a validation process are called consensus algorithms, such as Proof-of-Work (PoW), Proof-of-Stake (PoS), Delegated Proof-of-Stake (DPoS), Proof-of-Elapsed Time (PoET), Delegated Byzantine Fault Tolerance (DPFT), Proof-of-Weight (PoWeight), Proof-of-Burn (PoB), Proof-of-Capacity (PoC), Proof-of-Importance (PoI), and Proof-of-Activity (PoA) (Fernández-Caramés & Fraga-Lamas, 2018).

In the PoW method, the node should prove its computational capability. The node needs to spend more power and resources to achieve consensus. The miner node needs to increase the computing performance in solving the SHA256 Hash function to find a number inside the block called "nonce," a SHA256 hash number starting with zeros. Hash is a complex mathematical function used to verify the transactions saved inside the block. As a result, the attack on the system will be complex because of increasing computing resources (Lu et al., 2019). This mechanism is usually used in permissionless blockchain networks (Pal & Kant, 2021). In the PoS method, the miner node will be chosen by voting the network's nodes depending on their economic stake and grade of age. A node with a larger weight or age is expected to do mining to add the new block. In this type of consensus method, the miner node requires less computational performance than the PoW method (Dorri et al., 2019). In DPoS, the time of creation block is less and spent less than PoW computation consumption. This algorithm adopts a voting system by classifying nodes into witnesses, delegates, and workers to choose the best node to generate a block (Yang et al., 2019). The PoET was proposed by Intel Corporation in 2017. In this mechanism, every node gets a random waiting time, and the blockchain will choose the node with the shortest waiting time to be a miner. In this way of consensus, the blockchain network deals fairly with all nodes and uses a permission network (Pal & Kant, 2021).

The DPFT is proposed to solve the Byzantine problem using vote-system consensus algorithms. In this algorithm, the blockchain system can get consensus when the 2/3 majority of validators are dominated (Deng, 2019). The Po Weight algorithm is about the ownership of coins for every node in the blockchain. The network tries to create a random group for consensus depending on a weight-based node (Andrey & Petr, 2019). For the PoB, the node can create a block or transaction depending on its investment to burn coins virtually. This consensus method is like PoW but without real computational resources (Andrey & Petr, 2019). In the PoC, the decision to consider the miner node is related to the space in the hard disc that will be used for storing the next block instead of computing ability in PoW (Salimitari & Chatterjee, 2018). In the PoI method, the modified version of PoS in which the blockchain cares about the node reputation and the node activity inside the network to determine the node to make the mining of the next block rather than balance it has (Salimitari & Chatterjee, 2018). Lastly, in the PoA consensus, this algorithm combines PoW and PoS. The blockchain network uses PoW to determine the miner node according to computation ability, which can build the node header, and then the transaction can be added using the PoS algorithm (Salimitari & Chatterjee, 2018).

From an openness perspective and data management, the blockchain system can be categorised into permissioned and permissionless blockchains in which the blockchain opens publicly. Permissioned can be classified into private and consortium blockchains (Lu et al., 2019). In a private blockchain, access is limited to private participants and organisations. This type of blockchain supports auditability with less trust. A public blockchain, on the other hand, is open to anyone worldwide and is considered a clear personification of decentralised networks. In addition, any user can take part in the consensus process. A consortium blockchain is a blockchain limited in use by members of a specific group. Permission to use this type of blockchain is regulated according to the group's rules. In the oil and gas sector, the private blockchain is the best type to use to gain more privacy and limit access to the blockchain for specific members.

3.2   Leveraging blockchain for efficient asset management in Industry 5.0

According to a report by the Russian company, Gazprom Neft, technologies can increase productivity by almost 10–15% (Shigaev, 2020). Many operations and activities in these oil and gas companies need security, privacy, and data integration. Using blockchain is more efficient and transparent (Ahmad et al., 2022). Lu et al. (2019) classified the scenarios in which blockchain can be used in the oil and gas sector as oil trading, data management and decision-making, security, and supervision. They revealed that many oil companies applied blockchain in their operations, such as cybersecurity, management, trading, and decision-making. However, the use of technology is still rare, and their investment in it is still limited because of its infancy stage. Ajao (2019) explain how it can be used in distributed oil products by securing and monitoring locations in a database with a hash algorithm (SHA-1). On the other hand, Lu et al. (2019) reported that 72% of participants in Deloitte's 2018 global blockchain survey in the oil and gas sector realised that blockchain has a considerable impact on this sector. Despite this impact, Lakhanpal and Samuel (2018) stressed that many obstacles, such as trust, governance, data quality, and infrastructure, can prevent blockchain implementation.

Lakhanpal and Samuel (2018) pointed out that smart contracts can be used in oil and gas to operate the terms between parties digitally and automatically. This term execution can support the monitoring, tracking, and recording of all these terms to achieve the contractual purpose in goods and service delivery for the business. Smart contract features can serve as payment terms and enforce specific actions to be implemented according to the contract rules. In asset management, smart contracts can be used to monitor the materials inventory and improve the warehousing enhancement according to the terms of consumption materials in the operation cycle. In addition, the smart contract can be used to manage scheduling maintenance for assets in oil and gas facilities. Munim et al. (2022) asserted that the smart contract can minimise the need for a middle party between entities and prevent rules from breaking.

Christidis and Devetsikiotis (2016) concluded that the workflow operation time can be reduced when the smart contract is integrated with the asset management process in oil and gas facilities. In addition, the cost can be reduced significantly. Nugent et al. (2016) suggested that the characteristics of tampering resistance can prevent junk changing of the data regarding healthcare information. The same advantages can be used in oil and gas asset management. Nugent et al. (2016) proposed that integrating smart contracts with this characteristic can improve trust in the material data to make the best of related decision-making. Lu et al. (2019) argued that a smart contract should be designed carefully and that any mistake in the instructions can lead to a considerable loss. Similarly, Laneve and Coen (2021) argued that smart contracts caused the loss of billions of USD because some security holes in smart contract languages can lead to precise errors that are difficult to analyse inside the smart contract.

Numerous studies have investigated the use of blockchain in asset management. Zakhary et al. (2019) illustrate that financial assets can be used in permissioned and permissionless blockchains. They explained how a smart contract can register the user's assets in the blockchain network. They argued that using the smart contract within blockchain technology can prevent duplicating the spending of registering these assets. Kongezos and Jellum (2012) concluded that industrial asset management-based new technology would continue to develop to increase the productivity of oil and gas facilities, improve the safety of employees, and enhance environmental conditions. Bell et al. (2018) admitted that medical assets inside hospitals are a current issue in the healthcare sector. They pointed out that blockchain can be used in device tracking by manufacturers and healthcare institutions to solve the tracking issue.

3.3   Best practices in blockchain implementation for oil and gas assets

Iraq is one of the biggest oil producers in the world. It was one of the founders of the Organisation of the Petroleum Exporting Countries (OPEC), the oil producers' organisation responsible for 60% of the oil export internationally (Kisswani et al., 2022). The oil and gas sector is a primary source of the general budget in Iraq.

It supports almost 90% of government revenue and 74% of Iraq's gross domestic product (GPD) (Khdair et al., 2011). Many state companies manage the oil and gas sector in Iraq, for instance, Basra Oil Company (BOC), North Oil Company (NOC), and Thi Qar Oil Company (TOC), to name a few. Many giant oil fields, such as Majnoon, Rumaila, and West Qurna, are owned by these companies, especially BOC.

Many oil and gas companies are working on a new vision for oil fields by using new technologies to enhance their operations. They are trying to convert the oil field from the legacy form to the smart one (Unneland & Hauser, 2005). The oil and gas industry is a substantial consumable business for asset purchasing and maintenance in many oil and gas facilities, such as pipelines, drilling wells, and midstream and downstream departments. The improvement of asset management is remarkable in the oil and gas industry because of the expensive cost of assets and maintenance. The management of assets in the oil and gas sector should be secured to achieve existing equipment, increase productivity, and reduce the cost of maintenance (Ossai, 2012). Moreover, improving industrial asset management aids in securing safety, which is highly required in the oil and gas sector (Polenghi et al., 2022).

Two main types of asset maintenance can be noticeable in the enterprise asset management (EAM) process: corrective maintenance, in which the asset should be restored after its failure, and preventive maintenance, which is periodic maintenance to ensure full functionalities depending on the scheduled maintenance (Rastegari & Mobin, 2016). Real-time checking for the enterprise assets in oil and gas can support improving asset maintenance scheduling to avert the production process's shutdown (Kongezos & Jellum, 2012). Although technology such as bar code recognition is used in EAM, there are many challenges in implementing real-time tracking with data integrity for these assets. Consequently, more workforce costs should be added to warehouse management, and more computerisation level needs to develop in this process (Wang et al., 2015). The oil and gas sector is trying to benefit from blockchain, which is used downstream, midstream, and upstream. Asset management in oil and gas is one of the potential ways to use blockchain to manage maintenance tracking and digital identification to improve process performance and increase productivity.

EAM is one of the potential sectors that can apply blockchain to their management (Zakhary et al., 2019). Consequently, EAM in the oil and gas industry can benefit from private blockchain technology as a trusted system. Furthermore, this system can provide security and share data within a private blockchain network. One of the primary purposes of using this technology is to solve data security issues and to build a trusted system which can be traced and untamperable. In addition, all the information in the blockchain-based system is saved in decentralisation nodes instead of one central database (Lu et al., 2019). Many technologies, such as IoT, cloud computing, and blockchain, can enhance efficiency in the oil and gas sector. Many operations and activities in these oil and gas companies need more security, privacy, and data integration. Using blockchain in these activities is more efficient and transparent (Ahmad et al., 2022).

The oil and gas sector has become an essential factor in the country's development and has been affected politically worldwide in recent years. The rapid development of information technology in the oil and gas industry brings benefits to improve and optimise processes. From a marketing classification perspective, oil and gas can be classified into downstream, midstream, and upstream. Downstream, the oil needs to be stored and sold; midstream is related to transferring the oil and gas from producer to consumer, while the upstream is concerned with the exploration and production of the oil and gas. Using blockchain in different sectors has received much attention in recent years. However, the use of blockchain in oil and gas is not widely understood. Many studies focused on challenges in industrial asset management in many sectors, such as asset action monitoring, data management, and cost improvement (Parlikad & Jafari, 2016). Blockchain technology can improve assets-related processes and increase auditing and tracking (Kuhle et al., 2021). However, there are limited studies in the oil and gas sector about the impact of using blockchain technology in the industrial asset management process and what factors can support adopting this new technology in the oil and gas sector, specifically to manage assets inside this sector.

Managing enterprise assets has been very important in oil and gas production facilities in recent years. Practically, all maintenance requests are collected for many tasks. The start and period of maintenance can raise the cost of the production process and cause failure in this process (Achkar et al., 2019). Assets should be checked to see if they need corrective or preventive maintenance before accidents happen. Data integrity is paramount as a data security issue in asset management. In addition, the massive development of technology that deals with data brings more challenges to data security; more data produced needs more security, especially when using a centralised database (Yang et al., 2018). The data related to assets in the oil and gas warehouses can be tampered with by data warehouse management staff or hackers. The materials in oil and gas should continuously be tracked to check the validity of the oil and gas production process. Consequently, all materials should be registered digitally to improve data management, and all asset data should be secured to prevent data security issues. The current procedure to secure inventory data is dependent on using firewalls and multiple layers of security to prevent access to critical information. However, when a system breach happens, data can be accessed and hacked (Shrier et al., 2016). Blockchain technology can ensure non-tampering data since all data is distributed in a decentralised topology where any change in data can be discovered.

Blockchain technology can include many features, such as decentralisation, immutability, transparency, anonymity, and security. Blockchain has been adopted in multiple scenarios in the oil and gas industry, especially midstream, as an enabler for Industry 5.0 ecosystems. For example, carbon trading, security, and supply chain management (Kadry, 2020). However, the use of blockchain in oil and gas is still rare because the blockchain is still a new technology trend, and more research is needed to investigate the effect of this technology in the oil and gas sector (Lu et al., 2019). There has been less previous evidence for using ICT tools to manage data related to EAM in industries (Polenghi et al., 2022). The production process in oil and gas can be more efficient by preventing maintenance issues before they happen, which can decrease maintenance costs. For instance, any stop in production pumps in an oil field because there is no clear plan for scheduled maintenance due to unexpected asset issues. Maintenance scheduling and tracking can prevent sudden accidents in the oil production equipment. In oil and gas production, the maintenance process is crucial and should be implemented at a specific time and without repeated or can cause a lot of money loss. The maintenance process should be managed conveniently to improve production with less expense (Wenchi et al., 2015). Blockchain can play a significant role in the registration of production assets digitally inside the blockchain records. In addition, the maintenance schedule plan can be recorded as transactions inside the blockchain records. Consequently, all parties in the maintenance process can track this maintenance to prevent it from happening again. Moreover, this maintenance can be scheduled according to smart contracts technology if adopted with blockchain application by automating maintenance according to the maintenance plan of assets or by integrating IoT technology with smart contracts and blockchain together (Younus & Raju, 2021).

Limited studies have highlighted adopting blockchain technology in asset management in the oil and gas sector. Furthermore, few studies have focused on the performance of using smart contract-based blockchain in the oil and gas industry, such as using it in supply chain monitoring from production field to consumers, trading of oil and gas, and managing legitimate contracts between entities (Haque et al., 2021; Lakhanpal & Samuel, 2018). This lack of studies needs to improve, and more studies should be implemented to expand knowledge in this aspect. Many challenges can prevent the adoption of blockchain in different sectors, such as the e-government sector. Some of these challenges are technical challenges related to this new technology, such as scalability of data transactions, flexibility of use, cost-effectiveness, and immaturity. In addition, environmental challenges should be addressed in adopting the blockchain, for instance, weakness in legislation and regulatory support. Furthermore, organisational factors should be discovered, such as staff readiness, changes in business processes, trust, and auditing (Batubara et al., 2018). All these challenges can be discovered by adopting blockchain in asset management in the oil and gas sector. There is an impact of using blockchain technology, which can measure the performance inside oil and gas facilities. This impact can affect the adoption of blockchain technology in this industry. It is almost certain that these factors should be explored to understand the management-level perspective of opting for this technology in the oil and gas sector (Lu et al., 2019).

3.4   User adoption of blockchain in oil and gas assets management within Industry 5.0

User adoption of blockchain in oil and gas asset management within Industry 5.0 can be viewed from organisational, technological, and environmental dimensions. Successful implementation necessitates seamless integration with existing processes and demands an adaptive mindset, emphasising continuous learning and change management practices within the dynamic landscape of Industry 5.0. Many models have been proposed to understand how adopting new technology like blockchain can fit with the enterprise, like model technology-organisation-environment (TOE), unified theory of acceptance and use of technology (UTAUT), task-technology fit (TTF), and fit-viability model (FVM). These models explore how the organisation, technology, and environment can affect the adoption of new ICT. The TOE framework investigates three factors: organisational, technical, and environmental. This framework studies the factors of adopting new technology in the organisation according to the high management level instead of the individual level. This framework seeks to see how top levels of management can support new technology inside their organisation (Awa et al., 2017). On the other hand, the unified theory of acceptance and use of technology (UTAUT) measures new technology adoption connected with four elements: the performance of this technology that can be gained, the simplicity of usage, the social influence, and support availability. Later, the cost factor was added as one of the influence factors for adopting new technology. The weakness of this model is that it cannot deal with the organisational factors for adopting new technology (Liang et al., 2021).

The TTF framework was invented to explore how the new technology is accessible to implement tasks and how it is faster to achieve efficiency. This model supports the measurement of the performance impact on individuals. This model tries to find the connection between the technology features and task requirements. However, the TTF cannot deal with organisational and environmental factors (Liang et al., 2021). The FVM model tries to assess the successful impact of new technology on organisations (Liang et al., 2007). It aims to measure how the new technology is suitable to match tasks inside the organisation and how to make this organisation ready to use with less cost and more benefit (Liang et al., 2021). Blockchain is still a new technology that has not been widely implemented, so managers of information technology departments need to measure what value can be added by this technology before adopting it in the organisation. Many enterprises have used this technology and noticed a clear benefit can be made (Liang et al., 2021).

Liang et al. (2021) inferred that the model explores the adoption of new technology in industries that focus on technology itself, the organisation, and the environment. All these models need more investigation into the relationship between all these factors that affect adoption. The authors discussed many factors that explain the relationship between technology and organisation, which affect the adoption of new technology in any industry, such as technology functionalities, performance, process operation, and cost. In addition, they listed environmental factors that play a role in adopting the new technology, such as pressure from regulatory entities and competitors. The FVM model examines two dimensions to measure the adoption of new technology. The first dimension is measuring how the new technology fits with tasks inside the enterprise, adding benefits for the staff, and improving performance and productivity. The second dimension is viability, which cares about the cost of adoption, its benefits, and how the organisation is ready to use it.

Liang et al. (2007) constructed a measurement tool based on the FVM model. It investigated multiple factors that can lead to the successful adoption of mobile in commerce as a new technology. They concluded that the FVM model can really support assessing whether adopting mobile technology as new technology benefits enterprises. This research will adapt the FVM model to be compatible with blockchain technology in the oil and gas sector. The FIT direction will discover which blockchain characteristics like immutability, transparency, and security will serve asset management requirements in oil and gas, such as manipulation and changing data, maintenance tracking, and preventing failure of points for an asset management system. The model tries to discover if blockchain technology can achieve the tasks in asset management.

In the model's (viability) direction, the organisation's readiness to adopt new technology, such as blockchain, will be studied. Many factors will be inspected to measure this viability, such as the cost of technology, organisational infrastructure, and staff enablement. This chapter presents an extended FVM model to measure the adoption of the blockchain as a new technology in the oil and gas sector to manage assets for the maintenance process. The readiness factor influences the firm's ability to adopt new technology (Nugroho et al., 2017). A new category, human readiness, will be integrated, which can study some human factors that can affect adopting the new technology. User resistance can cause the failure of new technology when adopted in a company (Nov & Ye, 2008). The resistance to change is significant when the new technology is deployed within an organisation. It can cause more cost and delay in proceeding inside an organisation (Pardo Del Val & Martínez Fuentes, 2003).

On the other hand, the proposed model includes a senior-level awareness of new technology in the human awareness category, which can support the ICT plan strategy. The manager level in the organisation will support the adoption of new technology; they know this technology and its features (Claudy et al., 2010). The management needs to prepare an ICT plan strategy to discuss before adopting any new technology; it is challenging to include a blockchain plan without being aware. Finally, there is no evidence of using governmental rules to measure the adoption of blockchain in the oil and gas sector. The proposed factors, such as governmental rules, can be integrated into the FVM model's organisation category. This factor is crucial to match the adoption of new technology with organisational rules and how this factor can prevent this adoption. Figure 3.2 shows new factors such as governmental rules, resistance to change, and senior-level awareness included in the FVM model.

In recent years, the oil and gas sector has used information technology and communication to improve its operational process. One of these technologies is blockchain, which significantly enhances efficiency and security in this sector. EAM is one process that needs improvement depending on blockchain technology. Digital registration for materials, tracking them in real-time, and schedule maintenance are some advantages that can be performed using blockchain technology (Aslam et al., 2021). The FVM model, in its updated version, can be used to assess factors inside the organisation that affect the adoption of blockchain as a new technology inside the oil and gas sector, specifically in asset management.

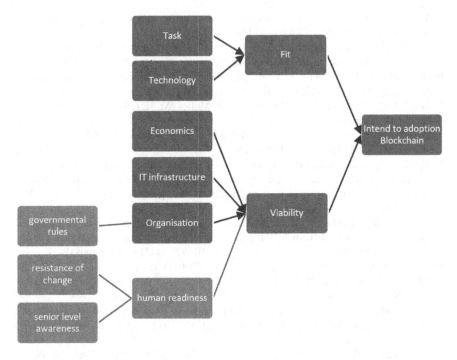

Figure 3.2 Fit-Viability research framework.

References

Achkar, V. G., Cafaro, V. G., Méndez, C. A., & Cafaro, D. C. (2019). Discrete-time MILP formulation for the optimal scheduling of maintenance tasks on oil and gas production assets. *Industrial & Engineering Chemistry Research, 58*(19), 8231–8245. https://doi.org/10.1021/acs.iecr.9b00861

Ahmad, R. W., Salah, K., Jayaraman, R., Yaqoob, I., & Omar, M. (2022). Blockchain in oil and gas industry: Applications, challenges, and future trends. *Technology in Society, 68*, 101941. https://doi.org/10.1016/j.techsoc.2022.101941

Ajao, L. (2019). A secure tracking automobile system for oil and gas distribution using telematics and blockchain techniques. *Balkan Journal of Electrical and Computer Engineering, 7*(3), 257–268. https://doi.org/10.17694/bajece.520979

Andrey, A., & Petr, C. (2019, September). Review of existing consensus algorithms blockchain. In 2019 International Conference "Quality Management, Transport and Information Security, Information Technologies" (IT&QM&IS) (pp. 124–127). IEEE.

Aslam, J., Saleem, A., Khan, N. T., & Kim, Y. B. (2021). Factors influencing blockchain adoption in supply chain management practices: A study based on the oil industry. *Journal of Innovation & Knowledge, 6*(2), 124–134. https://doi.org/10.1016/j.jik.2021.01.002

Awa, H. O., Ukoha, O., & Igwe, S. R. (2017). Revisiting technology-organisation-environment (TOE) theory for enriched applicability. *The Bottom Line, 30*(01), 2–22. https://doi.org/10.1108/BL-12-2016-0044

Batubara, F. R., Ubacht, J., & Janssen, M. (2018, May). Challenges of blockchain technology adoption for e-government: A systematic literature review. In *Proceedings of the 19th*

Annual International Conference on Digital Government Research: Governance in the Data Age (pp. 1–9). https://doi.org/10.1145/3209281.3209317

Bell, L., Buchanan, W. J., Cameron, J., & Lo, O. (2018). Applications of blockchain within healthcare. *Blockchain in Healthcare Today.* https://doi.org/10.30953/bhty.v1.8

Christidis, K., & Devetsikiotis, M. (2016). Blockchains and smart contracts for the internet of things. *IEEE Access, 4,* 2292–2303. https://doi.org/10.1109/ACCESS.2016.2566339

Claudy, M. C., Michelsen, C., O'Driscoll, A., & Mullen, M. R. (2010). Consumer awareness in the adoption of microgeneration technologies: An empirical investigation in the Republic of Ireland. *Renewable and Sustainable Energy Reviews, 14*(7), 2154–2160. https://doi.org/10.1016/j.rser.2010.03.028

Deng, Q. (2019). Blockchain economical models, delegated proof of economic value and delegated adaptive Byzantine fault tolerance and their implementation in artificial intelligence blockcloud. *Journal of Risk and Financial Management, 12*(4), 177. https://doi.org/10.3390/jrfm12040177

Dorri, A., Roulin, C., Jurdak, R., & Kanhere, S. S. (2019, October). On the activity privacy of blockchain for IoT. In 2019 IEEE 44th Conference on Local Computer Networks (LCN) (pp. 258–261). IEEE. https://doi.org/10.1109/LCN44214.2019.8990819

Fernández-Caramés, T. M., & Fraga-Lamas, P. (2018). A review on the use of blockchain for the internet of things. *IEEE Access, 6,* 32979–33001. https://doi.org/10.1109/ACCESS.2018.2842685

Haque, B., Hasan, R., & Zihad, O. M. (2021). SmartOil: Blockchain and smart contract-based oil supply chain management. *IET Blockchain, 1*(2–4), 95–104. https://doi.org/10.1049/blc2.12005

Kadry, H. (2020). Blockchain applications in midstream oil and gas industry. In International Petroleum Technology Conference (p. D033S067R003). IPTC. https://doi.org/10.2523/IPTC-19937-Abstract

Khdair, W. A., Shamsudin, F. M., & Subramanim, C. (2011). Improving safety performance by understanding relationship between management practices and leadership behavior in the oil and gas industry in Iraq: A proposed model. *Health, 22,* 23.

Kisswani, K. M., Lahiani, A., & Mefteh-Wali, S. (2022). An analysis of OPEC oil production reaction to non-OPEC oil supply. *Resources Policy, 77,* 102653. https://doi.org/10.1016/j.resourpol.2022.102653

Kongezos, V., & Jellum, E. (2012). Industrial asset management strategies for the oil & gas sector. IET & IAM Asset Management Conference 2012. https://doi.org/10.1049/cp.2012.1922

Kuhle, P., Arroyo, D., & Schuster, E. (2021). Building a blockchain-based decentralised digital asset management system for commercial aircraft leasing. *Computers in Industry, 126,* 103393. https://doi.org/10.1016/j.compind.2020.103393

Lakhanpal, V., & Samuel, R. (2018, September). Implementing blockchain technology in oil and gas industry: A review. In SPE Annual Technical Conference and Exhibition? (p. D031S032R003). SPE. https://doi.org/10.2118/191750-MS

Laneve, C., & Coen, C. S. (2021). Analysis of smart contracts balances. *Blockchain: Research and Applications, 2*(3), 100020. https://doi.org/10.1016/j.bcra.2021.100020

Liang, T. P., Huang, C. W., Yeh, Y. H., & Lin, B. (2007). Adoption of mobile technology in business: A fit-viability model. *Industrial Management & Data Systems, 107*(8), 1154–1169. https://doi.org/10.1108/02635570710822796

Liang, T. P., Kohli, R., Huang, H. C., & Li, Z. L. (2021). What drives the adoption of the blockchain technology? A fit-viability perspective. *Journal of Management Information Systems, 38*(2), 314–337. https://doi.org/10.1080/07421222.2021.1912915

Lu, H., Huang, K., Azimi, M., & Guo, L. (2019). Blockchain technology in the oil and gas industry: A review of applications, opportunities, challenges, and risks. *IEEE Access, 7,* 41426–41444. https://doi.org/10.1109/ACCESS.2019.2907695

Munim, Z. H., Balasubramaniyan, S., Kouhizadeh, M., & Hossain, N. U. I. (2022). Assessing blockchain technology adoption in the Norwegian oil and gas industry using Bayesian Best worst method. *Journal of Industrial Information Integration, 28,* 100346. https://doi.org/10.1016/j.jii.2022.100346

Nofer, M., Gomber, P., Hinz, O., & Schiereck, D. (2017). Blockchain. *Business & Information Systems Engineering, 59,* 183–187. https://doi.org/10.1007/s12599-017-0467-3

Nov, O., & Ye, C. (2008). Users' personality and perceived ease of use of digital libraries: The case for resistance to change. *Journal of the American Society for Information Science and Technology, 59*(5), 845–851. https://doi.org/10.1002/asi.20800

Nugent, T., Upton, D., & Cimpoesu, M. (2016). Improving data transparency in clinical trials using blockchain smart contracts. *F1000Research, 5.* https://doi.org/10.12688/f1000research.9756.1

Nugroho, M. A., Susilo, A. Z., Fajar, M. A., & Rahmawati, D. (2017). Exploratory study of SMEs technology adoption readiness factors. *Procedia Computer Science, 124,* 329–336. https://doi.org/10.1016/j.procs.2017.12.162

Ossai, C. I. (2012). Advances in asset management techniques: An overview of corrosion mechanisms and mitigation strategies for oil and gas pipelines. *International Scholarly Research Notices, 2012.* https://doi.org/10.5402/2012/570143

Pal, A., & Kant, K. (2021, June). DC-PoET: proof-of-elapsed-time consensus with distributed coordination for blockchain networks. In 2021 IFIP Networking Conference (IFIP Networking) (pp. 1–9). IEEE. https://doi.org/10.23919/IFIPNetworking52078.2021.9472787

Pardo del Val, M., & Martínez Fuentes, C. (2003). Resistance to change: A literature review and empirical study. *Management Decision, 41*(2), 148–155. https://doi.org/10.1108/00251740310457597

Parlikad, A. K., & Jafari, M. (2016). Challenges in infrastructure asset management. *IFAC-PapersOnLine, 49*(28), 185–190. https://doi.org/10.1016/j.ifacol.2016.11.032

Polenghi, A., Roda, I., Macchi, M., & Pozzetti, A. (2022). Information as a key dimension to develop industrial asset management in manufacturing. *Journal of Quality in Maintenance Engineering, 28*(3), 567–583. https://doi.org/10.1108/JQME-09-2020-0095

Rastegari, A., & Mobin, M. (2016, January). Maintenance decision making, supported by computerised maintenance management system. In *2016 Annual Reliability and Maintainability Symposium (RAMS)* (pp. 1–8). IEEE. https://doi.org/10.1109/RAMS.2016.7448086

Salimitari, M., & Chatterjee, M. (2018). A survey on consensus protocols in blockchain for IoT networks. *arXiv preprint arXiv:1809.05613.*

Shigaev, A. G. (2020, December). Digital Transformation of the Russian Oil and Gas Industry: Main Directions and Expected Results. In 2nd International Scientific and Practical Conference on Digital Economy (ISCDE 2020) (pp. 515–521). Atlantis Press.

Shrier, D., Wu, W., & Pentland, A. (2016). Blockchain & infrastructure (identity, data security). *Massachusetts Institute of Technology-Connection Science, 1*(3), 1–19.

Unneland, T., & Hauser, M. (2005). Real-time asset management: From vision to engagement—An operator's experience. In SPE Annual Technical Conference and Exhibition? (pp. SPE-96390). SPE.

Wang, M., Tan, J., & Li, Y. (2015, June). Design and implementation of enterprise asset management system based on IOT technology. In 2015 IEEE International Conference on Communication Software and Networks (ICCSN) (pp. 384–388). IEEE. https://doi.org/10.1109/ICCSN.2015.7296188

Wenchi, S., Wang, J., Wang, X., & Chong, H. Y. (2015, September). An application of value stream mapping for turnaround maintenance in oil and gas industry: Case study and lessons learned. In *Proceedings of 31st Annual ARCOM Conference* (pp. 7–9).

Yang, F., Zhou, W., Wu, Q., Long, R., Xiong, N. N., & Zhou, M. (2019). Delegated proof of stake with downgrade: A secure and efficient blockchain consensus algorithm with downgrade mechanism. *IEEE Access*, *7*, 118541–118555. https://doi.org/10.1109/ACCESS.2019.2935149

Yang, Z., Xie, W., Huang, L., & Wei, Z. (2018). Marine data security based on blockchain technology. In IOP Conference Series: Materials Science and Engineering (Vol. 322, No. 5, p. 052028). IOP Publishing. https://doi.org/10.1088/1757-899X/322/5/052028

Younus, A. M., & Raju, V. (2021). Resilient features of organisational culture in implementation of smart contract technology blockchain in Iraqi gas and oil companies. *International Journal for Quality Research*, *15*(2), 435. https://doi.org/10.24874/IJQR15.02-05

Zakhary, V., Amiri, M. J., Maiyya, S., Agrawal, D., & Abbadi, A. E. (2019). Towards global asset management in blockchain systems. *arXiv preprint arXiv:1905.09359*.

Zheng, Z., Xie, S., Dai, H. N., Chen, X., & Wang, H. (2018). Blockchain challenges and opportunities: A survey. *International Journal of Web and Grid Services*, *14*(4), 352–375. https://doi.org/10.1504/IJWGS.2018.095647

4 Blockchain consensus mechanism in named data networking

Enabling trust in Industry 5.0

Athirah Rosli[1,2], Suhaidi Hassan[1], and Mohd Hasbullah Omar[1]

[1] *InterNetWorks Research Laboratory, School of Computing, Universiti Utara Malaysia, Kedah, Malaysia*

[2] *Faculty of Computer Science and Mathematics, Universiti Malaysia Terengganu, Terengganu, Malaysia*

4.1 Understanding named data networking and its benefits for Industry 5.0

Industry 5.0 is a transformative approach to manufacturing that leverages connectivity, automation, and data-driven intelligence. However, the current networking architecture based on Transmission Control Protocol/Internet Protocol (TCP/IP) was not designed to meet the emerging requirements of Industry 5.0, such as massive machine-type communication, real-time control, and name-based data access. The Named Data Networking (NDN) is a networking architecture well-suited for Industry 5.0 requirements; it offers characteristics such as mobility, scalability, real-time control, and cybersecurity, which are essential for the successful implementation of Industry 5.0. One of the critical advantages of NDN is its ability to establish trust at the network, transport, and application layers, which is a crucial aspect in various fields, including sociology, psychology, economics, and computer science. Trust is commonly interpreted as the confidence level towards an entity in the control condition despite any conditions (Nepal et al., 2011).

As network services and applications have turned towards mobility and centric over the past two decades, the limits of the existing Internet have become increasingly apparent. Recently, projects relating to next-generation Internet architecture have been cultivated. Information-Centric Networking (ICN) is suggested to be the new distributed Internet paradigm instead of the existing host-based paradigm (Jmal & Fourati, 2020). Further, according to the National Institute of Standards and Technology (NIST), NDN is the recent ICN approach that has been one of the most promising future Internet technologies to succeed the current IP architecture (Salah et al., 2015). NDN is a cutting-edge network architecture that shifts from the conventional host-centric model to a data-centric paradigm. In NDN, data is uniquely named, and routers utilise this nomenclature to efficiently retrieve and deliver content to producers and consumers, with crucial components encompassing *interest packets, data packets, pending interest table (PIT), forwarding*

DOI: 10.1201/9781003479727-4

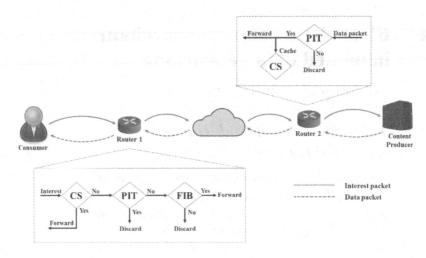

Figure 4.1 The architecture and components of NDN.

information based (FIB), and *content store (CS)* for caching frequently accessed information as illustrated in Figure 4.1.

In NDN, when a consumer needs to fetch any information on the network, named content is requested via *interest packets*. The flow process of the *interest packet* can be seen in Figure 4.2. The figure shows the forwarding process for the *interest packet* in NDN. When the lookups in any data structure return positive, it will transfer the *data packet* back to the consumer. However, if none of the lookups returns a positive result, the *interest packet* is not satisfied, and it proceeds to pass

```
Function PROCESS(Interest)
  Name <- Interest.Name
  if Data <- Cache.Find(Name) then
     return(Data)
  else if PitEntry <- PIT.Find(Name) then
     Record(PitEntry, Interest)
        else
            return Data
  else if FibEntry <- FIB.Find(Name) then
     Forward(FibEntry, Interest)
        else
            return Data
  else
     drop Interest (Interest cannot be satisfied)
  end if
end function
```

Figure 4.2 Forwarding process of the interest packet.

it on to other nodes. In NDN, forwarding strategies are used to select the best interface to be employed. This strategy determines the decision to send *interest* and *data packets* throughout the network (Sudiharto et al., 2017). Forwarding strategies will decide when, where, and whether the packets will be sent to the destination. Decision-making on forwarding strategies is done in this module.

Currently, the NDN distributes *interest packets* with unique names to the network. Once the *interest packet* arrives at the node with the required data, it will be returned to the consumer who requested it using the same route as the *interest packet* without having to authenticate the data. NDN allows users to publish and distribute content throughout the network. Therefore, anyone can send faked content and contaminated data that can affect the NDN network, as they will be kept in the cache memory and distributed to other nodes that request the content. They will fill up the spaces in the cache memory, leaving no room for storing valid content. In this situation, user authentication is crucial since everyone can be a producer and possibly publish contaminated and fake content. Authenticating the data that is being published is also essential since there is a possibility that the authenticated user will publish untrusted data. Hence, trusted producers and content are necessary for NDN to secure the network (Corujo et al., 2019). The content can be authenticated through a *data packet* signature, where the producer will use the key name to specify the public key to verify the generated packet signature to avoid disseminating bogus data (Lou et al., 2018).

4.2   Signature in named data networking

Signatures play a crucial role in ensuring the integrity of data in NDN while it is being transmitted and preventing unauthorised individuals from posing as producers or making unauthorised modifications to cached content. The producer cryptographically signs *data packets*, binding their names with payloads to verify their authenticity and prevent tampering. Then, a consumer fetches a *data packet* and verifies the signature to check its authenticity and integrity. The consumer uses the key locator in the *data packet* to retrieve the corresponding public key certificate. The packet is considered trustworthy only if the certificate chain is valid and anchored at a trusted certificate. This cryptographic approach enhances security in the network by providing a mechanism to confirm that the data retrieved matches the expected content and has not been tampered with during transit.

Signatures in NDN are produced through asymmetric cryptography techniques such as Rivest-Shamir-Adleman (RSA) or the Elliptic Curve Digital Signature Algorithm (ECDSA). In the process, the producer employs their private key to sign the content, while others can verify the authenticity of the content using the corresponding public key. The given information is subjected to hashing, where the name and content are transformed into a unique sequence of characters. This sequence is then authenticated by appending a signature. The value of the signature is incorporated within the *data packet* and can potentially encompass multiple signatures if it receives endorsement from others.

The inclusion of signatures in NDN architecture ensures both the integrity and authenticity of the transmitted data. The utilisation of digital signatures serves the purpose of verifying the integrity of data, guaranteeing that it has not been subjected to any unauthorised alterations, and confirming its origin from the anticipated producer. In addition to its primary function, signature servers prevent potential attackers' attempts to tamper with cached content or assume the identity of producers. The inclusion of signatures within the data-centric model of NDN facilitates the establishment of trust and ensures secure communication. This model allows for retrieval of data by name from any node. Figure 4.3 illustrates the process for signing and verifying the data in NDN.

NDN entities require four pieces of information to participate actively: (1) an assigned name, (2) a certificate binding the entity's name and public key, (3) a trust anchor represented as a certificate, and (4) trust policies. Everything in NDN can be encoded as a named piece of data. Therefore, certificates and trust policies can be encoded as secured *data packet* fetches like any other content. Trust management is a crucial aspect when it comes to the retrieval of data. This is because data is accessed based on its name rather than its physical location, and it may pass through multiple routers and caches during the process.

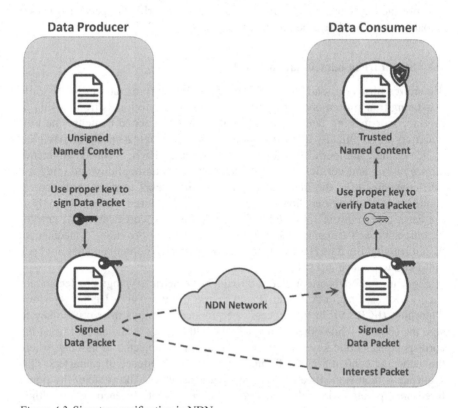

Figure 4.3 Signature verification in NDN.

4.3   The importance of trust in NDN for secure Industry 5.0 support

Trust in NDN can play a crucial role in securing Industry 5.0 support. The NDN architecture is a data-centric networking approach that prioritises content over the specific location of devices or endpoints. It provides a secure and efficient way of exchanging data, which can be beneficial for Industry 5.0 environments that heavily rely on data-driven processes and interactions between humans and machines. Trust is defined as "the degree to which one party is willing to engage in a particular activity with a given partner, taking into consideration the risks and rewards involved" (Ruohomaa & Kutvonen, 2005). Trust may be of three types: direct trust, third-party trust, and reputation trust. Both third-party and reputational trust are founded on direct trust. In comparison, direct trust is established via prior interactions with other entities. Figure 4.4 illustrates the trust components of network security.

Based on Figure 4.4, certification authorisation in third-party trust represents a trusted entity whose primary duties are to assure the authenticity of users. Using third-party trust, anyone trusting the certification authority will trust the user (Entrust, 2000). Certification authority combines the policies and physical elements to provide trust certification services that involve a third party in establishing trust. However, the certification authority does not vouch for the key owner's trustworthiness; it simply authenticates the owner's identity. A vouch can be obtained by having the assurance that the producer has had a successful connection with the other nodes. This action can be attested to their reputation based on their interaction history (Obada-Obieh & Somayaji, 2017). Certificates contain secure information, such as the public key that is utilised as a data encryptor and to verify the owner's identity (Ma et al., 2018). Meanwhile, cross-certification is exchanging information between two secured content authorisations to certify the trustworthiness of the owner's key (Turnbull, 2000).

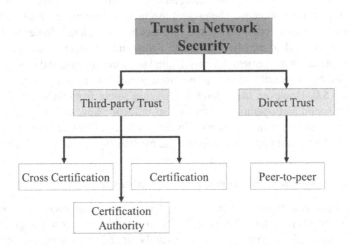

Figure 4.4 Trust component of network security.

NDN places high trust in *data packets* using a cryptographic signature placed at the time of generation to ensure that they retain their integrity and provenance attributes regardless of where and how they are stored or retrieved. It necessitates the possession by each entity of adequate authentication and trust mechanisms, which both local and global entities may utilise. Trust automation can be accomplished using trust schemas to ensure only trusted data is consumed by Industry 5.0 systems. NDN incorporates the concept of trust schemas, which are entities that vouch for the authenticity of data. Trust schemas are an automatic way of determining which keys should be used to authenticate individual *data packets* and provide data producers with an automatic decision about which keys should be used to sign *data packets*. If the keys are missing, trust schemas will be used to create keys while ensuring they are only used within a limited scope (Yu et al., 2015).

Due to the decentralised design of the NDN, the data is secured independently of the underlying communication routes. NDN data is immutable, and each entry is signed using the producer's cryptographic key (Abrar et al., 2022). This key is produced during the data generation process and is associated with the data's name and content. Unfortunately, since a digital signature and key are embedded in every content in the NDN architecture, poisoned content is disregarded if routers conduct signature verification. The digital signature also has a finite lifetime in which it is possible to get cracked and compromised or even reconstructed (Yu et al., 2017). Thus, to solve the issue of cryptographic keys, a new way of creating trust among the nodes in the NDN network needs to be built. The use of trust anchors has also been proposed. Nodes in the network need to share the same trust anchor to create a trusted connection between them. Moreover, by using appropriate trust rules, an application that does not have the same trust anchor can establish trust relations among them (Zhang et al., 2018). However, the time delay, especially for intermediary trust anchors, is the most significant concern (Meirovitch & Zhang, 2021).

In this perspective, it is evident that trust has been handled primarily in NDN via the use of credential-based trust mechanisms, which can be beneficial for securing Industry 5.0 environments. The present mechanism emphasises using public key cryptography to verify communications and tackling associated challenges such as establishing trust schemas, offering effective trust management solutions, and producing usable key management systems. Digital keys, certificates, and trust rules play a role in the NDN security system, providing a foundation for secure data exchange in Industry 5.0. However, trust alone is derivable solely from technical assurance. Additional social and operational factors also influence how trust is perceived and granted in Industry 5.0 environments. Consensus mechanisms have the potential to enhance the NDN in supporting the secure and trustworthy operations of Industry 5.0.

4.4   Exploring blockchain consensus mechanisms in NDN

Due to the growing blockchain ecosystem, there has been an increasing emphasis on creating trust and establishing credibility to provide more technologically possible solutions. Blockchain trust is inextricably linked to how people feel about technical aspects. A shared understanding or clarified affordance of key concerns

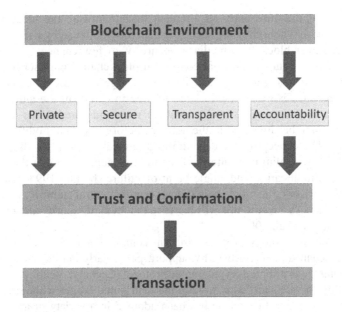

Figure 4.5 Features of blockchain.

motivates trust, not monetary benefits or other forms of compensation. In the context of Industry 5.0, the ability to place trust in blockchain technologies is a critical component of blockchain communication, which is on its way to becoming an alternative paradigm for the management and organisation of computational civilisations. By leveraging the features of blockchain technology, Industry 5.0 can benefit from enhanced trust and security in its operations. Several features in blockchain technology trigger user confidence and significantly develop trust in the network. Figure 4.5 shows the affordance that triggered the user's confidence. Blockchain can create trust in several ways, including private, secure, transparent, and accountable components.

In the current situation, the user's confidence is created by having the authentication mechanism. However, authentication mechanisms do not always deliver transparency and accountability. Some of the blockchain authentication mechanisms that researchers have proposed include BlockAuth (Conti et al., 2019). BlockAuth authenticates producers' prefixes to guarantee they will have the authority to advertise only handoff latency, increased packet loss, signalling overhead, and unprotected connections while managing the network forwarding information. Consequently, a protocol called BlockAuth is proposed and is expected to increase security, privacy, and access control (Conti et al., 2019).

The consensus mechanism can be seen as the most potential mechanism to develop trust that covers all the essential features that will trigger user's confidence in networks. It enables trust distribution and transparent network transactions by verifying transactions without the involvement of a third-party intermediary. Blockchain's decentralised structure has been praised due to the elimination of the third-party requirement to authenticate the identity of the other party with whom they transact. It is generally believed by users that sharing content over blockchain media is secure, with few chances of data leaks and other risks occurring. Mutual consent in blockchain from user to machine and machine to machine has made it an advantage over previous authentication mechanisms. No extra devices are needed to carry out the authentication in blockchain. Moreover, it will comprise numerous credentials from each consortium member involved in the network before any data modifications are performed. The concept of the decentralised blockchain network should be the focus, which will eliminate intermediary involvement and solve the issues of illegal data modification and single point of failure (Marsh, 1994). Unlike the host-based network, the blockchain did not require central authority or mediator authentication. As a result, this will increase the level of security and privacy on the network (Lamsal, 2001).

Blockchain technology promotes trust in communication networks due to its security mechanism and trustworthy support, particularly during transactions recorded using the distributed cryptographic protocol (Cachin & Vukolić, 2017). Due to its ability to safeguard data through the distributed ledger without any intervention by any party, blockchain has been adopted in a variety of areas such as agriculture, transportation, medical, finance, and many more (Ahmad et al., 2019; Kamilaris et al., 2019; Xia et al., 2017). Blockchain may be viewed as a platform that encourages confidence without revealing the identities of the producer and consortium members. Kim et al. (2019) proposed a trust management system based on blockchain to strengthen trust among Wireless Sensor Network (WSN) nodes. However, the notion is significantly different in this work since, in NDN, the location and identity of the nodes and routers are undisclosed.

The ability to ensure data integrity has elevated blockchain as a potential mechanism to be adapted in NDN. A consensus mechanism that blockchain offers can guarantee the data's purity and authenticity. A blockchain platform might become inefficient if an inadequate consensus method is chosen. As a result, the attacker jeopardises the network's data (Baliga, 2017). The role of the consensus layer is to get all nodes in the system to agree on the blockchain content. If a node appends or commits a block, the other nodes also append the same block to their copy of the blockchain (Tuan et al., 2017). The consensus mechanism maintains the sanctity of the data recorded on the blockchain. The blockchain system will safeguard the transaction and block order, thereby safeguarding all the critical properties of blockchain, such as immutability and auditability, only when the underlying assumptions are correct and the consensus model can uphold the state of the Blockchain under failure and adversarial conditions (Baliga, 2017). Table 4.1 compares the characteristics of the common types of blockchain consensus.

Poof-of-Trust (PoT) is depicted as the most promising consensus protocol among the others. Compared to Proof-of-Work (PoW), which requires much computational power to solve cryptographic puzzles, PoT requires less power consumption, which is essential in a resource-constrained environment. PoT is fast and can reduce communication overhead since it only retrieves and verifies trust data.

Table 4.1 Comparison between the common types of blockchain consensus

Characteristics	Proof-of-Work	Proof-of-Stake	Proof-of-Authority	Proof-of-Trust
Speed	Slowest	Average	Fastest	Fast
Power consumption	Inefficient	Efficient	Efficient	Efficient
Permission type	Permission-less	Permission-less	Permissioned	Permissioned
Finality	No finality	Finality (Possible)	Finality	Finality (Possible)
Maturity	Tested	Untested	Safe	Safe
Costs	Costly	Less costly	Free	Free

PoT used digital signatures to establish trust in the data (Zhu et al., 2020). In NDN, each piece of data is identified by its name, which serves as a unique identifier for the data. Digital signatures can be used to bind the data to its name and establish the authenticity and integrity of the data. This is particularly important in NDN, where data can be cached and distributed throughout the network, and it may not always be possible to trust the source of the data. Therefore, the PoT consensus protocol can potentially be used as the verification mechanism in NDN.

4.5   Enhancing data security and trust in Industry 5.0 through blockchain-NDN integration

Integrating blockchain PoT consensus into NDN can be simulated to emulate their collaborative dynamics, showcasing the potential for enhancing trust and security in content delivery. Within these simulated environments, the PoT mechanism is applied for authentication, providing a transparent and tamper-resistant network ecosystem that validates and secures the provenance of NDN data. NdnSIM and NDN Forwarding Daemon (NFD) codebase can be relevant for simulating the behaviour of NDN-based networks in Industry 5.0 scenarios. By utilising NdnSIM and following the strategies outlined in the "NFD Developer's Guide," researchers and practitioners can explore how NDN can be applied and optimised for Industry 5.0 use cases. This strategy is used to determine the methods for forward interest, and it is not expected to revoke any steps in forwarding pipelines of the NFD process. If there are new packet types that it needs to support other than *interest* and *data packets* or new fields in both packets, the action can be achieved by changes in forwarding pipelines in the *nfd::Forwarder class*. It is also applicable if there is a need to override some actions, and the changes can be made at the forwarding pipelines in the *nfd::Forwarder class*. A new strategy can be created by creating a new class; for example, *MyStrategy* can be derived from *nfd::fw::Strategy*.

Information or data that needs to be kept in the strategy must be decided if it relates to a namespace or an interest. If the data is related to a namespace, the data will be stored in the measurement's entries. Otherwise, if it is related to interest, the data will be kept in the PIT entries, PIT downstream records, or PIT upstream records. Following the conclusion of this choice, a data structure built from the

StrategyInfo class must be created and declared. Such data structures are specified as nested classes in the present implementation since this offers natural grouping and scope protection of the strategy-specific entity. However, adopting the same model is not mandatory. If timers are required, the EventId fields must be included in the data structure(s). When an *interest* is retrieved, passed all required checks, and is ready to be sent, the incoming interest pipeline activates this trigger with the PIT entry, incoming *interest packet*, and FIB entry, as shown in Figure 4.6.

A few requirements must be met for the *interest package* to be held. For instance, include the fact that the *interest* does not violate localhost scope, that it is not looped, that the *CS* does not fulfil it, and that the interest is located inside a namespace governed by this approach. After initiating the strategy, it should determine when and where to send this interest. If it chooses to forward the interest, it should call the send approach at least once. After initiating the strategy, it should

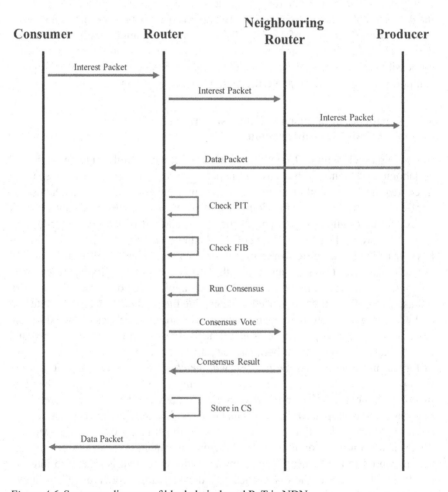

Figure 4.6 Sequence diagram of blockchain-based PoT in NDN.

determine when and where to send this *interest*. If it chooses to forward the *interest*, it should call the send *interest* action at least once. If the strategy determines that the *interest* cannot be transmitted, it should initiate the reject pending interest action, which will result in the deletion of the PIT record. Otherwise, if there is no information regarding the requested name, an *interest packet* will be sent to the neighbouring nodes until it reaches the nodes with the required data.

The proposed trust-based mechanism will start to generate when the *data packet* is returned after receiving the *interest packet*. A node in the consensus network will act as the authentication authority to run the consensus mechanism, which is the PoT. Forwarding strategies will blast the vote packet to the nearest node to vote whether the *data packet* should be received or not. The voting will be done before the catching happens. It will ensure that data integrity is preserved. The workflow of the proposed mechanism inside the forwarding strategy is illustrated in Figure 4.7.

Based on Figure 4.7, the proposed mechanism involves a consensus network of nodes that act as an authentication authority to run the consensus mechanism. When a *data packet* is returned after receiving an *interest packet*, the forwarding

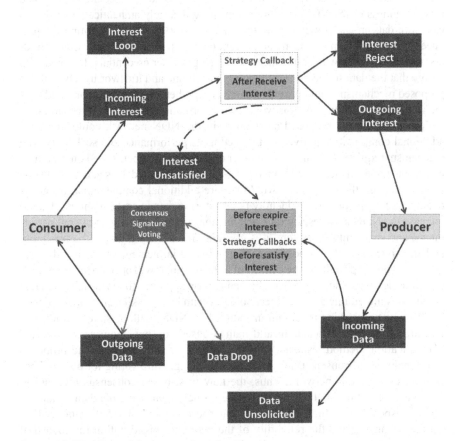

Figure 4.7 Workflow of the proposed mechanism.

```
# Verify the signature of the trusted blockchain data hash
    trust_payload = trust_data.content
    trust_signature = trust_data.signature
    if not self.keychain.verify_data(blockchain_data_name, trust_payload, trust_signature):
        return False
```

Figure 4.8 Verification of consensus signature voting.

strategy will blast a voting packet to the nearest node to vote whether the *data packet* should be received or not. The voting is done before caching happens to ensure data integrity is preserved, as shown in the code in Figure 4.8. The signature voting is based on the attributes of the nodes, and the result is retrieved to determine whether the *data packet* should be passed to the consumer or dropped. This mechanism creates trust in the NDN by ensuring that *data packets* are authenticated before being passed to the consumer.

The proposed trust-based consensus mechanism in NDN is expected to exhibit both potential advantages and disadvantages in its implementation, particularly in the context of Industry 5.0. The blockchain mechanism authenticates the producer's identity before storing the data in cache memory. It could enhance the security and trustworthiness of the NDN network by ensuring that only authenticated producers can store data in cache memory on the NDN network. By authenticating the producer's identity, the mechanism can prevent content poisoning attacks from intruders, especially those who stole other authorised producer credentials. It would help ensure that the data stored in cache memory is genuine and trustworthy. Overall, the proposed mechanism could provide a more comprehensive and focus-oriented trust management system to keep trustworthiness information from various resources.

Implementing the proposed mechanism in the NDN network could introduce additional complexity and overhead, affecting its performance and scalability. The mechanism requires the consensus of other consortium members based on the attributes of the nodes, which could lead to potential conflicts and delays in data transmission. Moreover, the mechanism would require additional computational resources to authenticate the producer's identity before storing data in cache memory. It could increase the NDN's processing time and memory usage, affecting its overall performance and scalability. Therefore, it is essential to carefully evaluate the feasibility and effectiveness of the proposed mechanism before implementing it in a real-world NDN network, especially in the context of Industry 5.0. It will open up more research opportunities since Industry 5.0 is a human-centric approach to industrialisation that emphasises integrating advanced technologies with human skills and capabilities.

The new networking paradigm introduced by NDN, with its stateful multipath forwarding plane with caching and named-based routing, requires a new data authentication method, especially in the context of Industry 5.0. The proposed blockchain-based consensus mechanism enables signature voting for user authentication in the NDN network. Thus, the new trust-based consensus mechanism for signature voting in NDN can encounter issues in ensuring the data is authenticated, especially in Industry 5.0. By incorporating Industry 5.0, data security can be enhanced, and the reliability of the data exchanged within the industrial environment can also be preserved.

Acknowledgements

This work was supported by the Ministry of Higher Education (MoHE) through the Fundamental Research Grant Scheme (Ref: FRGS/1/2020/ICT07/ UUM/01/1). The content of this chapter is solely the responsibility of the authors and does not necessarily represent the official views of the MoHE, Malaysia.

References

Abrar, A., Arif, A. S. C. M., & Zaini, K. M. (2022). Producer mobility support in information-centric networks: Research background and open issues. *International Journal of Communication Networks and Distributed Systems*, *28*(3), 312–336. https://doi.org/10.1504/ IJCNDS.2022.122183

Ahmad, F., Kerrache, C. A., Kurugollu, F., & Hussain, R. (2019). Realization of blockchain in named data networking-based internet-of-vehicles. *IT Professional*, *21*(4), 41–47. https://doi.org/10.1109/MITP.2019.2912142

Baliga, A. (2017). *Understanding Blockchain Consensus Models*. https://www.persistent. com/wp-content/uploads/2017/04/WP-Understanding-Blockchain-Consensus-Models.pdf

Cachin, C., & Vukolić, M. (2017). Blockchains Consensus Protocols in the Wild. *ArXiv Preprint ArXiv:1707.01873.*/https://doi.org/10.1109/EDCC.2017.36

Conti, M., Hassan, M., & Lal, C. (2019). BlockAuth: Blockchain based distributed producer authentication in ICN. *Computer Networks*, *164*, 106888. https://doi.org/10.1016/ j.comnet.2019.106888

Corujo, D., Guimarães, C., Quevedo, J., Ferreira, R., & Aguiar, R. L. (2019). Information-centric exchange mechanisms for IoT interoperable deployment. *User-Centric and Information-Centric Networking and Services: Access Networks, Storage and Cloud Perspective*, 71–139. https://doi.org/10.1201/9781315207650-3

Entrust (2000). The concept of trust in network security. Entrust Technologies White Paper.

Jmal, R., & Fourati, L. C. (2020). Distributed software defined information centric networking. *International Journal of High Performance Computing and Networking*, *16*(1), 14–25. https://doi.org/10.1504/IJHPCN.2020.110250

Kamilaris, A., Fonts, A., & Prenafeta-Boldú, F. X. (2019). The rise of blockchain technology in agriculture and food supply chains. *Trends in Food Science & Technology*, *91*, 640–652. https://doi.org/10.1016/j.tifs.2019.07.034

Kim, T. H., Goyat, R., Rai, M. K., Kumar, G., Buchanan, W. J., Saha, R., & Thomas, R. (2019). A novel trust evaluation process for secure localization using a decentralized blockchain in wireless sensor networks. *IEEE Access*, 7, 184133–184144. https://doi.org/10.1109/ ACCESS.2019.2960609

Lamsal, P. (2001). *Understanding trust and security*. Department of Computer Science, University of Helsinki.

Lou, J., Zhang, Q., Qi, Z., & Lei, K. (2018). A blockchain-based key management scheme for named data networking. In 2018 1st IEEE International Conference on Hot Information-Centric Networking (HotICN) (pp. 141–146). https://doi.org/10.1109/ HOTICN.2018.8605993

Ma, M., He, D., Kumar, N., Choo, K.-K. R., & Chen, J. (2018). Certificateless searchable public key encryption scheme for industrial internet of things. *IEEE Transactions on Industrial Informatics*, *14*(2), 759–767. https://doi.org/10.1109/TII.2017.2703922

Marsh, S. P. (1994). *Formalising trust as a computational concept*.

Meirovitch, D., & Zhang, L. (2021). *NSC–Named Service Calls, or a Remote Procedure Call for NDN*. Technical Report NDN-0074, Revision 1. NDN.

Nepal, S., Sherchan, W., & Paris, C. (2011). Strust: A trust model for social networks. In 2011 IEEE 10th International Conference on Trust, Security and Privacy in Computing and Communications (pp. 841–846). https://doi.org/10.1109/TrustCom.2011.112

Obada-Obieh, B., & Somayaji, A. (2017). Can I believe you?: Establishing trust in computer mediated introductions. In *Proceedings of the 2017 New Security Paradigms Workshop on ZZZ* (pp. 94–106). https://doi.org/10.1145/3171533.3171544

Ruohomaa, S., & Kutvonen, L. (2005). Trust management survey. In International Conference on Trust Management (pp. 77–92). https://doi.org/10.1007/11429760_6

Salah, H., Wulfheide, J., & Strufe, T. (2015). Coordination supports security: A new defence mechanism against interest flooding in NDN. In 2015 IEEE 40th Conference on Local Computer Networks (LCN) (pp. 73–81). https://doi.org/10.1109/LCN.2015.7366285

Sudiharto, D. W., Herutomo, A., & Rohmah, Y. N. (2017). The comparison of forwarding strategies between best route, multicast, and access on named data networking (NDN). Case study: A node compromised by the prefix hijack. *J. Commun, 12*(7), 426–432. https://doi.org/10.12720/jcm.12.7.426-432

Tuan, T., Dinh, A., Wang, J., Chen, G., Liu, R., Ooi, B. C., & Tan, K.-L. (2017). BLOCK-BENCH: A framework for analyzing private blockchains. In ACM International Conference on Management of Data (SIGMOD) 2017. https://doi.org/10.1145/3035918.3064033

Turnbull, J. (2000). Cross-certification and PKI policy networking. *Entrust, Inc*, 1–10.

Xia, Q. I., Sifah, E. B., Asamoah, K. O., Gao, J., Du, X., & Guizani, M. (2017). MeDShare: Trust-less medical data sharing among cloud service providers via blockchain. *IEEE Access, 5*, 14757–14767. https://doi.org/10.1109/ACCESS.2017.2730843

Yu, Y., Afanasyev, A., Clark, D., claffy, kc, Jacobson, V., & Zhang, L. (2015). Schematizing trust in named data networking. In *Proceedings of the 2nd International Conference on Information-Centric Networking - ICN '15* (pp. 177–186). https://doi.org/10.1145/2810156.2810170

Yu, Y., Afanasyev, A., Seedorf, J., Zhang, Z., & Zhang, L. (2017). NDN DeLorean: An authentication system for data archives in named data networking. In *Proceedings of the 4th ACM Conference on Information-Centric Networking* (pp. 11–21). https://doi.org/10.1145/3125719.3125724

Zhang, H., Li, Y., Zhang, Z., Afanasyev, A., & Zhang, L. (2018). NDN host model. *ACM SIGCOMM Computer Communication Review, 48*(3), 35–41. https://doi.org/10.1145/3276799.3276804

Zhu, X., Li, Y., Fang, L., & Chen, P. (2020). An improved proof-of-trust consensus algorithm for credible crowdsourcing blockchain services. *IEEE Access, 8*, 102177–102187. https://doi.org/10.1109/ACCESS.2020.2998803

5 Computational thinking technique for programmers

Empowering Industry 5.0 innovators

Asmalinda Adnan, Nur Hafiza Jamaludin, and Rohaida Romli

Data Management & Software Solutions Research Lab, School of Computing, Universiti Utara Malaysia, Kedah, Malaysia

5.1 Fundamentals of computational thinking and Industry 5.0

The studies in computational thinking (CT) were initiated by Seymour Papert (1996) and followed by Wing (2006). It began to grow rapidly in the scientific domain around 2013 (Selby, 2014), including in computer science, education, and instructional technologies (Ilic et al., 2018). Scholars from various perspectives have defined CT. For example, Wing (2006) stated that CT is a component of problem-solving skills related to an individual's attitude and skills and that the relationship between problem-solving activities and CT concepts should be considered together. According to Mannila et al. (2014), CT is defined as "the concepts and processes that assist in problem-solving and decision-making and involve the use of computers." Aside from that, ISTE (2018) defined CT as the ability to use technological methods to understand and solve problems. Although CT is perpetually ambiguous (Lyon & Magana, 2020), it can be defined as analysing and solving complex problems using a systematic approach.

The fifth industrial revolution (i.e., Industry 5.0) has been emerging with dominant visions as a theme, human-robot coworking, and bioeconomy (Demir et al., 2019). Industry 5.0 goes beyond profit in producing goods and services to counteract the asymmetrical innovation in the current Industry 4.0 paradigm by allowing research and innovation to drive the transition to human-centricity, resilience, and sustainability. Workers or humans are viewed as the main characters in the human-centric approach, as they will control the technology in manufacturing to improve production by practising problem-solving processes. In doing so, the technology used will be adapted based on the demand of industry workers. Furthermore, the industrial workers must upskill and reskill to advance in their careers and maintain a work-life balance. Another concept highlighted in Industry 5.0 is resilience. The collaboration among resilience, recovery, robustness, and sustainability provides a new and bright vision for manufacturing, business, the world, and society (Anderies et al., 2013). In general, Industry 5.0 allows for human-to-machine, machine-to-human, machine-to-machine, and human-to-human interaction and collaboration, which did not exist in Industry 4.0. Vulnerabilities related to humans and machines

DOI: 10.1201/9781003479727-5

Table 5.1 Main concepts of Industry 5.0

Human-centricity	Sustainability	Resilience
• Encourage the continuous development and renewal of human talents, diversity, and empowerment skills. • Adapt to the latest technologies. • Adapt to the basic requirements.	• Inculcate environmental concerns and promote eco-friendly manufacturing practices. • Customisation, resource efficiency, and waste reduction, higher resource effectiveness and efficiency.	• Agile and adaptable technology incorporates ideas and practices that allow industrial businesses to respond to issues effectively.

Source: Adapted from Narkhede et al. (2023).

are another resilience concern, especially during decision-making (Grafton et al., 2019). The resilient system must be adaptable to all circumstances to remain operational. In the context of Industry 5.0, the term "sustainability" refers to environmental protection. Table 5.1 depicts the key concepts of Industry 5.0, including human-centeredness, resilience, and sustainability (Narkhede et al., 2023).

Industry 5.0, according to Rada (2020), is the first human industrial revolution based on the 6R (Recognise, Reconsider, Realise, Reduce, Reuse, and Recycle) principles. Further, Nahavandi (2019) highlighted that Industry 5.0 fosters human-machine collaboration to increase production efficiency by integrating human critical thinking and creativity in intelligent systems. Hendry et al. (2020) proposed that human factors and technology are the primary considerations of various industry practitioners, information technologists, and philosophers. The main intention is to initiate orthogonal safe exits by separating hyperconnected automation systems for production and manufacturing. Lastly, Maddikunta et al. (2022) also defined Industry 5.0 as a human-centric approach that enables personalised autonomous manufacturing through enterprise social networks by cultivating the interaction between humans and robots (collaboration robots) with human resources. The presence of robots in the industrial world is not a programmable machine but exists as a collaborator with human creativity and critical thinking to be used in repetitive job and labour-intensive tasks.

Industry 5.0 has contributed to STEM education, where it stands for science, technology, engineering, and mathematics. Furthermore, Industry 5.0 has advanced the requirement of Education 5.0 from Industry 4.0, in which education is part of ongoing learning through formal and informal education. Nikum (2022) has highlighted the fourth key aspect of Education 5.0, including the teaching and learning process, technologies, infrastructure, skills, and capabilities. Nowadays, technological advancement has made education possible anywhere and anytime. Education 5.0 is considered more realistic to diminish the imbalance of Education 4.0, where technologies dominate humans and machines, creating a lack of human-to-human interactions. Education 5.0 has placed humans at the centre of education by advancing technology. Technologies aid in improving the teaching-learning experience, aiming to explore skills through education and learning consistency. Furthermore, the learning and development process allows for implementing critical thinking and problem-solving skills and preserving human values.

In the dynamic landscape of Industry 5.0, where the harmonious convergence of cutting-edge technologies defines the industrial narrative, CT emerges as the foundation for skilled programmers navigating the complex world of sophisticated programmes and systems. The foundation of this process is the art of decomposition, wherein developers systematically separate complex challenges into manageable components. This approach is not merely a technical strategy for addressing issues within smart environments, such as those characterising advanced manufacturing systems. Instead, it serves as a guiding philosophy that emphasises the significance of integrating CT into the education of future programmers during their university years. Considered not only a paradigm for industrial applications but also a pedagogical imperative, CT takes centre stage in the early stages of programmer education. This problem-solving approach nurtures the skills needed for young programmers to navigate the complicated intricacies of Industry 5.0. The skill set stimulates creativity across the STEM disciplines in a broader sense. Furthermore, because CT is built on the principles of abstraction and algorithmic design, programmers are able to create effective algorithms and abstract models. These skills extend beyond the boundaries of specific industrial applications, which is powerful in the broader landscape of STEM areas. Cultivating CT into novice programmer education will prepare them to meet the demands of Industry 5.0 and contribute significantly to the broader advancement of STEM disciplines.

5.2   Applying CT techniques in programmers development

Cultivating CT in programmers' training for STEM education and Education 5.0 is a critical agenda to support Industry 5.0. Thus, educational institutions that offer computing-related programmes must prepare students for future job requirements by teaching coding and exposing them to digital control devices (Maddikunta, 2022). In other words, future programmers must be trained in such a way that they are capable of supporting Industry 5.0. It requires the incorporation of computing teaching pedagogy suitable to educate the programmers at their early stage of training, including design thinking, and pair programming, to name a few. Another growing and demanding skill set is CT. It stands out as essential in programming, offering a universal problem-solving framework that transcends specific methodologies. CT also equips programmers with the ability to navigate complexity and innovate, which is crucial for adapting to the ever-evolving software development landscape in Industry 5.0. According to Csizmadia et al. (2015), CT skills are necessary for the programming discipline to facilitate problem-solving and algorithm-building skills in program development. As such, Guzdial (2008) defined CT as a problem-solving technique involving abstraction, analysis, automation, and modelling. Selby et al. (2014) also stated that CT concepts include abstraction, decomposition, algorithmic design, evaluation, and generalisation. Csizmadia et al. (2015)

support this definition by stating that CT processes include abstraction, generalisation, algorithm, and evaluation.

According to Wing and Stanzione (2016), problem-solving consists of six major steps: problem determination, data organising and analysis, abstraction of data representation, algorithmic thinking solution, recognising, examining, and implementing a possible solution, and finalising the solution. Furthermore, a recent study by Paucar-Curasma et al. (2023) has divided CT skills into five steps: decomposition, generalisation, algorithmic design, abstraction, and evaluation, with CT being associated with cognitive processes in problem-solving. Although the CT concept, process, set of skills, and techniques used vary, the techniques used are nearly consistent among scholars. Scholars frequently use the process of breaking down a complex problem (abstraction), data generalisation, designing the data solution (algorithm), and problem solution (evaluation) to demonstrate the problem-solving process. This is consistent with problem-solving steps as stated by the Organisation for Economic Co-operation and Development (OECD, 2005), which simplify the process into four key steps: exploring and understanding the complex problem (abstraction), generalising and summarising the problem (generalisation), designing the algorithm (algorithm), and reflecting on the result (evaluation).

Since CT is primarily concerned with problem-solving, many current studies use programming as their main reference to demonstrate that CT has a strong relationship with programming (Bocconi et al., 2016). Furthermore, Voogt et al. (2015) stated that programming is the primary platform for developing CT skills. Many studies have reported that CT concepts are effectively implemented in teaching programming by utilising various activities prior to coding to deliver the fundamental concept of programming (Castro et al., 2021; Giannakoulas & Xinogalos, 2018; Paucar-Curasma et al., 2023). On top of that, recent research has revealed an increasing trend in cultivating programming among novice programmers, particularly to support Industry 5.0 by introducing robotics programming (Ajaykumar et al., 2021; Díaz-Lauzurica & Moreno-Salinas, 2019; Kangungu & Yatim, 2020), Internet of Things (IoT) programming (Rahman et al., 2020), and digital twin and simulation programming (Liljaniemi & Paavilainen, 2020). Therefore, a study conducted by Güğerçin and Güğerçin (2021) has predicted that problem-solving skills will remain in demand, while the other three skills, including working with people/human-centric, technology use and development, and self-management will lead to in-demand skills for future industry.

5.3   CT techniques in programming for Industry 5.0

A review study was conducted to investigate the pivotal role of CT in training programmers, specifically to prepare them for the demands of Industry 5.0. The methodology involved a systematic review, including identifying relevant literature, analysing CT techniques implemented in educational environments, and aligning with Industry 5.0's core pillars of resilience, environmental sustainability, and human centricity. The review aimed to discern the in-demand programming skills necessary for Industry 5.0, shedding light on how CT shapes a workforce adept at navigating the intricacies of this emerging industrial paradigm. The systematic review will uncover insights into how CT, when integrated into programming training, contributes to developing skills crucial for Industry 5.0, thereby bridging the gap between educational practices and the evolving demands of the industrial landscape.

An analysis of the authors, publication year, and the classification of in-demand skills for programmers was made. There are four in-demand skills for programmers: problem-solving (PS), working with people (WP), technology use and development (TUD), and self-management (SM). On the other hand, the primary relevant pillars of Industry 5.0, which cover human centricity (HC), sustainability (ST), and resilience (RC), were also analysed. Further, the contribution of Industry 5.0 was a critical point for comparative analysis. All these key parameters were systematically assessed and deliberated within the studies of the selected articles, forming the basis for comprehensive conclusions in the context of this review study.

Humans and machines must interact and collaborate to achieve the key concepts of human-centricity, sustainability, and resilience in Industry 5.0. Programmers must also have sufficient knowledge and problem-solving skills to support technology and manufacturing by increasing production rate and profit. Table 5.2 lists the selected studies that support in-demand skill classification for future programmers. Güğerçin and Güğerçin (2021) support the core concept of Industry 5.0.

Table 5.2 In-demand skills classification for future programmers to support core concept of Industry 5.0

Author/Year	Programmer's skills classification				Supporting technology	Industry 5.0 concept			Contribution
	PS	WP	TUD	SM		HC	ST	RS	
Adorno et al. (2023)	/	/	/	/	Human-robot interaction	/	–	–	Instructional design to support Industry 5.0.
Li et al. (2023)	/	/	/	/	Augmented reality robot	/	/	–	Learning-based approach for Industry 5.0.
Ruppert et al. (2022)	/	/	/	–	IoT	/	/	/	Education skill towards Industry 5.0.
Maddikunta et al. (2022)	–	–	/	–	–	/	–	/	Technology, application and challenge of Industry 5.0.
Carayannis and Morawska-Jancelewicz (2022)	/	–	/	–	–	–	/	/	Digital innovation in the university practices and policies.

(Continued)

Table 5.2 (Continued)

Author/Year	Programmer's skills classification				Supporting technology	Industry 5.0 concept			Contribution
	PS	WP	TUD	SM		HC	ST	RS	
Adel (2022)	/	/	/	–	Cobot	/	–	/	Potential applications of Industry 5.0.
Bednar and Welch (2020)	/	–	/	–	Smart system	–	/	/	Technological and social systems work.
Neumann et al. (2022)	/	–	–	–	Low-code platform	–	/	–	Assistant system for low code programmers.
Kaarlela et al. (2022)	/	/	/	–	Digital twin	/	/	/	Robotics teleoperation platform supported by the Industry 5.0.
Poláková et al. (2023)	/	–	/	–	–	/	–	–	Provide a theoretical description of the significance of soft skills and their categorisation.
Mayr-Dorn et al. (2023)	/	–	/	–	Robot program	/	/	/	Provide a significant process of block programming for non-programmers.
Raudmäe et al. (n.d.)	/	–	/	–	Robot and digital twin	/	/	/	Robotont is an open-source omnidirectional mobile robot platform with physical hardware and a digital twin.
Kolade and Owoseni (2022)	–	–	/	–	–	/	–	–	Complementary insights on cross-cutting themes of technological unemployment, wage inequality and job polarisation.
Roveda et al. (2023)	/	–	/	–	Robotic	/	/	–	Propose and validate a human-centric approach to transfer humans' knowledge of a task into the robot controller.

(*Continued*)

Table 5.2 (Continued)

Author/Year	Programmer's skills classification				Supporting technology	Industry 5.0 concept			Contribution
	PS	WP	TUD	SM		HC	ST	RS	
Schmidbauer et al. (2020)	/	–	/	/	Cobot	/	/	/	An approach to teaching different levels of cobots and control addressing skill in a working environment.
Regassa Hunde and Debebe Woldeyohannes (2022)	/	–	/	/	AI and extended reality	/	/	/	Cooperation of AI with Computer Aided Design (CAD).
Smuts and Van der Merwe (2022)	/	/	/	/	–	/	/	/	Propose future work skills for software engineers and developers.
Cañas et al. (2020)	/	–	/	/	Robotics	/	/	/	A robot operating system (ROS)-based open tool for intelligent robotic education.
Zainal et al. (2021)	/	/	/	/	IoT	/	/	/	Review on design thinking approach in learning IoT programming.
Leonor et al. (2022)	/	–	/	–	IoT	/	/	/	Image acquisition for IoT projects and the AI service for facial recognition.

The primary goal of this review study is to examine the current in-demand programming skills to support the core concept of Industry 5.0. According to the analysis in Table 5.1, problem-solving skills are the most required to support the future revolution industry, followed by technology use and development, working with people, and self-management. This result is consistent with the findings of a study conducted by Güğerçin and Güğerçin (2021), who predict that problem-solving skills will continue to be in demand, while another three skills will lead to in-demand skills in the future industry. Furthermore, a review of the literature reveals that human-centricity has moved to the forefront of core concepts in Industry 5.0.

Industry 5.0 encourages the collaboration and creativity of human experts and machines to foster an efficient, powerful, and innovative manufacturing environment (Maddikunta et al., 2022). It demonstrates that the current implementation in all domains is moving towards a more human-centric approach in line with future evolution and supporting the other two pillars of Industry 5.0, resilience and sustainability. The analysis also suggested that the enabling technology used in current studies is moving forward to meet future demand. Most studies successfully integrated new technologies such as robots and cobot, IoT, digital twin and simulation, augmented reality, and AI.

Finally, from the result of the analysis, it is also clearly shown that the current technologies and machine, programming, and CT have become the core implementation in collaborating humans and machines, such as image acquisition for IoT projects and the AI service for facial recognition by Dorantes et al. (2022), co-operation AI with Computer Aided Design (CAD) by Hunde and Woldeyohannes (2022), and a robot operating system (ROS)-based open tool for intelligent robotic education by Cañas et al. (2020). This result is supported by Maddikunta et al.'s (2021) study, which stated that education for Industry 5.0 is equipped with changes to adapt to future Industry 5.0. They also mentioned blockchain, quantum computing, cognitive edge with AI, human-machine coworking policies, and continuous training as future directions.

In conclusion, future programmers are required to master programming concepts, especially problem-solving and critical thinking concepts, before pursuing their careers in the real working environment. According to Kamaruddin et al. (2021), in order to understand future technology, one must first master CT skills. Although CT is frequently associated with computers and coding, it is important to note that it can be taught without the use of a computer or coding. Advances in computer science and the application of CT skills in real life have also contributed to economic and social development (Nuar & Rozan, 2019). The use of CT in scientific sciences and humanities was also required in order to solve real-world problems and make decisions (Aho, 2012). Thus, whether the subject is science or non-science, CT is required to generate new scientific problems. As a result, future programmers must be well-equipped with programming and technology knowledge, and citizens should have a basic understanding of CT to support Industry 5.0 (Relkin et al., 2021).

5.4   CT and way forward

In the context of Industry 5.0, CT emerges as a crucial skill for programmers navigating the difficulties of interconnected systems. Practical applications of CT are evident in scenarios where programmers leverage problem decomposition to address complex challenges. For instance, in a smart manufacturing setting, CT allows programmers to break down complex processes into manageable components, such as optimising robotic control, sensor integration, and data processing. Pattern recognition, a key aspect of CT, finds practical application in Industry 5.0 when programmers design algorithms to recognise meaningful patterns from the vast streams of real-time data generated by the IoT. It is demonstrated in predictive maintenance algorithms that identify patterns representative of potential equipment failures, enabling proactive intervention. Moreover, the abstraction principle is vital for creating models that capture essential aspects of interconnected components without probing into unnecessary complexities. For instance, creating an abstract representation of a manufacturing process's workflow facilitates efficient problem-solving and system optimisation.

Looking forward, integrating CT in programmers' development for Industry 5.0 extends to fostering collaboration between disciplines. Programmers need to be skilled at designing algorithms, writing code, and possessing a holistic understanding of industrial processes and systems. This interdisciplinary approach ensures that CT is seamlessly applied to real-world challenges, contributing to developing intelligent systems that align with the principles of Industry 5.0.

Acknowledgement

The authors wish to thank the Data Management and Software Solutions Research Lab, Universiti Utara Malaysia (UUM), for funding the fees for this article.

References

Adel, A. (2022). Future of industry 5.0 in society: Human-centric solutions, challenges and prospective research areas. *Journal of Cloud Computing*, *11*(1). https://doi.org/10.1186/s13677-022-00314-5

Adorno, D. P., Ugras, T., Quaicoe, J. S., Jecheva, V., Ogunyemi, A. A., Bauters, M., Toshkov, A., Ortakci, Y., Ozacar, K., Atasoy, F., Peri, D., Kocijancic, S., Rihtaršič, D., Cerar, Š, & Uvet, H. (2023). An innovative tailored instructional design for computer programming courses in engineering. *U.Porto Journal of Engineering*, *9*(3), 209–222. https://doi.org/10.24840/2183-6493_009-003_001898

Aho, A. V. (2012). Computation and computational thinking. *Computer Journal*, *55*(7), 833–835. https://doi.org/10.1093/comjnl/bxs074

Ajaykumar, G., Stiber, M., & Huang, C. M. (2021). Designing user-centric programming aids for kinesthetic teaching of collaborative robots. *Robotics and Autonomous Systems*, *145*, 103845. https://doi.org/10.1016/j.robot.2021.103845

Anderies, J. M., Folke, C., Walker, B., & Ostrom, E. (2013). Aligning key concepts for global change policy: Robustness, resilience, and sustainability. *Ecology and Society*, *18*(2). http://dx.doi.org/10.5751/ES-05178-180208

Bednar, P. M., & Welch, C. (2020). Socio-technical perspectives on smart working: Creating meaningful and sustainable systems. *Information Systems Frontiers*, *22*(2), 281–298. https://doi.org/10.1007/s10796-019-09921-1

Bocconi, S., Chioccariello, A., Dettori, G., Ferrari, A., Engelhardt, K., Kampylis, P., & Punie, Y. (2016, June). Developing computational thinking: Approaches and orientations in K-12 education. In *EdMedia+ innovate learning* (pp. 13–18). Association for the Advancement of Computing in Education (AACE).

Cañas, J. M., Perdices, E., García-Pérez, L., & Fernández-Conde, J. (2020). A ROS-based open tool for intelligent robotics education. *Applied Sciences (Switzerland)*, *10*(21), 1–20. https://doi.org/10.3390/app10217419

Carayannis, E. G., & Morawska-Jancelewicz, J. (2022). The futures of Europe: Society 5.0 and industry 5.0 as driving forces of future universities. *Journal of the Knowledge Economy*, *13*(4), 3445–3471. https://doi.org/10.1007/s13132-021-00854-2

Castro, L. M. C., Magana, A. J., Douglas, K. A., & Boutin, M. (2021). Analysing students' computational thinking practices in a first-year engineering course. *IEEE Access*, *9*, 33041–33050. https://doi.org/10.1109/ACCESS.2021.3061277.

Csizmadia, A., Curzon, P., Dorling, M., Humphreys, S., Ng, T., Selby, C., & Woollard, J. (2015). *Computational thinking: A guide for teachers*.

Demir, K. A., Döven, G., & Sezen, B. (2019). Industry 5.0 and human-robot coworking. *Procedia Computer Science*, *158*(January), 688–695. https://doi.org/10.1016/j.procs. 2019.09.104

Díaz-Lauzurica, B., & Moreno-Salinas, D. (2019). Computational thinking and robotics: A teaching experience in compulsory secondary education with students with high degree of apathy and demotivation. *Sustainability*, *11*(18), 5109. https://doi.org/10.3390/ su11185109

Giannakoulas, A., & Xinogalos, S. (2018). A pilot study on the effectiveness and acceptance of an educational game for teaching programming concepts to primary school students. *Education and Information Technologies*, *23*, 2029–2052. https://doi.org/10.1007/ s10639-018-9702-x

Grafton, R. Q., Doyen, L., Béné, C., Borgomeo, E., Brooks, K., Chu, L., & Wyrwoll, P. R. (2019). Realising resilience for decision-making. *Nature Sustainability*, *2*(10), 907–913. https://doi.org/10.1038/s41893-019-0376-1

Güğerçin, S., & Güğerçin, U. (2021). How employees survive in the industry 5.0 era: In-demand skills of the near future. *International Journal of Disciplines Economics & Administrative Scienves Studies*, *7*(31), 524–533 (e-ISSN:2587-2168). http://dx.doi. org/10.26728/ideas.452

Guzdial, M. (2008). Education: Paving the way for computational thinking. *Communications of the ACM*, *51*(8), 25–27. https://doi.org/10.1145/1378704.1378713

Hendry, D., Umbrello, S., Van Den Hoven, J., & Yoo, D. (2020). The future of value sensitive design. In International Conference on the Ethical and Social Impacts of ICTI, *18*(June). www.unirioja.es

Ilic, U., Haseski, H., & Tugtekin, U. (2018). Publication trends over 10 years of computational thinking research. *Contemporary Educational Technology*, *9*(2), 131–153. https:// doi.org/10.30935/cet.414798

International Society for Technology in Education (ISTE). (2018). Computational Thinking for All. Retrieved from https://www.iste.org/explore/articleDetail?articleid=152

Kaarlela, T., Arnarson, H., Pitkäaho, T., Shu, B., Solvang, B., & Pieskä, S. (2022). Common educational teleoperation platform for robotics utilising digital twins. *Machines*, *10*(7), 1–21. https://doi.org/10.3390/machines10070577

Kamaruddin, A. R. C., Low, J., & Sarwar, A. (2021). Enhancing the adoption of computational thinking education among the Malaysians to prepare for future industrial revolution. In ACM International Conference Proceeding Series (pp. 81–85). https://doi.org/ 10.1145/3502434.3502448

Kangungu, S. M., & Yatim, M. H. M. (2020). Teaching programming using the robot-based learning approach. *International Journal of Artificial Intelligence*, *7*(2), 22–28. https:// doi.org/10.36079/lamintang.ijai-0702.145

Kolade, O., & Owoseni, A. (2022). Employment 5.0: The work of the future and the future of work. *Technology in Society*, *71*, 102086. https://doi.org/10.1016/j.techsoc.2022. 102086

Leonor Estévez Dorantes, T., Bertani Hernández, D., León Reyes, A., & Elena Miranda Medina, C. (2022, February). Development of a powerful facial recognition system through an API using ESP32-Cam and Amazon Rekognition service as tools offered by

Industry 5.0. In 2022 the 5th International Conference on Machine Vision and Applications (ICMVA) (pp. 76–81). https://doi.org/10.1145/3523111.3523122

Li, C., Zheng, P., Yin, Y., Pang, Y., & Shengzeng, H. (2023). An AR-assisted deep reinforcement learning-based approach towards mutual-congnitive safe human-robot interaction. *Robotics and Computer-Integrated Manufacturing, 80*, 102471. https://doi.org/10.1016/j.rcim.2022.102471https://doi.org/10.1016/j.rcim.2022.102471

Liljaniemi, A., & Paavilainen, H. (2020). Using digital twin technology in engineering education–course concept to explore benefits and barriers. *Open Engineering, 10*(1), 377–385. https://doi.org/10.1515/eng-2020-0040

Lyon, J. A., & Magana, A. J. (2020). Computational thinking in higher education: A review of the literature. *Computer Applications in Engineering Education, 28*(5), 1174–1189. https://doi.org/10.1002/cae.22295

Maddikunta, K. R., Pham, Q.-V., & Predevi, B. (2022). Industry 5.0: A survey on enabling technologies and potential applications. *Journal of Industrial Information Integration, 26.* https://doi.org/10.1016/j.jii.2021.100257

Mannila, L., Dagiene, V., Demo, B., Grgurina, N., Mirolo, C., Rolandsson, L., & Settle, A. (2014). Computational thinking in K-9 education. In ITiCSE-WGR 2014 - Working Group Reports of the 2014 Innovation and Technology in Computer Science Education Conference (pp. 1–29). https://doi.org/10.1145/2713609.2713610

Mayr-Dorn, C., Winterer, M., Salomon, C., Hohensinger, D., & Fürschuss, H. (2023). Assessing industrial end-user programming of robotic production cells: A controlled experiment. *Journal of Systems and Software, 195.* https://doi.org/10.1016/j.jss.2022.111547

Nahavandi, S. (2019). Industry 5.0 – a human-centric solution. *Sustainability (Switzerland), 11*(16). https://doi.org/10.3390/su11164371

Narkhede, G., Pasi, B., Rajhans, N., & Kulkarni, A. (2023). Industry 5.0 and the future of sustainable manufacturing: A systematic literature review. *Business Strategy and Development, August*, 0–20. https://doi.org/10.1002/bsd2.272

Neumann, E. M., Vogel-Heuser, B., Haben, F., Krüger, M., & Wieringa, T. (2022). Introduction of an assistance system to support domain experts in programming low-code to leverage industry 5.0. *IEEE Robotics and Automation Letters, 7*(4), 10422–10429. https://doi.org/10.1109/LRA.2022.3193728

Nikum, K. (2022). Answers to the societal demands with education 5.0: Indian higher education system. *Journal of Engineering Education Transformations, 36*(Special Issue 1), 115–127. https://doi.org/10.16920/jeet/2022/v36is1/22184

Nuar, A. N. A., & Rozan, M. Z. A. (2019). Benefits of computational thinking in entrepreneurship. In International Conference on Research and Innovation in Information Systems, ICRIIS, *December-2019*(October). https://doi.org/10.1109/ICRIIS48246.2019.9073671

OECD (2005). *Trends in migration.* In OECD Fact Book.

Papert, S. (1996). An exploration in the space of mathematics educations metaphorical intentions. *International Journal of Computers for Mathematical Learning, 1* (1), 95–123.

Paucar-Curasma, R., Cerna-Ruiz, L. P., Acra-Despradel, C., Villalba-Condori, K. O., Massa-Palacios, L. A., Olivera-Chura, A., & Esteban-Robladillo, I. (2023). Development of computational thinking through STEM activities for the promotion of gender equality. *Sustainability (Switzerland), 15*(16). https://doi.org/10.3390/su151612335

Poláková, M., Suleimanová, J. H., Madzík, P., Copuš, L., Molnárová, I., & Polednová, J. (2023). Soft skills and their importance in the labour market under the conditions of industry 5.0. *Heliyon, 9*(8). https://doi.org/10.1016/j.heliyon.2023.e18670

Rada, M. Industry 5.0 Definition. 2020. URL https://michael-rada.medium.com/industry-5-0-definition-6a2f9922dc48

Rahman, N. A., Idris, M. R., & Baharudin, K. S. (2020). Development of educational kit for IoT online learning. *International Journal of Technology, Innovation and Humanities*, *1*(1), 26–32. https://doi.org/10.29210/881001

Raudmäe, R., Schumann, S., Vunder, V., Oidekivi, M., Nigol, K., Valner, R., Masnavi, H., Singh, A. K., Aabloo, A., & Kruusamäe, K. (n.d.). *ROBOTONT-Open-source and ROS-supported omnidirectional mobile robot for education and research*. https://doi.org/10.5281/zenodo.7897546

Regassa Hunde, B., & Debebe Woldeyohannes, A. (2022). Future prospects of computer-aided design (CAD) – A review from the perspective of artificial intelligence (AI), extended reality, and 3D printing. In *Results in engineering* (Vol. 14). Elsevier B.V. https://doi.org/10.1016/j.rineng.2022.100478

Relkin, E., de Ruiter, L. E., & Bers, M. U. (2021). Learning to code and the acquisition of computational thinking by young children. *Computers and Education, 169*(September 2020), 104222. https://doi.org/10.1016/j.compedu.2021.104222

Roveda, L., Veerappan, P., Maccarini, M., Bucca, G., Ajoudani, A., & Piga, D. (2023). A human-centric framework for robotic task learning and optimization. *Journal of Manufacturing Systems, 67*, 68–79. https://doi.org/10.1016/j.jmsy.2023.01.003

Ruppert, T., Darányi, A., Medvegy, T., Csereklei, D., & Abonyi, J. (2022). Demonstration laboratory of industry 4.0 retrofitting and operator 4.0 solutions: Education towards industry 5.0. *Retrofitting and Operator 4.0 Solutions: Education towards Industry 5.0. Sensors, 23*(1), 283.

Schmidbauer, C., Komenda, T., & Schlund, S. (2020). Teaching cobots in learning factories – user and usability-driven implications. *Procedia Manufacturing, 45*, 398–404. https://doi.org/10.1016/j.promfg.2020.04.043

Selby, C., Dorling, M., & Woollard, J. (2014). Evidence of assessing computational thinking.

Selby, C. C. (2014). *UNIVERSITY OF SOUTHAMPTON FACULTY OF SOCIAL AND HUMAN SCIENCES Southampton Education School How Can the Teaching of Programming Be Used to Enhance Computational Thinking Skills?*

Smuts, H., & Van der Merwe, A. (2022). Knowledge management in society 5.0: A sustainability perspective. *Sustainability (Switzerland), 14* (11), 6878. MDPI. https://doi.org/10.3390/su14116878

Voogt, J., Fisser, P., Good, J., Mishra, P., & Yadav, A. (2015). Computational thinking in compulsory education: Towards an agenda for research and practice. *Education and Information Technologies, 20*, 715–728. https://doi.org/10.1007/s10639-015-9412-6

Wing, J. M. (2006). Computational thinking. *Communications of the ACM, 49*(3), 33–35. https://doi.org/10.1145/1118178.1118215

Wing, J. M., & Stanzione, D. (2016). Progress in computational thinking, and expanding the HPC community. *Communications of the ACM, 59*(7), 10–11. Association for Computing Machinery. https://doi.org/10.1145/2933410

Zainal, S., Che Mohd Yusoff, R., Abas, H., Yaacub, S., & Megat Zainuddin, N. (2021). Review of design thinking approach in learning IoT programming. *International Journal of Advanced Research in Future Ready Learning and Education, 24*(1), 28–38.

6 Agile software test

Optimising quality assurance
in Industry 5.0 projects

*Samera Obaid Barraood[1], Haslina Mohd[2],
Fauziah Baharom[2], and Shafinah Farvin
Packeer Mohamed[2]*

[1] *Department of Computer Science, College of Computers
and Information Technology, Hadhramout University,
Hadhramout, Yemen*

[2] *School of Computing, Universiti Utara Malaysia, Kedah, Malaysia*

6.1 Agile software development

The agile software development (ASD) methodology is a workable software process that divides a project into smaller, manageable units that deal with time items, time control, and change risks (Rajasekhar & Shafi, 2014). The continuous changes in ASD methods require many efforts to be performed on testing activities (Beer & Felderer, 2018). The best way to ensure software quality is to do extensive software testing to discover faults in the system by executing a test case (TC). The quality of testing activities primarily depends on test case quality (TCQ), which is directly related to the quality of testing (Lai, 2017). The nature of TC construction is to obtain the necessary software coverage under testing, which produces quality software (Tran et al., 2019). Although the primary purpose of ASD methods is to get defect-free software, assessing TCQ is essential to understand how much testing is required and where potential testing attempts should be carried out (Ahmed et al., 2016).

A quality TC refers to a TC with a high chance of revealing defects with a minimum effort, providing more detailed results, and increasing system performance at a smaller cost (Gómez et al., 2016). Although TCQ is a promising approach for detecting software defects, software quality remains challenging for many organisations (Sekgweleo & Iyamu, 2022). Tricentis (2017) reported that the companies revealed more than $1.7 trillion in financial losses in 2017 caused by software failures. Moreover, in 2020, the cost of poor software in the United States was $2.08 trillion (Ba-Quttayyan et al., 2022; Krasner, 2021). Reviewing past studies on TCQ open issues in ASD is essential for several reasons, such as allowing researchers and development teams to learn from past studies for future optimisation of the TCQ. Although prior review studies primarily focus on TCQ in general, the studies on TCQ in ASD are lacking. Therefore, this chapter is an attempt to bridge this gap.

DOI: 10.1201/9781003479727-6

Agile testing still has issues that must be studied and addressed for reasons such as requirement changes (Rehman et al., 2020; Sekgweleo & Iyamu, 2022). In addition, because of the short iterations, there is not enough time for the testers to achieve their tasks, which results in failing some TCs. Due to the errors, identifying and mitigating them in the early stages of the development process need less cost for corrections than when the errors are detected later (Stradowski & Madeyski, 2022), which is one of the testing sustainability goals. Again, because of testers' fatigue as a result of the long hours of work and, consequently, poor quality testing (Sekgweleo & Iyamu, 2022). The software that delivers with some bugs adversely impacts some of its functionalities that are not working very well, leading to customer dissatisfaction with the software quality, which is significant in Industry 5.0 (Fischbach et al., 2020).

Industry 5.0 primarily enhances customer satisfaction (Maddikunta et al., 2022). Since a good TCQ is essential to eliminate errors, defects, or misinterpretations (Juhnke et al., 2021), it is crucial to identify the shortcomings of TCQ in the agile testing process, which leads to increased software quality and sustainability, and this is one of Industry 5.0 advantages. With such an intention, this chapter tries to answer the following research question: What are the problems in TCs in agile testing? Thoroughly searching and reviewing the published works to identify and extract the problems that lead to poor-quality software testing and address them will increase software sustainability in Industry 5.0.

In the IT industry, project management has grown increasingly complex. Short deadlines, constant technical advancements, and shifting needs have driven the profession to provide competitive software to the market at an ever-increasing rate (Lalic et al., 2022). As a result, the project managers knew that their projects needed a different method to develop than the traditional method. Therefore, a new method (i.e., ASD) has arisen for project management (Lalic et al., 2022). Tiny multidisciplinary teams incorporated into the Toyota Lean production system boosted customer satisfaction and quality by generating small, efficient systems and eliminating unneeded ones in the 1980s, marking the beginning of the ASD method. The Agile Manifesto was published in 2001, explaining the four agile values, as well as 12 core principles, because the values alone are insufficient to build a foundational philosophy for software development (which details four values) (Chovanova et al., 2020). Agile is defined by Boehm and Turner (2005) as "a lightweight software development approach which emphasises iterative, incremental, self-organising and emergent practices." Nowadays, businesses operate in a global, rapidly changing environment (StateOfAgile, 2020).

Since managing projects in the IT area has grown difficult with the waterfall method, ASD has made an official appearance on the global stage (Gorgadze, 2021). As a result, rapid software development and delivery, known as ASD, is the most critical requirement for most business systems. They are meant to quickly produce and deliver useful software (Padmini et al., 2018). The agile framework is an umbrella term for software development methodologies with several iterative and incremental development patterns (Padmini et al., 2018). Agile means moving easily and quickly, and when it comes to software development, it refers to the sharp focus on short iterations (Padmini et al., 2018). Nowadays, around 20 ASD methods are known, utilised for different goals, have further specifics, and are used at varying frequencies (Gorgadze, 2021). The company can use a suitable method based on the type of project, the resources, constraints, tools, the client, personnel, and deadlines (Orlov et al., 2021). The most common ASD method used is scrum, based on the survey conducted by the authors in 2020 and by Gorgadze (2021).

6.2 Agile software testing methodologies

Software testing is a crucial component of every project that raises the quality and productivity of agile projects (Gil et al., 2016; Nawaz & Malik, 2008). It is a sequence of procedures that starts with the requirements phase during the early stages of the product's life cycle (Nawaz & Malik, 2008). Poor-quality TCs will fail to serve their purpose in the first defensive line in bug prevention (Grano, 2019). It may also negatively impact program comprehension and maintenance (Lucr et al., 2023). In the agile approach, testing practices adhere to agile principles and are appropriately planned to accommodate constant changes in requirements (Yu, 2018). It also refers to testing an application to learn about it and integrate it into the agile development process, unlike traditional testing, in which the testing is a phase (Harichandan et al., 2014). Agile testing shares similar goals with traditional testing but differs in team structure. All team members are involved in agile testing, with professional testers making remarkable contributions (Kayes et al., 2016).

Agile quadrants are used to identify and plan the team's testing needs (Crispin & Gregory, 2009). The quadrants help to emphasise the whole team's responsibility for testing to build software products with high quality in agile (Yu et al., 2021). Agile testing uses continuous feedback, which allows users to redirect the process during software development. The agile testing framework can be divided into business-facing and technology-facing tests (Yu et al., 2021). Business-facing tests describe test scenarios and their results, where software quality is critiqued to discover inadequacies without focusing on the technical coding of software (Yu et al., 2021). Technology-facing tests are more concerned with non-functional requirements than functional ones (Crispin & Gregory, 2009), as in Figure 6.1.

The agile testing process is based on iterative methodologies and overcomes the disadvantages of sequential models (Gil et al., 2016). After constant testing, all errors are fixed in each iteration, resulting in continuously maintained clean code (Gil et al., 2016). The TCs in agile must be developed as the requirements evolve (Black, 2017). Continuous requirements change and project duration calls for changing and increasing TCs (Beer & Felderer, 2018). Testing tasks are carried out in each iteration, starting with creating a test plan, arranging user stories by priority in the product backlog, and establishing acceptance criteria for testable user stories. Then, TCs are developed according to the acceptance criteria, as shown in Figure 6.2.

TCs are designed using one of the testing techniques, and the standard techniques are black box and white box, where each has some techniques for creating

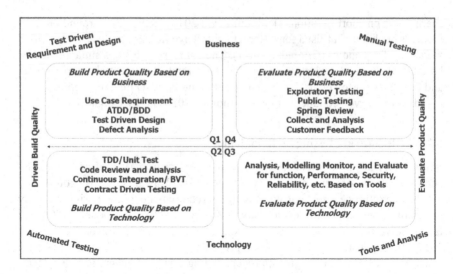

Figure 6.1 Business and technology layers of agile testing.

TCs (Barraood et al., 2021; Black, 2017). These techniques are also used in traditional methodologies and agile methods, but in agile, the documentation way is different (Black, 2017). Black box testing assesses the system's compliance with specific functional requirements (Galin, 2004). It is also called functionality or specified-based testing, which identifies errors only based on software defects discovered through its wrong output. In contrast, this type of testing ignores the internal calculation paths of a component (Galin, 2004). The reliance will be on

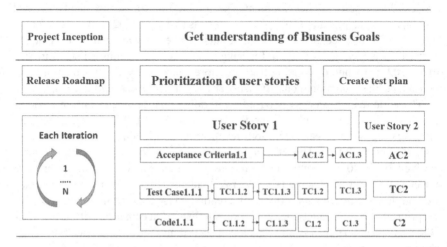

Figure 6.2 Testing activities during iteration.

Source: Adapted from Rajasekhar and Shafi (2014).

the testers' experience, knowledge, and skill to carry out the tests (Black, 2017). In the ASD context, TCs can be created from the test bases and acceptance criteria of user stories by using black box test design techniques (Black, 2017). The methods for designing TCs in a black box include equivalence class partitioning, boundary value analysis, and decision tables (Black, 2017). On the other hand, white-box testing provides information about the system's internal workings and enables the tester to clearly understand the application's structure and source code (Honest, 2019). Techniques for creating TCs based on the system's internal workings include control flow, basis path, data flow, and loop testing (Nidhra & Dondeti, 2012).

6.3 Agile test case issues

The swift transition towards Industry 5.0 has revealed considerable promise and notable challenges in establishing sustainable software engineering practices (Anbarkhan, 2023). Testing is a fundamental software development process with significant potential to promote sustainability in software development. Agile testing can overcome the limitations of traditional testing by conducting testing frequently, early testing, adapting to frequent changes in requirements, and working in short iterations and releases (Stradowski & Madeyski, 2022). In addition, continuous feedback redirects the development process (Gil et al., 2016). However, these benefits of agile can cause some challenges. As reported by Padmini et al. (2018) and Rehman et al. (2020), the testing challenges are (1) fixed time of testing activities, (2) welcomed requirement changes, (3) insufficient test coverage, (4) code breakage frequently, (5) deferring essential tests, (6) lack of requirements documentation, (7) the communication between developers and customers creates testing activities challenges, (8) testing infrastructure, (9) insufficient API testing, and (10) lacking focused testing.

However, the testing is generally neglected and not tracked (Unudulmaz & Kalıpsız, 2020). As TC is an essential part of testing, we will focus on its issues to increase testing sustainability in Industry 5.0. Industry 5.0 is expected to solve this issue through increased human participation. Since a TC represents the test instructions for a tester, it consists of a group of conditions or variables that a tester uses to determine whether a system meets the requirements and functions correctly (Olausson et al., 2013). In ASD, TCs are written based on the acceptance criteria by the tester in an initial sprint phase. The tester illustrates the requirements for user stories one by one shortly before commencing the coding, typically just a few days or hours prior (Kayes et al., 2016).

Good enough testing should have a sufficient quality assessment at a reasonable cost (Goeschl et al., 2010). The quality TCs are very important for assuring and gaining the benefits in six aspects: (1) reducing defects, (2) development cost, (3) the delivery time of the product, (4) improving testing adequacy, (5) meeting customer requirements, and 6) the most important is improving the software quality (Barraood et al., 2022). In writing TCs, it is crucial to ensure that testing reaches a certain level of comprehensiveness, specification, and code coverage

Table 6.1 Agile test case issues

TC Issues	Source
Elaborating requirements insufficiently	Kārkliņa and Pirta (2018)
Inconsistent, incomplete, incorrect requirements	Beer et al. (2017)
Undefined user stories and acceptance criteria properly	Fischbach et al. (2020), Padmini et al. (2018)
It does not refer to quality standards of software testing	Fischbach et al. (2020), Padmini et al. (2018)
TCs not written upfront with requirements	Uikey and Suman (2012)
Lack of traceability between TCs and acceptance criteria	Fischbach et al. (2020)
Incomplete TCs	Fischbach et al. (2020)
Flaky TCs	Rahman and Rigby (2018), Sundaram (2021)
Insufficient test coverage	Padmini et al. (2018), Rehman et al. (2020)
Lack of documentation on the requirements	Padmini et al. (2018), Rehman et al. (2020)

(Romli et al., 2020). Missing test targets, procedures, or expected results reduce TCQ (Jovanovikj et al., 2018). The issues of TCs in ASD are listed in Table 6.1.

6.4   Implementing agile testing practices in Industry 5.0 environments

In the software industry, the incorporation of ASD methodologies has transpired progressively. ASD methods need testing practices to support their implementation. Testing in agile has been extensively employed in a range of testing practices. Testing in the context of ASD heavily relies on the expertise of testers and developers when performing testing process activities and crafting TCs (Black, 2017). It is particularly crucial in today's Industry 5.0, which seeks to boost production through the application of critical thinking by humans. The typical techniques employed in testing practice are test-driven development (TDD), acceptance test-driven development (ATDD), behaviour-driven development (BDD), and exploratory testing (ET) (Barraood et al., 2021).

TDD is one of the second quadrants of the agile testing framework (Yu et al., 2021). This method follows the sequence of writing TCs before coding, meaning testing starts before the actual programming. TDD is the preferred development methodology among most ASD methods. It seems suitable for rapidly changing contexts and, thus, good support for the ASD methodology (Thi & Tra, 2020). ATDD depends on the cooperation of testers, developers, and customers to create testable requirements, define acceptance tests and expedite the production of high-quality software. The customer pays attention to the problem, and the developer focuses on how to solve the problem while the tester checks what could go wrong. Cooperation and knowledge sharing are crucial in Industry 5.0. ATDD is centred around predetermining acceptance criteria and acceptance TCs. Each program component must pass an acceptance test before it can be merged into the main branch (Atawneh, 2019).

The testing depends on the software's expected behaviour in the BDD method. BDD starts with specifying the wanted software behaviour and then programming the implementation to produce the desired behaviour. BDD and ATDD are in the first quadrant of the agile testing framework, which clarifies, verifies, and builds high-quality requirements and design products (Yu et al., 2021). ET is a significant activity testing in quadrant 4 (see Figure 6.1). In this method, the learning, design, and execution go together in one test approach (Crispin & Gregory, 2009). ET can immediately continue from the program's interesting point, saving time and redundant work (Atawneh, 2019). This capability proves highly efficient within the framework of Industry 5.0, which strives to optimise efficiency while minimising costs and maximising precision (Maddikunta et al., 2022).

Most studies utilise traditional development approaches but cannot tackle the challenges and limitations of balancing software quality and rapid delivery. Previous research has also commonly faced an issue with no well-defined description of measuring and accessing the quality factors of TCs. Therefore, first, there is a need for further research on effective TCQ based on apparent requirements and organisational goals. Secondly, since ASD emphasises organisational goals and human expertise, more research is needed to investigate a more comprehensive organisational artefact that may strengthen future findings.

6.5 Maximising efficiency and quality through agile testing in Industry 5.0

ISO-IEC 25010 (2011) defines software quality as "the degree to which a software product satisfies stated and implied needs when used under specified conditions." Identifying and addressing problems before delivering the system and defining and assessing software quality before deploying the system will benefit the software, decrease maintenance costs, and improve the company's reputation that developed the software, which is critical in Industry 5.0 projects. As a result, this research focuses on optimising testing quality by identifying the issues of TCQ, which will affect the entire quality of the testing process, affecting the product quality. Software testing is an essential activity in the ASD environment in Industry 5.0. Agile testing contributes to sustainability by promoting resource efficiency and responsible resource management (Beer et al., 2021). The testing process is heavily influenced by how TCs are written and managed.

Agile teams must understand the weaknesses of TCs, as this helps to write effective ones quickly. That is why this research focused on pinpointing the problems with TCQ in the agile testing process in Industry 5.0 and providing areas of research opportunities in software testing. In the context of Industry 5.0, the synergy between humans and machines is harnessed to enhance operational efficiency by incorporating human cognitive abilities and innovation into seamlessly integrating workflows with intelligent systems (Maddikunta et al., 2022).

The TCQ in ASD projects faces some challenges. It is better to identify the factors of TCQ to address these challenges. Examples of the essential quality factors that make TCQ better are TC readability, understandability, specified purpose, efficiency, independence, repeatability, and correctness. The matters of TCQ are identified in this chapter as the source for developing our proposed model, which aids in assessing the TCQ in ASD projects.

Acknowledgement

This work was supported by the Ministry of Higher Education (MoHE) of Malaysia through The Fundamental Research Grant Scheme for Research Acculturation of Early Career Researchers (RACER/1/2019/ICT01/UUM//1).

References

Ahmed, I., Gopinath, R., Brindescu, C., Groce, A., & Jensen, C. (2016). Can testedness be effectively measured? In *Proceedings of the 2016 24th ACM SIGSOFT International Symposium on Foundations of Software Engineering* (pp. 547–558). https://doi.org/10.1145/2950290.2950324

Anbarkhan, S. H. (2023). A fuzzy-TOPSIS-based approach to assessing sustainability in software engineering: An industry 5.0 perspective. *Sustainability, 15*(18), 13844. https://doi.org/10.3390/su151813844

Atawneh, S. (2019). The analysis of current state of agile software development. *Journal of Theoretical and Applied Information Technology, 97*(22), 3197–3208.

Ba-Quttayyan, B., Mohd, H., & Yusof, Y. (2022). A critical analysis of swarm intelligence for regression test case prioritization. *Journal of Theoretical and Applied Information Technology, 100*(12), 3997–4025.

Barraood, S. O., Mohd, H., & Baharom, F. (2021). A comparison study of software testing activities in agile methods. In Knowledge Management International Conference (KMICe) Virtual Conference (pp. 130–137). https://soc.uum.edu.my/kmice/proceedings/2021/pdf/CR168.pdf

Barraood, S. O., Mohd, H., & Baharom, F. (2022). An initial investigation of the effect of quality factors on agile test case quality through experts review. *Cogent Engineering, 9*(1), 1–26. https://doi.org/10.1080/23311916.2022.2082121

Beer, A., & Felderer, M. (2018). Measuring and improving testability of system requirements in an industrial context by applying the goal question metric approach. In *5th International Workshop on Requirements Engineering and Testing Measuring* (pp. 25–32). https://doi.org/10.1145/3195538.3195542

Beer, A., Felderer, M., Lorey, T., & Mohacsi, S. (2021). Aspects of sustainable test processes. In *2021 IEEE/ACM International Workshop on Body of Knowledge for Software Sustainability (BoKSS)* (pp. 9–10). https://doi.org/10.1109/BoKSS52540.2021.00012

Beer, A., Junker, M., Femmer, H., & Felderer, M. (2017). Initial investigations on the influence of requirement smells on test-case design. In 2017 IEEE 25th International Requirements Engineering Conference Workshops (REW) (pp. 323–326). https://doi.org/10.1109/REW.2017.43

Black, R. (2017). *Agile testing foundations an ISTQB foundation level agile tester guide*. BCS Learning & Development Ltd.

Boehm, B., & Turner, R. (2005). Management challenges to implement agile processes. *Traditional Development Organizations, 22*(5), 30–39. https://doi.org/10.1109/MS.2005.129

Chovanova, H. H., Husovic, R., Babcanova, D., & Makysova, H. (2020). Agile project management—what is it? In 2020 18th International Conference on Emerging eLearning Technologies and Applications (ICETA) (pp. 167–175). https://doi.org/10.1109/ICETA51985.2020.9379181

Crispin, L., & Gregory, J. (2009). *Agile testing: A practical guide for testers and agile teams* (1st ed.). Pearson Education, Inc.

Fischbach, J., Femmer, H., Mendez, D., Fucci, D., & Vogelsang, A. (2020). What makes agile test artifacts useful? An activity-based quality model from a practitioners' perspective. *ESEM '20*, 1–10. https://doi.org/10.1145/3382494.3421462

Galin, D. (2004). *Software quality assurance from theory to implementation*. Pearson Education Limited.

Gil, C., Diaz, J., Orozco, M., de la Hoz, A., de la Hoz, E., & Morales, R. (2016). Agile testing practices in software quality: State of the art review. *Journal of Theoretical and Applied Information Technology, 92*(1), 28–36. http://hdl.handle.net/11323/727

Goeschl, S., Herp, M., & Wais, C. (2010). When agile meets OO testing: A case study. In *Proceedings of the 1st Workshop on Testing Object-Oriented Systems* (p. 10). https://doi.org/10.1145/1890692.1890702

Gómez, O. S., Monte, B., & Monte, B. (2016). Impact of CS programs on the quality of test cases generation: An empirical study categories and subject descriptors. *ICSE '16 Companion*, 374–383. http://dx.doi.org/10.1145/2889160.2889190

Gorgadze, N. (2021). Agile project management approach, methods and its application in Georgia. *Globalization and Business, 12*, 191–196. https://doi.org/10.35945/gb.2021.12.027

Grano, G. (2019). A new dimension of test quality: Assessing and generating higher quality unit test cases. In *The 28th ACM SIGSOFT International Symposium on Software Testing and Analysis (ISSTA '19)* (July 15–19). https://doi.org/10.1145/3293882.3338984

Harichandan, S., Panda, N., & Acharya, A. A. (2014). Scrum testing with backlog management in agile development environment. *International Journal of Computer Science and Engineering, 2*(3), 187–192. http://www.ijcseonline.org/pub_paper/38-IJCSE-00144.pdf

Honest, N. (2019). Role of testing in software development life cycle. *International Journal of Computer Sciences and Engineering, 7*(5), 886–889. https://doi.org/10.26438/ijcse/v7i5.886889

ISO-IEC 25010. (2011). *ISO-IEC 25010: 2011 systems and software engineering-systems and software quality requirements and evaluation (SQuaRE)-system and software quality models*. ISO. https://doi.org/DOI:10.3403/30215101

Jovanovikj, I., Narasimhan, V., Engels, G., & Sauer, S. (2018). Context-specific quality evaluation of test cases. *MODELSWARD*, 594–601. https://doi.org/10.5220/0006724405940601

Juhnke, K., Tichy, M., & Houdek, F. (2021). Challenges concerning test case specifications in automotive software testing: Assessment of frequency and criticality. *Software Quality Journal, 29*(1), 39–100. https://doi.org/10.1007/s11219-020-09523-0

Kārkliņa, K., & Pirta, R. (2018). Quality metrics in agile software development projects. *Information Technology & Management Science (RTU Publishing House), 21*, 54–59. https://doi.org/10.7250/itms-2018-0008

Kayes, I., Sarker, M., & Chakareski, J. (2016). Product backlog rating: A case study on measuring test quality in scrum. *Innovations in Systems and Software Engineering, 12*(4), 303–317. https://doi.org/10.1007/s11334-016-0271-0

Krasner, H. (2021). The cost of poor software quality in the US: A 2020 report. In *Consortium Inf. Softw. Quality^{TM} (CISQ^{TM})*.

Lai, S.-T. (2017). Test case quality management procedure for enhancing the efficiency of IID continuous testing. *Journal of Software, 12*(10), 794–806. https://doi.org/10.17706/jsw.12.10.794-806

Lalic, D. C., Lalic, B., Delić, M., Gracanin, D., & Stefanovic, D. (2022). How project management approach impact project success? From traditional to agile. *International Journal of Managing Projects in Business*. https://doi.org/10.1108/IJMPB-04-2021-0108

Lucr, D., Marcelo, A., Vincenzi, R., Almeida, E. S. D., & Ahmed, I.. (2023). *Test case quality: An empirical study on belief and evidence*. 1–12. https://doi.org/10.48550/arXiv.2307.06410

Maddikunta, P. K. R., Pham, Q. V., B, P., Deepa, N., Dev, K., Gadekallu, T. R., Ruby, R., & Liyanage, M. (2022). Industry 5.0: A survey on enabling technologies and potential applications. *Journal of Industrial Information Integration, 26*(February). https://doi.org/10.1016/j.jii.2021.100257

Nawaz, A., & Malik, K. M. (2008). Software testing process in agile development. In *Computer Science Master Thesis*. Blekinge Institute of Technology.

Nidhra, S., & Dondeti, J. (2012). Black box and white box testing techniques—A literature review. *International Journal of Embedded Systems and Applications (IJESA), 2*(2), 29–50. https://doi.org/10.5121/ijesa.2012.2204

Olausson, M., Rossbreg, J., Ehn, J., & Sköld, M. (2013). Pro team foundation service. In *Apress* (illustrate). Apress.

Orlov, E. V., Rogulenko, T. M., Smolyakov, O. A., Oshovskaya, N. V., Zvorykina, T. I., Rostanets, V. G., & Dyundik, E. P. (2021). Comparative analysis of the use of Kanban and Scrum methodologies in it projects. *Universal Journal of Accounting and Finance, 9*(4), 693–700. https://doi.org/10.13189/ujaf.2021.090415

Padmini, K. V. J., Kankanamge, P. S., Bandara, H. M. N. D., & Perera, G. (2018). Challenges faced by agile testers: A case study. In *2018 Moratuwa Engineering Research Conference (MERCon)* (pp. 431–436). https://doi.org/10.1109/MERCon.2018.8421968

Rahman, M. T., & Rigby, P. C. (2018). The impact of failing, flaky, and high failure tests on the number of crash reports associated with Firefox builds. In *Proceedings of the 2018 26th ACM Joint Meeting on European Software Engineering Conference and Symposium on the Foundations of Software Engineering* (pp. 857–862). https://doi.org/10.1145/3236024.3275529

Rajasekhar, P., & Shafi, R. M. (2014). Agile software development and testing: Approach and challenges in advanced distributed systems. *Global Journal of Computer Science and Technology, 14*(1), 7–10.

Rehman, A. U., Nawaz, A., & Abbas, M. (2020). Agile methods: Testing challenges, solutions & tool support. In *2020 14th International Conference on Open Source Systems and Technologies (ICOSST)* (pp. 1–5). https://doi.org/10.1109/ICOSST51357.2020.9332965

Romli, R., Sarker, S., Omar, M., & Mahmod, M. (2020). Automated test cases and test automated test cases and test data generation for dynamic structural testing in automatic programming assessment using MC/DC. *International Journal on Advanced Science, Engineering and Information Technology, 10*(1), 120. https://doi.org/10.18517/ijaseit.10.1.10166

Sekgweleo, T., & Iyamu, T. (2022). Understanding the factors that influence software testing through moments of translation. *Journal of Systems and Information Technology, 24*(3), 202–220. https://doi.org/10.1108/JSIT-07-2021-0125

StateOfAgile. (2020). *The 14th annual state of agile report*. https://www.qagile.pl/wp-content/uploads/2020/06/14th-annual-state-of-agile-report.pdf

Stradowski, S., & Madeyski, L. (2022). Exploring the challenges in software testing of the 5G system at Nokia: A survey. *Information and Software Technology*, 107067. https://doi.org/10.1016/j.infsof.2022.107067

Sundaram, A. (2021). Technology based overview on software testing trends, techniques, and challenges. *International Journal of Engineering Applied Sciences and Technology*, 6(1). https://doi.org/10.33564/ijeast.2021.v06i01.011

Thi, L., & Tra, B. (2020). *BDD in agile testing: An experimental study*. 130–136. https://doi.org/10.1108/JSIT-07-2021-0125

Tran, H. K. V., Ali, N. B., Börstler, J., & Unterkalmsteiner, M.. (2019). Test-case quality–understanding practitioners' perspectives. In International Conference on Product-Focused Software Process Improvement (pp. 37–52). https://doi.org/10.1007/978-3-030-35333-9_3

Tricentis. (2017). *Software fail watch: 5th edition*.

Uikey, N., & Suman, U. (2012). An empirical study to design an effective agile project management framework. In *Proceedings of the CUBE International Information Technology Conference* (pp. 385–390). https://doi.org/10.1145/2381716.2381788

Unudulmaz, A., & Kalıpsız, O. (2020). TMMI integration with agile and test process. In ACM EASE Conference (EASE'20). https://doi.org/10.1145/3383219.3386124

Yu, J. (2018). Design and application of a testing framework of online course based on agile. *IOP Conference Series: Materials Science and Engineering*, 394(3), 32099. https://doi.org/10.1088/1757-899X/394/3/032099

Yu, J., Zhu, S., Zhang, J., Chen, Y., Wu, N., & Mei, Y. (2021). An agile testing framework of four quadrants. *Journal of Physics: Conference Series* https://doi.org/10.1088/1742-6596/1792/1/012004

7 Smartphone penetration test

Securing Industry 5.0 mobile applications

*Eka Wahyu Aditya[1], Nur Haryani Zakaria[2],
Fazli Azzali[2], and Mohamad Nazim Jambli[3]*

[1]*School of Computing and Informatics, Albukhary
International University, Kedah, Malaysia*

[2]*School of Computing, Universiti Utara Malaysia,
Kedah, Malaysia*

[3]*Faculty of Computer Science and Information
Technology, Universiti Malaysia Sarawak,
Sarawak, Malaysia*

7.1 Introduction

In the era of Industry 5.0, characterised by the seamless integration of digital technologies into industrial processes, the role of mobile applications has become pivotal. As Industry 5.0 emphasises the convergence of cyber-physical systems, the reliance on smartphones for various industrial applications has witnessed a significant impact. However, with this increased integration comes an inherent vulnerability, demanding a proactive approach to ensure the robust security of mobile applications (Chan, 2020). This brings us to the focus of this chapter, which is on using smartphones to conduct penetration tests. In the realm of Industry 5.0, where the boundaries between the digital and physical are blurred, securing mobile applications becomes a paramount concern. Penetration testing, a practice employed to assess the vulnerabilities of systems, takes on a new significance when applied to smartphones in the industrial context.

This chapter explores the intricacies of smartphone penetration testing and its critical role in fortifying mobile applications within the framework of Industry 5.0. As we navigate the evolving landscape of industrial digitisation, understanding how to secure mobile applications on the ubiquitous smartphone becomes a necessity and a strategic imperative. In the subsequent sections, we will unravel the importance of penetration testing for smartphone applications, highlighting how the penetration test can be done via smartphones. This chapter will then highlight some advantages and disadvantages of using smartphones to conduct penetration tests compared to usual personal computers. This chapter ends with a discussion to conclude the topic with some future work being shared for interested researchers in the same domain.

DOI: 10.1201/9781003479727-7

7.2 Understanding the importance of penetration testing for smartphone applications

In the contemporary digital landscape, where smartphones have seamlessly integrated into the fabric of our daily lives, the importance of penetration testing for smartphone applications cannot be overstated. This process of evaluating the security of mobile applications by simulating real-world attacks is not merely a technical exercise but a vital safeguard against an array of threats (Reuvid, 2021). Penetration testing for smartphone applications is essential for protecting sensitive data. Smartphone applications often collect and store sensitive information, such as user credentials, payment details, and personal identification. On the other hand, penetration testing rigorously assesses the security of data storage and transmission mechanisms within the app, identifying vulnerabilities that could lead to data breaches. By pre-emptively discovering and addressing these issues, organisations can prevent unauthorised access to sensitive data, protecting users and the business. Secondly, penetration testing for smartphone applications is vital for mitigating financial risks. The aftermath of a security breach can be financially devastating. Costs may include legal fees, regulatory fines, customer compensation, and expenses associated with investigating the breach. Penetration testing helps mitigate these financial risks by identifying vulnerabilities before attackers can exploit them. Addressing these issues proactively is often far less expensive than dealing with the fallout of a data breach (Xichen et al., 2022).

Besides that, penetration testing also helps to maintain users' trust, which is paramount for the success of any smartphone application. Users expect their data to be handled securely. A security breach can shatter this trust, leading to users uninstalling the app or leaving negative reviews (Jang et al., 2013). Penetration testing helps ensure the app remains secure, preserving user confidence and loyalty. Many industries are subject to strict regulations governing the protection of user data, such as the General Data Protection Regulation (GDPR) in Europe or the Health Insurance Portability and Accountability Act (HIPAA) in the healthcare industry (Lee et al., 2023). Penetration testing helps organisations comply with these regulations by identifying and addressing vulnerabilities that could result in data breaches. Non-compliance can lead to substantial fines and legal consequences.

Cyber threats evolve rapidly. New attack techniques and vulnerabilities are constantly emerging. Regular penetration testing keeps an application's security posture current. It allows organisations to adapt to new threats by identifying and mitigating vulnerabilities that may not have been known when the app was initially developed. Many smartphone applications rely on third-party services or APIs for functionality, such as payment processing or location services (Engel et al., 2022). These integrations can introduce security risks if not adequately assessed. Penetration testing ensures that security is maintained across all aspects of the application, including external connections.

An application's reputation is closely tied to its security. Users are more likely to trust and engage with an app they perceive as secure. By proactively addressing vulnerabilities through penetration testing, organisations enhance their reputation, attracting more users and building brand loyalty. Even if unintentional, data leaks can lead to significant consequences, including legal actions and loss of trust. Penetration testing helps to identify potential weaknesses that could result in data leaks, allowing organisations to implement safeguards to prevent such incidents. Penetration testing for smartphone applications is a multifaceted process that safeguards sensitive data, mitigates financial risks, maintains user trust, ensures regulatory compliance, adapts to evolving threats, secures third-party integrations, enhances reputation, and prevents data leaks (Carranza & DeCusatis, 2016). It is a strategic investment in security and the application's long-term success. As the digital landscape continues to evolve, the importance of robust security measures, including regular penetration testing, will only grow.

7.3   Performing comprehensive penetration testing on Industry 5.0 mobile applications

In order to perform comprehensive penetration testing, Kali NetHunter Lite is available on the official Kali Linux website (KaliLinux, 2023). It was then installed on all rooted Android devices with a custom recovery. The whole NetHunter experience requires a device-specific kernel that has been purpose-built for Kali NetHunter. The NetHunter GitLab repository contains over 164 kernels for over 65 devices. Kali Linux publishes over 25 images for the most popular devices on their official NetHunter download page. Before installing the NetHunter on top of our Android smartphone, we need to download the NetHunter image. Official release NetHunter images for specific supported devices can be downloaded from the Kali Linux page at the URL "kali.org/get-kali/". Check that the SHA256 checksum of the NetHunter zip image matches the values listed on the download page once the zip file has been completely downloaded. If the SHA256 hash sums do not match, the installation process must not be continued.

Once the software has been downloaded, the next step is to prepare the Android devices, which includes:

1 Installing "Team Win Recovery Project" as a custom recovery.
2 Installing "Magisk" to root the device.
3 Disabling force encryption may be required if TWRP cannot access the data partition.
4 If a user has a custom recovery, all that remains is to flash the NetHunter installer zip file onto the Android device.

Once everything is prepared, the installation process will begin. The complete process of installation can be found in Callaham (2023), whereby the steps are summarised below:

1 Once the smartphone and the Kali NetHunter Lite ROM are prepared, a user should extract the Zip file. Then go to/data/app and install the applications in that folder.

2 Open up the preferred root explorer app, and go to "/data/data/com.offsec. nethunter/files/scripts".

3 Copy all the files and paste them into/system/bin (if the folder is unavailable or content is not in files/scripts, open the NetHunter app and then close it and check again).

4 Open the NetHunter app, go to the Kali Chroot Manager, and install Minimal Chroot.

5 Open Terminal Emulator or nh-terminal and choose KALI. It will open up the Kali shell. The user may be prompted to allow root permission.

6 Run the following commands in the terminal one by one: "apt-get update", "apt-get upgrade", "apt-get dist-upgrade", and "apt-get install kali-linux-nethunter".

There are multiple ways of installing Kali NetHunter Lite on smartphones, and the steps chosen in this study are due to its simplicity and the safest way to install the Kali NetHunter inside our smartphone. In order to mitigate any error and malware that could occur after installing, we suggest downloading all the software and images from the official website of Kali Linux NetHunter Lite. Kali NetHunter Lite offers several features and tools summarised in Tables 7.1 and 7.2, respectively.

Table 7.1 The features of Kali NetHunter

Feature	Description
App Store	A feature that allows users to download and install additional tools and utilities within the Kali NetHunter environment.
Kali CLI	The command-line interface for Kali Linux provides access to a wide range of security and penetration testing tools.
KeX Manager	A feature that enables users to access the Kali Linux desktop environment from their Android device.
Custom Commands	A feature that allows users to create custom commands for the Kali NetHunter command-line interface.
Home Screen	The main screen of the Kali NetHunter interface provides access to various tools and features.
NetHunter App	A collection of mobile penetration testing and security assessment tools specific to the Kali NetHunter environment.
Kali Chroot Manager	A feature that enables users to manage the chroot environment, which is used to run Kali Linux on an Android device.
Kali Services	A set of services included in the Kali NetHunter environment, such as SSH and FTP, can be used for various security and penetration testing tasks.

Table 7.2 The Kali NetHunter's attack tools

Attack's tool	Description
Searchsploit	A tool that allows users to search for and exploit known vulnerabilities in various software and systems.
NMAP scan	A tool that allows users to scan networks and hosts for open ports and services, which can be used to identify potential security vulnerabilities.
DuckHunter HID	A tool that allows users to perform "HID attacks" by emulating a USB keyboard and sending pre-defined keystrokes to a target system.
MAC Changer	A tool that allows users to change the Media Access Control (MAC) address of a network interface, which can be used to evade detection or impersonate another device.
MITM Framework	A tool that allows users to perform "man-in-the-middle" attacks by intercepting and modifying network traffic between two parties.
Mana Wireless Toolkit	A set of tools allows users to perform various wireless attacks, such as rogue access point creation and wireless sniffing.
Bluetooth Arsenal	A collection of tools that allows users to perform various Bluetooth attacks, such as Bluetooth sniffing and device spoofing.
Social Engineer Toolkit	A tool that allows users to perform various social engineering attacks, such as phishing and pretexting.
Metasploit Payload Generator	A tool that allows users to generate payloads for the Metasploit Framework, which can be used to exploit known vulnerabilities in various software and systems.

7.4   Mitigating security risks and ensuring robustness in smartphone applications for Industry 5.0

In the context of Industry 5.0, which emphasises integrating technology with human-centric processes, examining strategies for enhancing smartphone applications' security becomes crucial. To shed light on this, we must consider the pros and cons of utilising smartphones for penetration testing, as outlined in Table 7.3. This analysis provides insights into how the evolving landscape of Industry 5.0 intersects with the challenges and advantages of smartphone-based penetration testing in ensuring robust cybersecurity practices.

Further, a comparative analysis of using PCs or laptops versus smartphones for penetration tests was made. The investigation underscores the distinct advantages that PCs and laptops bring to penetration testing, presenting a nuanced perspective on the capabilities of each platform. One pivotal aspect lies in the superior processing power endowed by PCs and laptops. These devices facilitate the execution of intricate and resource-intensive penetration testing tasks and are equipped with more robust processors and memory capacities than smartphones. This enhanced processing capability is a fundamental asset in tackling complex security assessments. Moreover, the broader spectrum of functionality offered by PCs and laptops stands out prominently. Specialised penetration testing software and tools are

Table 7.3 The advantages and disadvantages of using smartphones to perform penetration testing

Categories	Advantages	Disadvantages
Portability	A smartphone allows for easy mobility and can be used to conduct penetration testing in various locations.	Because of its size, the components inside of the smartphone are not as good as those of a personal computer (PC) or laptop.
Usability	A smartphone can be used as one device, as it can be used to run Kali NetHunter Lite, a penetration testing platform, as well as other tools and applications.	Even though we can use our smartphones to do other things, the smartphone's performance will be worse over time.
Storage	With evolving technology, there is a high possibility that a smartphone will have more storage in the future.	Smartphones have limited storage capacity, which can be an issue when dealing with large data sets or storing multiple tools and payloads.
Tools	Kali NetHunter Lite, a penetration testing platform that can be run on a smartphone, offers various tools for testing various network and system security aspects.	Smartphones may not have the same connectivity options as dedicated penetration testing devices, such as multiple Ethernet ports or support for various wireless protocols.
Security	Conducting penetration testing on a smartphone can be less conspicuous than using a laptop or other larger device.	Smartphones are personal devices often used for sensitive activities such as banking and communication, and using them for penetration testing can put personal information at risk.

predominantly tailored for compatibility with these devices, endowing practitioners with a more extensive repertoire of functionalities and capabilities than their smartphone counterparts can provide.

The disparity extends to storage capacities as well. PCs and laptops, characterised by larger storage capacities, prove indispensable for storing substantial volumes of data and test results. This attribute becomes particularly crucial in scenarios where comprehensive testing necessitates handling considerable amounts of information. Furthermore, the connectivity options inherent in PCs and laptops add another advantage. With features like Ethernet and USB ports, these devices seamlessly accommodate specialised testing hardware and equipment. This enhanced connectivity empowers testers to employ diverse tools and peripherals in their assessments, thereby enriching the testing environment. A notable consideration is the disparity in battery life, where PCs and laptops emerge as the more enduring options. The extended battery life of these devices translates into prolonged testing sessions without interrupting recharging. This longevity proves invaluable, especially in instances requiring sustained and uninterrupted testing efforts.

The advantages of employing PCs or laptops in penetration testing are manifold: superior processing power, expansive functionality, larger storage capacity, diverse connectivity options, and extended battery life. These attributes collectively contribute to the overall efficacy of PCs and laptops in executing thorough and resource-intensive ·penetration tests. However, contrasting this paradigm, smartphones offer distinctive advantages in penetration testing.

Firstly, their portability is a notable asset, enabling testers to efficiently conduct assessments across diverse locations. Smartphones' compact and easily transportable nature facilitates testing network and system vulnerabilities in various environments. Secondly, smartphones are a cost-effective alternative and relatively inexpensive compared to the more resource-intensive PCs and laptops. Finally, the inherent mobility of smartphones, omnipresent in our daily lives, allows for on-the-go testing. This immediate and spontaneous testing capability starkly contrasts the stationary nature of PCs or laptops, rendering smartphones advantageous in scenarios demanding real-time assessments. Ultimately, the choice between a smartphone, PC, or laptop will depend on the specific needs of the penetration testing project and the resources available to the tester. Moving on to mitigative strategies to overcome security risks in smartphone applications, our study would recommend some possible ways, as summarised in Table 7.4.

Table 7.4 Mitigative strategies to overcome security risks in smartphone applications

Recommendations	*Strategies*
Data Encryption	• Implement end-to-end encryption to protect sensitive data during transmission. • Employ strong encryption algorithms to secure data stored on the device.
Secure Authentication	• Utilise biometric authentication methods, such as fingerprint or facial recognition, alongside strong passwords. • Implement multi-factor authentication for an additional layer of security.
Regular Software Updates	• Ensure that the smartphone applications receive regular security updates to patch vulnerabilities. • Prompt users to update their applications to the latest version for enhanced security.
Secure APIs	• Implement secure communication channels for APIs to prevent unauthorised access. • Use API keys and tokens with proper access controls to restrict data access.
Application Permissions	• Adopt a least privilege approach for app permissions, only requesting access to necessary functionalities. • Clearly communicate to users why certain permissions are required.
Secure Cloud Integration	• Ensure secure communication and storage practices if the application relies on cloud services. • Use strong authentication mechanisms for cloud access.
Compliance with Standards	• Ensure that the application complies with industry-specific security standards and regulations; also regularly conduct auditing.

7.5   Way to move forward towards Industry 5.0

The use of smartphones for penetration testing has gained significant attention in recent years as these devices have become increasingly powerful and versatile. Smartphones can be a highly effective tool for penetration testing that quickly and easily identifies vulnerabilities in the networks and applications we tested. It is handy for small businesses and individuals who may not have the resources to invest in expensive penetration testing equipment. However, some limitations of smartphone penetration testing include smartphones' limited processing power and storage capacity, making testing complex networks and systems challenging. Additionally, using smartphones for penetration testing raises ethical concerns, as unauthorised testing of networks and systems could be considered a form of hacking.

Smartphone applications for penetration testing align with the principles of Industry 5.0, offering the potential to enhance the accessibility and efficiency of security testing significantly. Integrating smartphones into cybersecurity professionals' toolkits can elevate the effectiveness and efficiency of their tasks. Transforming smartphones into penetration testing tools is facilitated by readily available operating system images and documentation on the official Kali Linux website. Despite encountering multiple challenges during smartphone-based penetration testing, a discernible prospect exists for smartphones to emerge as primary instruments for conducting cybersecurity tests.

Future investigations towards devising methodologies that address the constraints associated with employing smartphones for penetration testing within the context of Industry 5.0 can be an excellent way to strengthen the device's capability. It could involve the development of more robust testing applications or exploring the integration of cloud computing to augment the limited resources of smartphones. Furthermore, ethical considerations surrounding the use of smartphones for penetration testing should be a focal point for future research, aiming to establish best practices for responsible and legal utilisation of these devices. It is imperative to recognise that while smartphones contribute significantly to penetration testing, they should not be the sole method in an overall security strategy. Combining various tools and methodologies alongside smartphone-based testing ensures a comprehensive and thorough network and system security assessment. The adoption of smartphones for penetration testing in Industry 5.0 holds great promise for enhancing accessibility and efficiency in security testing. However, acknowledging the limitations and ethical considerations is crucial. Continued research is essential to explore these aspects and formulate best practices, ensuring that smartphones become a valuable addition to the security professional's toolkit and complementing other methods for a holistic security assessment.

As we navigate towards Industry 5.0, integrating smartphones into cybersecurity frameworks becomes pivotal. Industry 5.0 emphasises the symbiotic relationship between humans and technology, and smartphones, ubiquitous in our daily lives, exemplify this integration. Moving forward, it is imperative to develop advanced cybersecurity solutions that leverage the capabilities of smartphones for penetration testing while addressing their inherent constraints. It entails harnessing artificial intelligence and machine learning algorithms to enhance the processing capabilities of smartphones and adopting innovative approaches to secure data storage and transmission. Embracing a comprehensive strategy that aligns with the principles of Industry 5.0 will fortify cybersecurity measures, ensuring the resilience of interconnected systems in our increasingly digitised and interconnected world.

Acknowledgement

This work was supported by the Ministry of Education Malaysia under the Fundamental Research Grant Scheme (Ref: FRGS/1/2020/ICT03/UUM/02/1).

References

Callaham, J. (2023, September 5). *Here's How to Install KaliNetHunter on any Android Devices*. https://www.androidauthority.com/how-to-install-kali-nethunter-android-896887/

Carranza, A., & DeCusatis, C. M. (2016). Wireless network penetration testing using Kali Linux on BeagleBone Black. In The Fourteen LACCEI International Multi-Conference for Engineering, Education, and Technology: 'Engineering Innovations for Global Sustainability'. https://doi.org/10.18687/laccei2016.1.1.095

Chan, B. C. (2020). Cyber Security: Learn All the Essentials and Basic Ways to Avoid Cyber Risk for Your Business (Cybersecurity Guide for Beginners). Independently Published.

Engel, M. M., Ramashan, A., Abduracham, E., & Trisetyarso, A. (2022). Mobile device security: A systematic literature review on research trends, methods and datasets. *Journal of System and Management Science, 12*(3), 66–78. https://doi.org/10.33168/JSMS.2022.0204

Jang, Y. T., Chang, S. E., & Tsai, Y. J. (2013). Smartphone security: Understanding smartphone users' trust in information security management. *Security and Communication Networks, 7*(9), 1313–1321. https://doi.org/10.1002/sec.787

KaliLinux. (2023, June 23). *Kali NetHunter | Kali Linux Documentation*. https://www.kali.org/docs/nethunter/#20-nethunter-supported-devices-and-roms

Lee, T. F., Chang, I. P., & Su, G. J. (2023). Compliance with HIPAA and GDPR in certificateless-based authentication key agreement using extended chaotic maps. *Electronics, 12*(5), 1108. https://doi.org/10.3390/electronics12051108

Reuvid, J. (2021). *Be cyber secure: Tales, tools and threats*. Legend Press Ltd.

Xichen, Z., Mohammad, M. Y., Sajjad, D., Haruna, I., Duc-Phong, L., & Ali, A. G. (2022). Data breach: Analysis, countermeasures and challenges. *International Journal of Information and Computer Security (IJICS), 19*(3/4), 1–27. https://doi.org/10.1504/IJICS.2023.10050154

8 Digital signature

Enabling trust and security in Industry 5.0 transactions

Norliza Katuk[1], Noradila Nordin[2], and Adib Habbal[3]

[1]*School of Computing, Universiti Utara Malaysia, Kedah, Malaysia*

[2]*School of Games & Creative Technology, University for the Creative Arts, Farnham, United Kingdom*

[3]*Computer Engineering Department, Faculty of Engineering, Karabuk University, Karabuk, Türkiye*

8.1 The significance of digital signatures in Industry 5.0

In the dynamic landscape of Industry 5.0, trust and security are foundational elements, especially as cyber-physical systems and advanced technologies reach unprecedented levels of integration. In this evolving digital ecosystem, digital signatures become paramount, acting as a linchpin to ensure the integrity, authenticity, and confidentiality of information exchanged between entities (Kaur & Kaur, 2012). The emergence of Industry 5.0 signifies a paradigm shift, emphasising the convergence of physical and digital realms. This evolution demands a robust trust infrastructure to facilitate secure transactions within an interconnected environment where technologies like the Internet of Things (IoT), artificial intelligence (AI), and blockchain play pivotal roles.

Digital signatures are crucial in this trust infrastructure as they are digital counterparts to traditional handwritten signatures. Leveraging cryptographic algorithms, they bind a unique identifier to digital data, ensuring the authenticity of the sender and the integrity of the information exchanged. In the fast-paced transactions of Industry 5.0, where data is a valuable currency, the significance of digital signatures cannot be overstated. One primary contribution of digital signatures is their ability to secure transactions in a decentralised and interconnected environment (Anthony Jr, 2023). As Industry 5.0 fosters collaboration and autonomous machine communication, the assurance that transmitted messages remain untampered during transit is fundamental. Digital signatures create a cryptographic seal, verifying the transmitted data's origin and integrity.

Signing and verifying messages using digital signatures involve several cryptographic components (Prasad & Kaushik, 2019). To sign a message, the sender first creates a hash of the message using a cryptographic hash function. The sender then encrypts this hash value with their private key using a digital signature algorithm (DSA), generating the digital signature. This signature and the original message

DOI: 10.1201/9781003479727-8

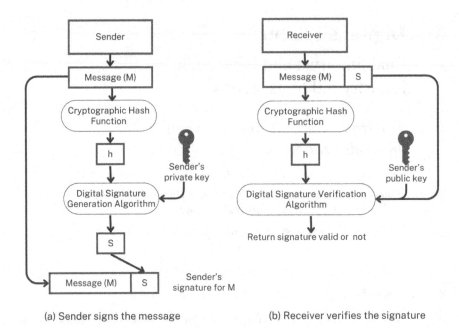

(a) Sender signs the message   (b) Receiver verifies the signature

Figure 8.1 (a) Demonstrates the process of generating a signature; (b) Demonstrates the process for verifying a digital signature on a message.

are sent to the receiver. Upon receiving the message, the receiver uses the sender's public key to decrypt the digital signature, obtaining the hash value. Subsequently, the receiver independently computes the hash of the received message using the same cryptographic hash function. If the computed hash matches the decrypted hash from the digital signature, and the signature is valid using the digital signature verification algorithm, the receiver can confidently confirm the message's integrity and authenticity. This comprehensive process ensures that the message has not been tampered with during transmission and originated from the legitimate sender with the corresponding private key. Figure 8.1(a) demonstrates the process of generating a signature while Figure 8.1(b) demonstrates the process for verifying a digital signature on a message.

Digital signatures are instrumental in fostering trust and ensuring data integrity, confidentiality, and non-repudiation in electronic communication. Across diverse sectors, these cryptographic mechanisms are vital in verifying message authenticity and protecting against tampering during transmission. Digital signatures provide a secure foundation by employing robust algorithms and key management practices. They instil confidence in the sender's credibility and assure confidentiality by safeguarding sensitive information. Additionally, the non-repudiation aspect ensures that senders cannot deny their involvement in the communication. This comprehensive approach establishes a resilient and reliable digital environment, enhancing trust and integrity while addressing confidentiality and non-repudiation.

Confidentiality and non-repudiation are imperative aspects of trust in Industry 5.0. Digital signatures, through the use of public and private key pairs, encrypt sensitive information, safeguarding it from unauthorised access (Prasad & Kaushik, 2019). Simultaneously, they ensure that the sender cannot deny involvement in a transaction, establishing a foundation for secure and accountable digital interactions. In delving deeper into Industry 5.0, the role of digital signatures becomes increasingly indispensable. An integral part of the cryptographic landscape is the DSA. The DSA has a significant place in the evolution of cryptographic techniques for ensuring the authenticity and integrity of digital messages. The history of DSA dates back to the early 1990s, when the need for secure digital communication became more pronounced. In 1991, the National Institute of Standards and Technology (NIST) initiated a competition to develop a secure digital signature standard (DSS). This competition led to the selection of the DSA as the DSS in 1993.

The DSA was proposed by the National Security Agency (NSA) and designed by David Kravitz, who played a key role in its development (Landau, 2015). DSA relies on the mathematical properties of modular exponentiation and the discrete logarithm problem for its security. One of the key features of DSA is its reliance on a pair of keys—a private key for signing and a corresponding public key for verification. In 1994, the DSA became a Federal Information Processing Standard (FIPS PUB 186) (Data Encryption Standard, 1999), solidifying its status as a government-approved DSA. Over the years, DSA has found applications in various domains, including government communications, financial transactions, and secure digital identities. DSA is a widely used algorithm for creating digital signatures and is mainly known for its efficiency in ensuring data integrity and authentication. It operates on the principles of public-key cryptography, utilising a pair of asymmetric keys—a private key for signing and a public key for verification. Despite its historical significance, DSA has faced some scrutiny due to concerns about the potential vulnerability of its parameters (Blake & Garefalakis, 2002). As a result, other DSAs like Rivest–Shamir–Adleman (RSA) (Aufa & Affandi, 2018) and the Elliptic Curve Digital Signature Algorithm (ECDSA) (Johnson et al., 2001) have gained popularity in certain applications. Nevertheless, the history of DSA marks a crucial milestone in developing secure cryptographic protocols for digital signatures.

8.2 Implementing digital signature technologies for secure transactions

In the context of Industry 5.0, the application of digital signatures plays a pivotal role in securing transactions and operations within the rapidly advancing landscape of smart manufacturing and beyond. As Industry 5.0 embraces integrating cyber-physical systems, the secure exchange of data and instructions between interconnected machines becomes paramount. Digital signatures, with their ability to ensure authenticity, integrity, confidentiality, and non-repudiation, become a linchpin in safeguarding critical transactions and operational commands.

In a smart factory setting, digital signatures play a pivotal role in ensuring the security, integrity, and efficiency of operations (Tuptuk & Hailes, 2018). These cryptographic mechanisms are employed across various facets of smart manufacturing, providing a robust layer of authentication and verification. One notable application is authorising and validating digital documents governing manufacturing processes. Digital signatures authenticate production orders, quality control specifications, and supply chain instructions, instilling confidence in the legitimacy of the data and instructions exchanged between interconnected machines and systems. Moreover, digital signatures contribute to the establishment of a secure communication framework within the smart factory. From machine-to-machine interactions to human-machine interfaces, digital signatures verify the origin of messages, ensuring that commands are legitimate and have not been tampered with during transmission (Alshowkan et al., 2022). It is particularly crucial in preventing unauthorised machinery adjustments and guaranteeing the integrity of production data. The non-repudiation aspect of digital signatures becomes essential in a smart factory environment (Yalcinkaya et al., 2020), providing an indisputable record of actions taken by machines or operators. This feature is invaluable in accountability, audit trails, and dispute-resolution scenarios.

Beyond smart factories, using digital signatures extends to financial systems and online businesses, where secure transactions and data integrity are paramount (Saghafi et al., 2009). In the financial sector, digital signatures are instrumental in validating electronic transactions, including fund transfers, contract agreements, and digital identities. By employing public and private key pairs, digital signatures verify the authenticity of financial documents and ensure the integrity of critical information, preventing fraudulent activities and unauthorised alterations. Online businesses leverage digital signatures to establish trust in electronic communications and transactions. From e-commerce platforms to digital contracts, digital signatures authenticate the parties' identities and secure the exchange of sensitive information, such as customer details and payment data. It safeguards businesses from cyber threats and instils consumer confidence, fostering a secure online marketplace (Bhasin, 2006). Furthermore, the non-repudiation feature of digital signatures is crucial in the legal and regulatory context of financial transactions and online business operations. It provides an indisputable record of the parties involved, their consent, and the integrity of the exchanged data, which is essential for compliance and dispute resolution.

In the IoT environment, the application of digital signatures becomes increasingly vital as connected devices proliferate (Lalem et al., 2023). Digital signatures are crucial in ensuring the authenticity, integrity, and security of data exchanged between IoT devices. Each device is equipped with its unique set of public and private keys, allowing it to create digital signatures for the data it generates. Digital signatures in the IoT context authenticate the source of data, verifying that it originates from a legitimate device and has not been tampered with during transmission. It is particularly crucial for critical applications such as healthcare monitoring, smart home systems, and industrial IoT, where the accuracy and trustworthiness of data are paramount. Additionally, digital signatures contribute to the establishment of a secure communication framework among IoT devices (Sousa et al., 2021). Whether it's sensors in a smart city infrastructure or interconnected machinery in an industrial IoT setting, digital signatures verify the legitimacy of commands and updates, preventing unauthorised access and ensuring the integrity of the entire IoT ecosystem. The non-repudiation aspect of digital signatures is precious in the IoT environment (Alagheband & Mashatan, 2022). It provides an indisputable record of actions taken by specific devices, offering accountability and traceability. This becomes essential in scenarios where regulatory compliance and auditability are critical considerations.

In Industry 5.0, the role of digital signatures as a key element for security cannot be overstated. As smart manufacturing systems evolve, interconnected devices, collaborative robots, and real-time data exchanges become integral components. Digital signatures are a robust safeguard, ensuring the authenticity, integrity, confidentiality, and non-repudiation of critical information exchanged within this sophisticated industrial ecosystem. The secure application of digital signatures in Industry 5.0 translates into trusted communication among cyber-physical systems, enabling smart factories to operate efficiently and securely. Whether validating production orders, verifying quality control specifications, or securing supply chain instructions, digital signatures create a foundation of trust in the digital domain. Furthermore, the non-repudiation aspect ensures accountability for actions taken by machines or operators, offering a verifiable record of events. It proves invaluable for compliance, auditing, and dispute resolution, addressing the stringent requirements of modern industrial practices.

8.3   Algorithms for digital signatures in Industry 5.0

The efficacy of digital signatures in ensuring security relies heavily on the underlying cryptographic algorithms. Two primary components define the algorithms associated with digital signatures: the hash function for creating a digest of the message and the asymmetric encryption algorithm for generating and verifying the digital signature.

- **Hash function:** At the heart of digital signatures lies the hash function, a one-way cryptographic algorithm that transforms an input message into a fixed-length string of characters, known as a hash or digest. This process is irreversible, meaning that even a small change in the original message will produce a vastly different hash value (Yang et al., 2017). Popular hash functions include Secure Hash Algorithm 256-bit (SHA-256) and SHA-3, renowned for their resistance to collision attacks, where two different inputs produce the same hash output. The hash function ensures data integrity by providing a unique and secure message representation, making it a cornerstone in DSAs. Figure 8.2 illustrates the processes of calculating hash values for checking the message integrity.
- **Asymmetric encryption algorithm:** Digital signatures employ asymmetric encryption algorithms to create a pair of keys: a private key for signing and a corresponding public key for verification. The RSA algorithm, Elliptic Curve Cryptography (ECC), and Diffie–Hellman Key Exchange fall under this category. The private key, held securely by the signer, is used to generate the digital signature, while the public key, distributed openly, is used by others to verify the signature's authenticity (Shankar et al., 2023). The security of these algorithms

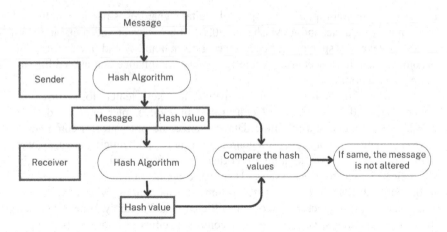

Figure 8.2 Hash functions.

lies in the computational complexity of deriving the private key from the public key, making them fundamental in securing digital communication and ensuring non-repudiation. Symmetric and asymmetric encryptions are two fundamental cryptographic techniques that differ in their key management and application. In symmetric encryption, the same key is used for encryption and decryption, making communication more straightforward but requiring a secure channel for key exchange. On the other hand, asymmetric encryption employs a pair of keys—a public key for encryption and a private key for decryption (Yassein et al., 2017). Refer to Figures 8.3(a) and (b) for an illustration of the two types of encryption; the asymmetric and symmetric respectively. Asymmetric encryption eliminates the need for a secure key exchange channel but is computationally more intensive than symmetric encryption.

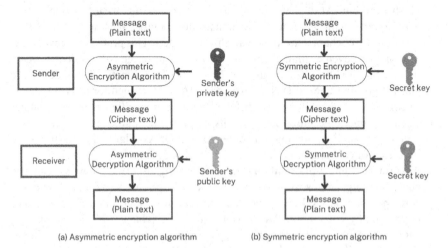

Figure 8.3 (a) Asymmetric encryption algorithms; (b) Symmetric encryption algorithms.

DSAs, crucial for ensuring the authenticity and integrity of digital messages, often utilise asymmetric encryption because asymmetric encryption provides a unique advantage in the context of verification and non-repudiation. The private key, used for creating the digital signature, remains confidential with the signer, while the public key, employed for signature verification, can be openly distributed. It ensures that anyone with access to the public key can verify the signature but cannot forge it, enhancing the security of the digital signature process. The asymmetry in the key pair addresses the challenges of key distribution and provides a more secure foundation for digital signatures. Asymmetric encryption's unique characteristics make it particularly suitable for scenarios where secure key exchange is challenging, as is often true in digital communication over open networks (Rao & Deebak, 2023). The use of asymmetric encryption in digital signatures establishes a secure and reliable framework for authentication and non-repudiation, essential in various domains, including secure financial transactions, legal documents, and smart manufacturing processes. Integrating robust hash functions and asymmetric encryption algorithms in digital signature processes fortifies security. As technology advances, there is a continuous evolution in cryptographic algorithms to address emerging threats and maintain the resilience of digital signatures in safeguarding the integrity and authenticity of electronic communications and transactions.

8.4   Practical applications of digital signatures in Industry 5.0

Digital signatures, cryptographic tools that validate the authenticity and integrity of electronic documents or transactions, play a pivotal role in the transformative landscape of Industry 5.0. The need for secure, transparent, and efficient digital interactions becomes paramount as digital technologies and physical systems convergence shape a new era of industrial practices. In response to this demand, blockchain technology has emerged as a critical enabler, offering a decentralised and tamper-resistant framework that synergises seamlessly with digital signatures. This symbiotic relationship holds immense potential, revolutionising how transactions and interactions are secured and verified across the spectrum of Industry 5.0 applications. In the context of Industry 5.0, where interconnected devices, smart manufacturing processes, and cross-industry collaborations are prevalent, the reliability of digital signatures becomes foundational. These cryptographic techniques assure the signer's identity and safeguard against tampering, providing a secure means for conducting electronic transactions in the dynamic and complex environments that characterise the industrial landscape (Asare, 2022).

Blockchain, the underlying technology of cryptocurrencies like Bitcoin, is a trustworthy ledger. It operates as a decentralised and distributed database that ensures transparency and immutability of records. In the context of digital signatures, blockchain acts as a secure repository where signed transactions are recorded chronologically and securely. Each block in the chain contains a unique identifier, a timestamp, and a reference to the previous block, creating an unalterable chain of blocks that establishes a credible and decentralised ledger (Katuk, 2019). Figure 8.4 shows the blockchain data structure.

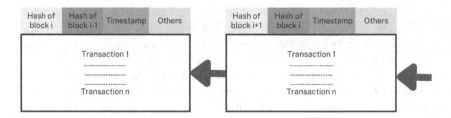

Figure 8.4 Blockchain data structure.

Source: Katuk (2019). Adapted with permission.

Practically applying this fusion of digital signatures and blockchain in Industry 5.0 yields a spectrum of transformative applications. One such application lies in supply chain visibility (Saberi et al., 2019). Applying digital signatures on the blockchain ensures the authenticity of crucial documents, such as shipping manifests and quality certifications, fostering transparency and traceability throughout the supply chain. Additionally, this integration empowers smart contracts, which are self-executing contracts with predefined conditions, to automate and secure various transactions (De Giovanni, 2020) in Industry 5.0, from equipment maintenance agreements to payment settlements. The authentication of the involved parties through digital signatures ensures the trustworthiness of these automated agreements (Kawaguchi, 2019). Figure 8.5 illustrates the blockchain-based digital signature in supply chain management, covering producers, processors, retailers, and consumers.

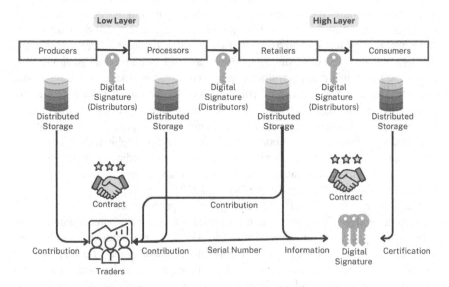

Figure 8.5 Blockchain-based digital signature in supply management.

Source: Kawaguchi (2019). Adapted with permission.

Decentralised identity management (Liu et al., 2020), another significant application, addresses the collaborative nature of Industry 5.0 by providing secure authentication through digital signatures. Each participant can possess a unique digital identity, verified through cryptographic signatures, reducing dependence on central authorities and enhancing security in collaborative endeavours. Furthermore, blockchain's transparent and immutable nature and digital signatures facilitate comprehensive audit trails, ensuring regulatory compliance in Industry 5.0 processes. In the expansive ecosystem of the IoT within Industry 5.0, secure communication and authentication of transactions among interconnected devices are critical. Blockchain and digital signatures provide a decentralised and secure framework, ensuring the authenticity of messages and transactions between devices in this interconnected landscape (Fang et al., 2020).

The amalgamation of blockchain technology and digital signatures in Industry 5.0 unfolds myriad possibilities across diverse applications. One such area is the optimisation of manufacturing processes. By utilising digital signatures on the blockchain, manufacturers can secure and authenticate critical documents related to production orders, quality control specifications, and equipment maintenance schedules (Leng et al., 2020). This ensures the integrity of essential data and streamlines the production workflow, reducing the risk of errors and unauthorised alterations. Blockchain-based digital signatures offer a robust solution in intellectual property and innovation management (Ito & O'Dair, 2019). Research and development teams can securely timestamp and sign their discoveries on the blockchain, creating an immutable record of innovation. This fosters a transparent and secure environment for intellectual property protection, providing a verifiable trail of ownership and invention timelines.

In the context of financial transactions within Industry 5.0, blockchain and digital signatures contribute to the evolution of secure and efficient payment systems. Digital signatures authenticate payment requests, and blockchain's decentralised nature ensures the integrity of financial records (Kabra et al., 2020). It is particularly crucial in global transactions, where cross-border payments can be streamlined, secure, and transparent, reducing the risk of fraud and ensuring compliance with financial regulations. The combination of blockchain and digital signatures proves invaluable for regulatory compliance and auditability in industries subject to stringent standards. Whether in healthcare (Mehbodniya et al., 2022), where patient records need to be securely accessed and audited or in environmental compliance (Gangwani et al., 2021), where emissions data requires transparent verification, the integration ensures a tamper-proof record that meets regulatory requirements.

Moreover, in the burgeoning field of additive manufacturing or 3D printing (Alkaabi et al., 2020), where digital designs are integral, the use of digital signatures on the blockchain safeguards the authenticity and integrity of these designs. This is crucial in maintaining the trustworthiness of the digital files as they traverse the supply chain, from design to production. Blockchain-based digital signatures are also poised to revolutionise energy management and distribution (Pawan, 2023). With the increasing integration of renewable energy sources and smart grids, secure and authenticated transactions on the blockchain enable efficient energy trading, grid management, and transparent tracking of energy sources. In human resources and identity verification, blockchain and digital signatures can be utilised to establish secure and immutable employee records (Madaan et al., 2023). Each record can be digitally signed and timestamped, from hiring documents to training certifications on the blockchain, creating a trustworthy and verifiable employment history.

As Industry 5.0 continues to evolve, the applications of blockchain-based digital signatures are set to expand, influencing how industries approach security, transparency, and collaboration in the digital age. From manufacturing and finance to intellectual property and energy management, the integration of these technologies shapes a future where trust and efficiency coalesce, paving the way for a more secure and interconnected industrial landscape. In conclusion, integrating blockchain technology and digital signatures in Industry 5.0 signifies a paradigm shift, redefining how trust, security, and transparency are established in digital interactions. As industries embrace these technologies, the applications extend beyond traditional boundaries, fostering a secure and collaborative environment in the era of interconnected, intelligent systems.

References

Alagheband, M. R., & Mashatan, A. (2022). Advanced digital signatures for preserving privacy and trust management in hierarchical heterogeneous IoT: Taxonomy, capabilities, and objectives. *Internet of Things*, *18*, 100492. https://doi.org/10.1016/j.iot.2021.100492

Alkaabi, N., Salah, K., Jayaraman, R., Arshad, J., & Omar, M. (2020). Blockchain-based traceability and management for additive manufacturing. *IEEE Access*, *8*, 188363–188377. https://doi.org/10.1109/ACCESS.2020.3031536

Alshowkan, M., Evans, P. G., Starke, M., Earl, D., & Peters, N. A. (2022). Authentication of smart grid communications using quantum key distribution. *Scientific Reports*, *12*(1), 12731. https://doi.org/10.1038/s41598-022-16090-w

Anthony, B. Jr (2023). Deployment of distributed ledger and decentralized technology for transition to smart industries. *Environment Systems and Decisions*, *43*(2), 298–319. https://doi.org/10.1007/s10669-023-09902-5

Asare, B. T. (2022). *A cryptographic technique for authentification of multimedia data in internet-of-things using blockchain*. Ghana Communication Technology University, École doctorale Mathématiques et sciences et technologies de l'information et de la communication (Rennes), Laboratoire en sciences et techniques de l'information, de la communication et de la connaissance.

Aufa, F. J., & Affandi, A. (2018). Security system analysis in combination method: RSA encryption and digital signature algorithm. In 2018 4th International Conference on Science and Technology (ICST). https://doi.org/10.1109/ICSTC.2018.8528584

Bhasin, M. L. (2006). Guarding privacy on the internet. *Global Business Review*, *7*(1), 137–156. https://doi.org/10.1177/097215090500700109

Blake, I. F., & Garefalakis, T. (2002). On the security of the digital signature algorithm. *Designs, Codes and Cryptography*, *26*, 87–96. https://doi.org/10.1023/A:1016549024113

Data Encryption Standard. (1999). Federal information processing standard FIPS PUB 46-3. National Institute of Standards and Technology. https://csrc.nist.gov/files/pubs/fips/46-3/final/docs/fips46-3.pdf

De Giovanni, P. (2020). Blockchain and smart contracts in supply chain management: A game theoretic model. *International Journal of Production Economics*, *228*, 107855. https://doi.org/10.1016/j.ijpe.2020.107855

Fang, W., Chen, W., Zhang, W., Pei, J., Gao, W., & Wang, G. (2020). Digital signature scheme for information non-repudiation in blockchain: A state of the art review. *EURASIP Journal on Wireless Communications and Networking*, *2020*(1), 1–15. https://doi.org/10.1186/s13638-020-01665-w

Gangwani, P., Perez-Pons, A., Bhardwaj, T., Upadhyay, H., Joshi, S., & Lagos, L. (2021). Securing environmental IoT data using masked authentication messaging protocol in a DAG-based blockchain: IOTA tangle. *Future Internet*, *13*(12), 312. https://doi.org/10.3390/fi13120312

Ito, K., & O'Dair, M. (2019). A critical examination of the application of blockchain technology to intellectual property management. In H. Treiblmaier & R. Beck (Eds.), Business Transformation through Blockchain (pp. 317–335). Palgrave Macmillan. https://doi.org/10.1007/978-3-319-99058-3_12

Johnson, D., Menezes, A., & Vanstone, S. (2001). The elliptic curve digital signature algorithm (ECDSA). *International Journal of Information Security*, *1*, 36–63. https://doi.org/10.1007/s102070100002

Kabra, N., Bhattacharya, P., Tanwar, S., & Tyagi, S. (2020). MudraChain: Blockchain-based framework for automated cheque clearance in financial institutions. *Future Generation Computer Systems*, *102*, 574–587. https://doi.org/10.1016/j.future.2019.08.035

Katuk, N. (2019). The application of blockchain for halal product assurance: A systematic review of the current developments and future directions. *International Journal of Advanced Trends in Computer Science and Engineering*, *8*(5), 1893–1902.

Kaur, R., & Kaur, A. (2012). Digital signature. In 2012 International Conference on Computing Sciences. https://doi.org/10.1109/ICCS.2012.25

Kawaguchi, N. (2019). Application of blockchain to supply chain: Flexible blockchain technology. *Procedia Computer Science*, *164*, 143–148. https://doi.org/10.1016/j.procs.2019.12.166

Lalem, F., Laouid, A., Kara, M., Al-Khalidi, M., & Eleyan, A. (2023). A novel digital signature scheme for advanced asymmetric encryption techniques. *Applied Sciences*, *13*(8), 5172. https://doi.org/10.3390/app13085172

Landau, S. (2015). NSA and Dual EC_DRBG: Déjà vu all over again? *The Mathematical Intelligencer*, *37*, 72–83. https://doi.org/10.1007/s00283-015-9543-z

Leng, J., Ruan, G., Jiang, P., Xu, K., Liu, Q., Zhou, X., & Liu, C. (2020). Blockchain-empowered sustainable manufacturing and product lifecycle management in industry 4.0: A survey. *Renewable and Sustainable Energy Reviews*, *132*, 110112. https://doi.org/10.1016/j.rser.2020.110112

Liu, Y., He, D., Obaidat, M. S., Kumar, N., Khan, M. K., & Raymond Choo, K.-K. (2020). Blockchain-based identity management systems: A review. *Journal of Network and Computer Applications*, *166*, 102731. https://doi.org/10.1016/j.jnca.2020.102731

Madaan, V., Singh, R., & Dhawan, A. (2023). Use and applications of blockchain technology in human resource management functions. In *Effective AI, blockchain, and e-governance applications for knowledge discovery and management* (pp. 130–142). IGI Global. https://doi.org/10.4018/978-1-6684-9151-5.ch009

Mehbodniya, A., Webber, J. L., Neware, R., Arslan, F., Pamba, R. V., & Shabaz, M. (2022). Modified Lamport Merkle digital signature blockchain framework for authentication of internet of things healthcare data. *Expert Systems*, *39*(10), e12978. https://doi.org/10.1111/exsy.12978

Pawan, W. (2023). 11 - Peer-to-peer energy trading with blockchain: A case study. In S. Padmanaban, R. K. Dhanaraj, J. B. Holm-Nielsen, S. Krishnamoorthi, & B. Balusamy (Eds.), *Blockchain-based systems for the modern energy grid* (pp. 171–188). Academic Press. https://doi.org/10.1016/B978-0-323-91850-3.00004-4

Prasad, A., & Kaushik, K. (2019). Digital signatures. In *Emerging security algorithms and techniques* (pp. 249–272). Taylor & Francis.

Rao, P. M., & Deebak, B. D. (2023). A comprehensive survey on authentication and secure key management in internet of things: Challenges, countermeasures, and future directions. *Ad Hoc Networks, 146,* 103159. https://doi.org/10.1016/j.adhoc.2023.103159

Saberi, S., Kouhizadeh, M., Sarkis, J., & Shen, L. (2019). Blockchain technology and its relationships to sustainable supply chain management. *International Journal of Production Research, 57*(7), 2117–2135. https://doi.org/10.1080/00207543.2018.1533261

Saghafi, F., NasserEslami, F., & Esmaili, M. (2009). Ranking secure technologies in security provision financial transactions mobile commerce. In Proceedings of the 2nd International Conference on Interaction Sciences: Information Technology, Culture and Human. https://doi.org/10.1145/1655925.1655986

Shankar, G., Ai-Farhani, L. H., Anitha Christy Angelin, P., Singh, P., Alqahtani, A., Singh, A., & Samori, I. A. (2023). Improved multisignature scheme for authenticity of digital document in digital forensics using Edward-curve digital signature algorithm. *Security and Communication Networks, 2023,* 2093407. https://doi.org/10.1155/2023/2093407

Sousa, P. R., Magalhães, L., Resende, J. S., Martins, R., & Antunes, L. (2021). Provisioning, authentication and secure communications for IoT devices on FIWARE. *Sensors, 21*(17), 5898. https://doi.org/10.3390/s21175898

Tuptuk, N., & Hailes, S. (2018). Security of smart manufacturing systems. *Journal of Manufacturing Systems, 47,* 93–106. https://doi.org/10.1016/j.jmsy.2018.04.007

Yalcinkaya, E., Maffei, A., & Onori, M. (2020). Blockchain reference system architecture description for the ISA95 compliant traditional and smart manufacturing systems. *Sensors, 20*(22), 6456. https://doi.org/10.3390/s20226456

Yang, Y., chen, F., Zhang, X., Yu, J., & Zhang, P. (2017). Research on the hash function structures and its application. *Wireless Personal Communications, 94*(4), 2969–2985. https://doi.org/10.1007/s11277-016-3760-4

Yassein, M. B., Aljawarneh, S., Qawasmeh, E., Mardini, W., & Khamayseh, Y. (2017). Comprehensive study of symmetric key and asymmetric key encryption algorithms. In 2017 International Conference on Engineering and Technology (ICET). https://doi.org/10.1109/ICEngTechnol.2017.8308215

9 Revolutionising Industry 5.0 with the Internet of Things

Norliza Katuk[1], Ijaz Ahmad[2], Ekaterina Chzhan[3], and Derar Eleyan[4]

[1]*School of Computing, Universiti Utara Malaysia, Kedah, Malaysia*

[2]*Faculty of Information Technology and Electrical Engineering, University of Oulu, Oulu, Finland*

[3]*School of Information and Space Technology, Siberian Federal University, Krasnoyarsk, Russia*

[4]*Applied Computing Department, Palestine Technical University, Kadoorie, Palestine*

9.1 Introduction to the IoT and its role in Industry 5.0

The Internet of Things, or IoT, is an advanced technological concept that creates a network of physical objects capable of interacting and sharing data through the Internet (Chander & Kumaravelan, 2020). These objects, often embedded with sensors, software, and other forms of technology, can communicate, consequently fostering a smart and responsive environment. IoT has evolved everyday objects into 'smart' devices that generate and exchange data. Its scope has broadened over time, enabling machine-to-machine communication, the creation of smart wearable devices, and even the development of smart homes and cities. The potential of IoT is further amplified with big data analytics and cloud computing, which provide the infrastructure to manage vast amounts of data generated by these connected devices. IoT is not just a technology but a pivotal element in advancing Industry 5.0, where it facilitates connectivity and data exchange between physical and digital systems. IoT is a transformative force in the industrial realm, from monitoring workers' health to adjusting manufacturing processes based on real-time data.

The IoT is integral in Industry 5.0, the digital backbone enabling seamless interaction between humans and machines. IoT devices range from sensors and wearables to smart appliances and machinery (Javaid et al., 2021). They are designed to measure specific conditions or changes in their environment, such as temperature, humidity, light, motion, or pressure. They convert these physical quantities into electronic signals that can be processed and interpreted by a computer system. Further, sensors collect vast amounts of environmental data, making machines 'aware' of their surroundings. Advanced sensors can monitor variables such as temperature, pressure, and vibrations, enabling machines to respond to changes in real time. For instance, a vibration sensor on a manufacturing machine can detect

DOI: 10.1201/9781003479727-9

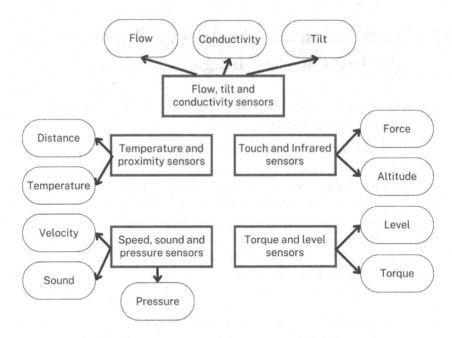

Figure 9.1 Typical types of sensors.

Source: Javaid et al. (2021). Adapted with permission.

abnormal vibrations, which may indicate a potential fault. They are pivotal in predictive maintenance, where real-time monitoring allows for early detection and resolution of potential faults, minimising downtime and enhancing productivity.

Refer to Figure 9.1 for examples of sensors in our daily lives. These sensors, from simple temperature and pressure sensors to more sophisticated motion and image sensors, are the elemental components of data acquisition and can capture and disseminate real-time information. These devices gather vast amounts of data from their environment, which are then analysed to drive automation, predictive capabilities, and decision-making (Liang & Shah, 2023). In Industry 5.0, sensors help create intelligent machines that can talk to each other and make quick decisions together. This teamwork happens because machines with various sensors can easily share information in real time, leading to a smooth flow of data and resources. This connection makes industries more flexible and integrated.

IoT aids in creating a more responsive, efficient, and connected industrial process (Mantravadi et al., 2022). For instance, it makes seamless coordination possible between factory parts or real-time remote control of heavy machinery. It enhances the agility and flexibility of industrial processes, essential elements in today's fast-paced industrial landscape. IoT is pivotal in fostering human-machine collaboration using advanced sensors, and AI-equipped machines can understand and respond to human actions in real time, enhancing safety and efficiency in the workplace. It is a technological tool and a transformative force in

Industry 5.0. Its ability to collect, analyse, and leverage data makes it integral to the growth and evolution of this new era of industrialisation.

This collaborative approach is not limited to traditional manufacturing industries; it extends across diverse sectors, including agriculture and services. In agriculture, for instance, smart sensors on farming equipment can collect data about soil conditions, crop health, and weather patterns. This information enables farmers to make informed decisions, optimise irrigation schedules, and predict crop yields. Integrating IoT and sensors enhances efficiency and customer experiences in the services realm. In smart cities, for instance, sensors in public transportation systems can provide real-time data on routes, helping commuters plan their journeys more effectively. Additionally, in healthcare services, wearable sensors can monitor patients' vital signs, facilitating proactive and personalised medical care.

The application of IoT and sensors across various industries exemplifies the versatility and transformative potential of Industry 5.0. By fostering connectivity and data-driven decision-making, these technologies contribute to a more efficient, responsive, and integrated industrial landscape, spanning agriculture, services, and beyond. As we continue to advance in this era, the collaborative synergy between humans and intelligent machines holds the promise of unlocking unprecedented possibilities for innovation and sustainable development.

Connectivity, on the other hand, refers to the ability of these sensors and other IoT devices to communicate with each other and central systems. It is achieved through various communication protocols and networks, including Wi-Fi, Bluetooth, LoRaWan, NB-IoT, Zigbee, cellular networks, or even complex systems like 5G (Mantravadi et al., 2022) (refer to Table 9.1 for a list of the technology). For example, a smart factory's sensor that detects a fault could send this information to a central system via a network. The system could instantly alert the maintenance team or shut the machine down to prevent further damage. 5G's high-speed data transfer and low latency enable real-time remote control of heavy machinery and

Table 9.1 Technology for connectivity in IoT

Technology	Features	Applications
Wi-Fi	High data rates, wide adoption, wide range and coverage	Smart homes, offices, industrial automation
Bluetooth	Low energy consumption, easy pairing, low cost	Beacons, monitors, network connectivity
LoRaWAN	Extended range, low power, deep indoor penetration	Smart agriculture, smart cities, asset tracking
NB-IoT	Low power, reliable connectivity, high security	Smart meters, remote monitoring, logistics
Zigbee	Mesh networking, low interference, scalable	Home automation, lighting control, sensor networks
5G	High data rates, low latency, massive device connectivity	Home and industrial applications

Source: Hardesty (2023).

seamless coordination between factory parts (Longo et al., 2021). This level of connectivity fosters a more responsive and efficient industrial process, which is essential in the fast-paced landscape of Industry 5.0.

9.2   Harnessing IoT technologies and applications for Industry 5.0 advancements

In the dynamic evolution of Industry 5.0, there is a pivotal emphasis on harnessing the potential of IoT technologies across a spectrum of sectors, including healthcare, smart cities, smart transportation, smart vehicles, smart buildings, smart manufacturing, and smart agriculture. A focus should be given to collaborative robots (cobots) and advanced predictive maintenance strategies. Integrating IoT through sensors on existing machines fosters connectivity and intelligent decision-making and introduces collaborative synergy between human workers and cobots. Simultaneously, IoT applications extend innovative solutions for real-time data acquisition and monitoring in traditionally challenging areas, enhancing the adaptability and responsiveness of industrial systems, healthcare practices, city infrastructure, transportation networks, building management, manufacturing processes, and agricultural practices. As we explore the multifaceted applications of IoT in the broader context of Industry 5.0, the potential for heightened efficiency, proactive predictive maintenance, and seamless collaboration across these diverse sectors becomes even more promising, heralding a transformative era characterised by innovation and sustainable development across industries and societal domains.

- **Cobot:** In the landscape of Industry 5.0, cobots emerge as transformative agents, offering innovative solutions that redefine industrial processes. Cobots allow seamless integration with the IoT, enabling a new level of connectivity and intelligence in industrial operations (Vermesan et al., 2022). These cobots are designed to work collaboratively with human counterparts, combining human intelligence and dexterity with the precision and efficiency of robotic automation, all while leveraging the power of IoT. One compelling example of this synergy is found in smart manufacturing environments. Cobots equipped with IoT sensors are integrated into assembly lines to perform intricate tasks alongside human workers in these settings. For instance, in the automotive industry, cobots with IoT capabilities can precisely weld components, ensuring the quality and accuracy of the welding process. The IoT sensors embedded in these cobots continuously collect data on operational parameters, enabling real-time monitoring and predictive maintenance, thereby minimising downtime and optimising overall efficiency.

  Cobots with IoT integration play a vital role in surgical procedures in healthcare (Gürce et al., 2023). These advanced robots are equipped with sensors that enhance the precision of tasks and collect data on surgical parameters. This data is transmitted through the IoT network, providing valuable insights to surgeons and contributing to continuous improvement in surgical techniques and patient outcomes. Smart cities are also leveraging IoT-enabled cobots to enhance public services. For example, cobots equipped with IoT sensors can intelligently sort and segregate recyclables in waste management. The data collected by these cobots is transmitted in real time, facilitating efficient recycling practices and contributing to sustainable urban environments. In agriculture, cobots with IoT integration navigate fields equipped with sensors to collect data on crop health, soil moisture, and nutrient levels. This real-time information is transmitted through IoT networks, empowering farmers to make data-driven decisions for optimising crop yield and resource utilisation.

- **Predictive maintenance:** It is a game-changer across diverse sectors. In Industry 5.0 settings, IoT-enabled sensors continuously collect and transmit real-time data from machinery and equipment. This data is then processed through advanced analytics, allowing for predicting potential failures or maintenance needs before they escalate. In manufacturing, IoT-driven predictive maintenance ensures that production lines operate optimally. By monitoring equipment health and performance in real time, manufacturers can schedule maintenance activities precisely when needed, reducing downtime and preventing costly breakdowns (Soori et al., 2023). This proactive approach extends the machinery's lifespan and enhances overall operational efficiency. The healthcare sector also benefits significantly from IoT-driven predictive maintenance in medical equipment management (Manchadi et al., 2023). Connected sensors on devices such as MRI machines and X-ray equipment allow healthcare providers to monitor usage patterns and performance metrics. Predictive analytics based on this data enable healthcare providers to schedule maintenance activities efficiently, ensuring the continuous functionality of critical medical equipment.

In smart cities, infrastructure components such as bridges, roads, and utilities leverage IoT for predictive maintenance (Hassebo & Tealab, 2023). Sensors embedded in structures monitor factors like wear and tear, structural integrity, and environmental conditions. By analysing this data, municipalities can predict and address maintenance needs before they become critical, ensuring the longevity and safety of urban infrastructure. Predictive maintenance also benefits the agriculture sector and embraces IoT devices for farm equipment (Prabha & Pathak, 2023). Connected sensors on tractors, harvesters, and other machinery monitor usage and performance parameters. Predictive analytics help farmers schedule maintenance tasks, reducing equipment downtime during crucial periods such as planting and harvesting seasons. Other than that, transportation sectors, including aviation and logistics, harness the power of IoT for predictive maintenance. Connected sensors on aircraft engines or delivery vehicles track performance metrics, allowing for the early detection of potential issues. Airlines and logistics companies can then schedule maintenance activities strategically, minimising disruptions and ensuring the safety and reliability of their fleets.

The overarching impact of predictive maintenance with IoT extends beyond individual sectors, fostering a holistic approach to operational efficiency, cost reduction, and sustainability (Bibri et al., 2024). By anticipating maintenance needs and addressing them proactively, industries in the era of Industry 5.0 set new standards for reliability, resource utilisation, and overall system resilience across manufacturing, healthcare, smart cities, agriculture, and transportation sectors. As predictive maintenance continues to evolve, driven by the capabilities of IoT, it becomes a cornerstone in building intelligent and interconnected ecosystems that define the future of industrial and societal landscapes.

9.3   Real-world examples of IoT integration in Industry 5.0

In the unfolding landscape of Industry 5.0, the integration of IoT technologies stands as a cornerstone, reshaping the operational paradigms of leading entities like Rolls-Royce and Bosch. These industry giants exemplify the transformative power of IoT, showcasing how real-time data and predictive analytics redefine traditional practices. By delving into their applications, particularly in predictive maintenance and smart manufacturing, we gain valuable insights into how IoT integration fuels innovation, sustainability, and efficiency across diverse industrial sectors. Let us explore the concrete manifestations of Industry 5.0's vision through the experiences of Rolls-Royce and Bosch.

Rolls-Royce has strategically embraced Microsoft Azure IoT to address challenges in the aviation industry, focusing mainly on predictive maintenance and fuel efficiency (RTInsights, 2016). The aviation sector, characterised by high operating and maintenance costs, prompted Rolls-Royce to leverage IoT technologies to analyse data generated by various sensors in aircraft engines. This data encompasses real-time signals related to engine performance, wear-and-tear, and fuel efficiency. Rolls-Royce's TotalCare Services, which is responsible for engine reliability and maintenance, integrates Microsoft's Azure IoT Suite to collect and aggregate data from various sources. Rolls-Royce can proactively identify potential issues through predictive maintenance, ensuring optimal engine performance and minimising costly downtime. Additionally, analysing new data against forecasts allows for a deeper understanding of fuel efficiency factors, contributing to significant operational savings (Lee et al., 2019). The initiative showcases how IoT integration, specifically in predictive maintenance, can revolutionise industries with complex and high-cost operational structures.

The use of IoT in the industry has long been demonstrated by Bosch's (Bosch, 2018). The company's embrace of the IoT is evident in its goal to web-enable all Bosch electronic devices by 2020, creating a merged reality of virtual and physical worlds. With over 60 products and services in its portfolio, Bosch has successfully implemented connected solutions in nearly all of its 280 plants. The envisioned factory of the future is characterised by intelligent machines and human creativity, where data-driven insights enhance productivity, safety, and resource efficiency. Bosch recognises the evolving skill requirements in the era of digital transformation, emphasising the importance of interdisciplinary collaboration, information and communication technology (ICT) know-how, and social skills such as flexibility and lifelong learning. The company actively engages in education and training worldwide, establishing innovation centres. The seamless integration of data, analytics, and intelligent machines at Bosch leads to significant benefits, including increased productivity, reduced stock levels, and enhanced flexibility within plants.

Bosch's Nexeed software platform further exemplifies its commitment to simplifying and optimising manufacturing and logistics operations.

Intelligent machines, including collaborative robots, will enhance productivity and safety in future factories. Bosch's evaluation of collected data informs the continuous development and improvement of these technical assistants. Moreover, the increasing use of robots in industry, with global sales growing by 29 per cent in 2017, addresses workforce shortages while contributing to manufacturing process advancements. The success of Industry 4.0 implementation relies heavily on high-performance connectivity infrastructure. Bosch identifies 5G as a key technology, serving as the central nervous system in the factory of the future. Andreas Müller from Bosch, who chairs the 5G Alliance for Connected Industries and Automation (5G-ACIA), emphasises the importance of open standards, cross-industry collaborations, and global interdisciplinary cooperation in shaping the future of manufacturing. Bosch's forward-thinking approach lays the foundation for a transformative and interconnected industrial landscape.

These examples from Rolls-Royce and Bosch illustrate the tangible benefits of IoT integration in Industry 5.0. By leveraging real-time data and predictive analytics, these companies exemplify how IoT technologies are not just futuristic concepts but practical tools driving efficiency, sustainability, and innovation in the contemporary industrial landscape. These outcomes show that integrating IoT within Industry 5.0 can lead to substantial cost savings, efficiency improvements, and sustainability. These advancements make organisations more competitive and contribute to better products and services for customers.

9.4   Challenges in implementing IoT within Industry 5.0

Implementing the IoT within the paradigm of Industry 5.0 presents a revolutionary shift in industrial operations, fostering connectivity, data-driven decision-making, and intelligent automation. However, this transformative journey has challenges, as integrating IoT technologies into existing industrial frameworks requires overcoming several hurdles. One prominent challenge lies in the complexity of IoT infrastructure (Thilakarathne et al., 2022). As industries evolve towards more excellent connectivity, the sheer volume and diversity of devices, sensors, and data streams can become overwhelming. Establishing a coherent and standardised framework for IoT devices to communicate seamlessly is crucial. Interoperability issues between devices and platforms (Rane, 2023) must be addressed to ensure a harmonious integration for efficient data exchange and analysis.

Security emerges as another critical concern in the implementation of IoT within Industry 5.0 (Maddikunta et al., 2022). With more connected devices, the attack surface for potential cyber threats expands. Securing the vast network of IoT devices becomes paramount to prevent unauthorised access, data breaches, and potential disruptions to critical industrial processes. Robust security protocols, encryption standards, and continuous monitoring are imperative to safeguard data integrity and interconnected systems' reliability. Data privacy is intricately linked to security challenges (Ahmed & Khan, 2023). The sheer volume of data generated by IoT devices raises concerns about how this information is collected, stored, and utilised. Industries must navigate the delicate balance between leveraging data for operational insights and protecting the privacy of individuals, particularly as regulations surrounding data protection become more stringent. Implementing transparent data governance practices and adhering to privacy regulations is vital to building trust with consumers and stakeholders.

The scalability of IoT solutions poses yet another challenge (Breivold & Sandström, 2015). Industries often need to scale their operations, introducing more devices and sensors to accommodate growing demands. Ensuring IoT infrastructure can seamlessly scale to support these expansions is crucial for long-term success. Additionally, the cost associated with scaling IoT implementations, both in terms of hardware and connectivity, must be carefully managed to maintain the economic viability of these solutions. Reliability and resilience in technological failures or disruptions constitute significant challenges for Industry 5.0 (Khan et al., 2023). Industrial processes are often mission-critical, and any downtime resulting from IoT malfunctions can have severe consequences. Implementing redundant systems, failover mechanisms, and robust contingency plans becomes imperative to minimise disruptions and ensure the continuous operation of essential processes.

The need for a skilled workforce further compounds the complexity of integrating IoT technologies (Ozkan-Ozen & Kazancoglu, 2022). Industry 5.0 demands a workforce with IoT technologies, data analytics, and cybersecurity expertise. The shortage of skilled professionals in these domains poses a significant obstacle to the effective implementation of IoT solutions. Investing in training programmes, partnerships with educational institutions, and talent acquisition strategies becomes essential to bridge this skill gap. Interdisciplinary collaboration is a crucial aspect that cannot be overlooked. The convergence of ICT and operational technology requires collaboration between traditionally siloed departments within organisations (Farahani & Monsefi, 2023). Bridging the gap between ICT and operational technology teams, each with unique expertise and objectives, is crucial for implementing IoT within Industry 5.0. Establishing effective communication channels and fostering a collaborative culture is vital to overcoming this organisational challenge.

A robust and reliable communication infrastructure is another significant challenge in implementing IoT within Industry 5.0 (Ghosh et al., 2022). The success of IoT relies heavily on seamless communication between devices, sensors, and systems. High-bandwidth communication becomes essential as the number of connected devices proliferates, ensuring low latency (Fazel et al., 2023). The deployment of 5G technology holds promise in addressing this challenge by providing faster and more reliable connectivity. However, the widespread adoption of 5G and the associated infrastructure upgrades pose logistical and investment challenges for industries. Furthermore, the issue of standardisation emerges as a critical consideration. The absence of universally accepted standards for IoT devices and communication protocols can hinder interoperability and the seamless integration of diverse IoT ecosystems. Developing and adhering to common standards is vital to fostering a cohesive IoT environment where devices from different manufacturers can work together seamlessly. Industry consortia and international collaborations are crucial in establishing and promoting these standards.

Energy efficiency is a significant concern as the number of connected devices rises (He et al., 2022). Many IoT devices operate on limited power sources or rely on batteries, making energy consumption a critical factor. Striking a balance between the functionality of devices and their energy efficiency is a challenge that industries must address to ensure sustainable and cost-effective IoT implementations. Innovations in low-power devices, energy harvesting technologies, and optimised communication protocols are avenues to explore in mitigating this challenge. The concept of edge computing has become increasingly relevant in the context of IoT within Industry 5.0. Edge computing involves processing data closer to the source, reducing latency and the need to transmit large volumes of data to centralised cloud servers. While this approach offers advantages regarding real-time processing and bandwidth optimisation, managing and securing distributed edge computing environments pose challenges (Kong et al., 2022). Establishing robust edge computing architectures and ensuring data integrity and security at the edge become critical considerations for Industry 5.0 implementations.

Ethical considerations also come to the forefront in the era of IoT (Kizza, 2023). As devices become more interconnected and capable of collecting vast amounts of personal and sensitive data, ethical guidelines for data usage and transparency become imperative. Industries must navigate the ethical implications of IoT implementations, considering issues such as consent, data ownership, and the responsible use of technology. Establishing ethical frameworks and guidelines for IoT deployments is crucial to fostering trust among users and stakeholders. The dynamic nature of technology and the rapid pace of innovation contribute to the challenge of future-proofing IoT implementations. As new technologies and standards emerge, industries must ensure that their IoT infrastructure can seamlessly adapt to and integrate these advancements. Building flexible and scalable IoT architectures that evolve with technological developments is a strategic imperative for long-term success (Allioui & Mourdi, 2023).

As industries forge ahead with the integration of IoT within the framework of Industry 5.0, several additional challenges come to the forefront, shaping the landscape of intelligent and interconnected systems. The challenge arises in managing vast amounts of data generated by IoT devices (Azbeg et al., 2022). The sheer volume of data necessitates sophisticated data management strategies, including efficient storage, retrieval, and analysis mechanisms. Implementing advanced analytics and machine learning algorithms to derive actionable insights from the deluge of data becomes a critical undertaking. Moreover, ensuring data quality, accuracy, and relevance is paramount for making informed decisions, and industries must invest in data governance frameworks to address these concerns.

The longevity and sustainability of IoT devices pose environmental challenges. As connected devices increase, so does electronic waste (Rahmani et al., 2023).

Ensuring responsible disposal and recycling practices for obsolete or malfunctioning IoT devices becomes crucial. Industry 5.0 must prioritise sustainable design principles, including energy-efficient devices and environmentally friendly materials. Circular economy models, where components can be reused or recycled, should be embraced to minimise the environmental impact of IoT implementations.

In regulatory compliance, navigating diverse and evolving standards poses a challenge. Different regions and industries may have distinct regulations governing data privacy, security, and IoT device certifications (Rizvi et al., 2023). Harmonising these regulations and ensuring compliance across borders become complex tasks. Collaborative efforts between industry stakeholders and regulatory bodies are essential to establish coherent and globally applicable standards that promote responsible IoT deployments. The potential for unintended consequences and ethical dilemmas in AI-driven decision-making is an emerging challenge. As industries rely on machine learning algorithms to analyse IoT data and make autonomous decisions, issues related to bias, transparency, and accountability arise (Aldoseri et al., 2023). Addressing these challenges requires a multidisciplinary approach involving ethicists, data scientists, and policymakers to develop frameworks that ensure fair and ethical AI applications within Industry 5.0.

An often-overlooked challenge is integrating legacy systems with modern IoT infrastructure (Ivo et al., 2023). Many industries operate with existing technologies and equipment that are not designed to be part of a connected ecosystem. Retrofitting these legacy systems to accommodate IoT connectivity without disrupting ongoing operations poses a considerable challenge. Industries must develop seamless integration strategies, considering backward compatibility and scalability, to bridge the gap between legacy and modern technologies. The issue of trust in IoT systems presents a significant challenge. For Industry 5.0 to flourish, stakeholders, including consumers, employees, and business partners, must trust interconnected systems' reliability, security, and privacy. Establishing transparency in how data is collected, processed, and utilised and providing clear channels for recourse in case of issues is essential for building and maintaining trust in IoT implementations.

The economics of IoT deployment require careful consideration. While the potential benefits of increased efficiency, productivity, and innovation are substantial, the upfront costs of implementing IoT infrastructure can be significant. Industries must conduct thorough cost-benefit analyses to justify investments and ensure a favourable return on investment. Developing sustainable business models that align with the economic realities of Industry 5.0 is imperative for long-term success (Narkhede et al., 2023). The journey of implementing IoT within Industry 5.0 unfolds against a backdrop of multifaceted challenges that demand strategic and collaborative solutions. Addressing the challenges is essential for industries to fully harness IoT's transformative potential. Industries can propel themselves into a future where intelligent, connected systems redefine the landscape of industrial operations by navigating these challenges with foresight and adaptability.

References

Ahmed, S., & Khan, M. (2023). Securing the internet of things (IoT): A comprehensive study on the intersection of cybersecurity, privacy, and connectivity in the IoT ecosystem. *AI, IoT and the Fourth Industrial Revolution Review, 13*(9), 1–17.

Aldoseri, A., Al-Khalifa, K. N., & Hamouda, A. M. (2023). Re-thinking data strategy and integration for artificial intelligence: Concepts, opportunities, and challenges. *Applied Sciences, 13*(12), 7082. https://doi.org/10.3390/app13127082

Allioui, H., & Mourdi, Y. (2023). Exploring the full potentials of IoT for better financial growth and stability: A comprehensive survey. *Sensors, 23*(19), 8015. https://doi.org/10.3390/s23198015

Azbeg, K., Ouchetto, O., & Jai Andaloussi, S. (2022). BlockMedCare: A healthcare system based on IoT, blockchain and IPFS for data management security. *Egyptian Informatics Journal, 23*(2), 329–343. https://doi.org/10.1016/j.eij.2022.02.004

Bibri, S. E., Krogstie, J., Kaboli, A., & Alahi, A. (2024). Smarter eco-cities and their leading-edge artificial intelligence of things solutions for environmental sustainability: A comprehensive systematic review, *Environmental Science and Ecotechnology, 19*, 100330. https://doi.org/10.1016/j.ese.2023.100330

Bosch. (2018). *Industry 4.0 at Bosch: The power of an idea.* https://www.bosch-presse.de/pressportal/de/en/industry-4-0-at-bosch-the-power-of-an-idea-177024.html

Breivold, H. P., & Sandström, K. (2015). Internet of things for industrial automation–challenges and technical solutions. In 2015 IEEE International Conference on Data Science and Data Intensive Systems. https://doi.org/10.1109/DSDIS.2015.11

Chander, B., & Kumaravelan, G. (2020). Internet of things: Foundation. *Principles of Internet of Things (IoT) Ecosystem: Insight Paradigm*, 3–33. https://doi.org/10.1007/978-3-030-33596-0_1

Farahani, B., & Monsefi, A. K. (2023). Smart and collaborative industrial IoT: A federated learning and data space approach. *Digital Communications and Networks, 9*(2), 436–447. https://doi.org/10.1016/j.dcan.2023.01.022

Fazel, E., Najafabadi, H. E., Rezaei, M., & Leung, H. (2023). Unlocking the power of mist computing through clustering techniques in IoT networks. *Internet of Things, 22*, 100710. https://doi.org/10.1016/j.iot.2023.100710

Ghosh, S., Dagiuklas, T., Iqbal, M., & Wang, X. (2022). A cognitive routing framework for reliable communication in IoT for industry 5.0. *IEEE Transactions on Industrial Informatics, 18*(8), 5446–5457. https://doi.org/10.1109/TII.2022.3141403

Gürce, M. Y., Wang, Y., & Zheng, Y. (2023). Artificial intelligence and collaborative robots in healthcare: The perspective of healthcare professionals. In A. Saini & V. Garg (Eds.), *Transformation for sustainable business and management practices: Exploring the spectrum of industry 5.0* (pp. 309–325). Emerald Publishing Limited. https://doi.org/10.1108/978-1-80262-277-520231022

Hardesty, G. (2023). *IIoT top six wireless technologies compared: Industrial internet of things.* Data Alliance. https://www.data-alliance.net/blog/iiot-top-six-wireless-technologies-compared-industrial-internet-of-things/

Hassebo, A., & Tealab, M. (2023). Global models of smart cities and potential IoT applications: A review. *IoT, 4*(3), 366–411. https://doi.org/10.3390/iot4030017

He, P., Almasifar, N., Mehbodniya, A., Javaheri, D., & Webber, J. L. (2022). Towards green smart cities using internet of things and optimization algorithms: A systematic and bibliometric review. *Sustainable Computing: Informatics and Systems, 36*, 100822. https://doi.org/10.1016/j.suscom.2022.100822

Ivo, A. A., Ribeiro, S. G., Mattiello-Francisco, F., & Bondavalli, A. (2023). Towards conceptual analysis of cyber-physical systems projects focusing on the composition of legacy systems. *IEEE Access, 11*, 58136–58158. https:/doi.org/10.1109/ACCESS.2023.3284039

Javaid, M., Haleem, A., Rab, S., Singh, R. P., & Suman, R. (2021). Sensors for daily life: A review. *Sensors International, 2*, 100121. https://doi.org/10.1016/j.sintl.2021.100121

Khan, M., Haleem, A., & Javaid, M. (2023). Changes and improvements in industry 5.0: A strategic approach to overcome the challenges of industry 4.0. *Green Technologies and Sustainability, 1*(2), 100020. https://doi.org/10.1016/j.grets.2023.100020

Kizza, J. M. (2023). New frontiers of ethics and security: Internet of things (IoT). In *Ethical and social issues in the information age* (pp. 287–302). Springer. https://doi.org/10.1007/978-3-031-24863-4_15

Kong, L., Tan, J., Huang, J., Chen, G., Wang, S., Jin, X., & Das, S. K. (2022). Edge-computing-driven internet of things: A survey. *ACM Computing Surveys, 55*(8), 1–41. https://doi.org/10.1145/3555308

Lee, S. M., Lee, D., & Kim, Y. S. (2019). The quality management ecosystem for predictive maintenance in the industry 4.0 era. *International Journal of Quality Innovation, 5*, 1–11. https://doi.org/10.1186/s40887-019-0029-5

Liang, C., & Shah, T. (2023). IoT in agriculture: The future of precision monitoring and data-driven farming. *Eigenpub Review of Science and Technology, 7*(1), 85–104.

Longo, F., Padovano, A., Aiello, G., Fusto, C., & Certa, A. (2021). How 5G-based industrial IoT is transforming human-centered smart factories: A quality of experience model for operator 4.0 applications. *IFAC-PapersOnLine, 54*(1), 255–262. https://doi.org/10.1016/j.ifacol.2021.08.030

Maddikunta, P. K. R., Pham, Q.-V., B, P., Deepa, N., Dev, K., Gadekallu, T. R., & Liyanage, M. (2022). Industry 5.0: A survey on enabling technologies and potential applications. *Journal of Industrial Information Integration, 26*, 100257. https://doi.org/10.1016/j.jii.2021.100257

Manchadi, O., Ben-Bouazza, F.-E, & Jioudi, B.. (2023). Predictive maintenance in healthcare system: A survey. *IEEE Access. 11*, 61313–61330. https://doi.org/10.1109/ACCESS.2023.3287490

Mantravadi, S., Møller, C., Li, C., & Schnyder, R. (2022). Design choices for next-generation IoT-connected MES/MOM: An empirical study on smart factories. *Robotics and Computer-Integrated Manufacturing, 73*, 102225. https://doi.org/10.1016/j.rcim.2021.102225

Narkhede, G., Pasi, B., Rajhans, N., & Kulkarni, A. (2023). Industry 5.0 and the future of sustainable manufacturing: A systematic literature review. *Business Strategy & Development, 6*(4), 704–723. https://doi.org/10.1002/bsd2.272

Ozkan-Ozen, Y. D., & Kazancoglu, Y. (2022). Analysing workforce development challenges in the industry 4.0. *International Journal of Manpower, 43*(2), 310–333. https://doi.org/10.1108/IJM-03-2021-0167

Prabha, C., & Pathak, A. (2023). Enabling technologies in smart agriculture: A way forward towards future fields. In 2023 International Conference on Advancement in Computation & Computer Technologies (InCACCT). https://doi.org/10.1109/InCACCT57535.2023.10141722

Rahmani, H., Shetty, D., Wagih, M., Ghasempour, Y., Palazzi, V., Carvalho, N. B., & Alimenti, F. (2023). Next-generation IoT devices: Sustainable eco-friendly manufacturing, energy harvesting, and wireless connectivity. *IEEE Journal of Microwaves, 3*(1), 237–255. https://doi.org/10.1109/JMW.2022.3228683

Rane, N. (2023). Enhancing customer loyalty through artificial intelligence (AI), internet of things (IoT), and big data technologies: Improving customer satisfaction, engagement, relationship, and experience. *Internet of Things (IoT), and Big Data Technologies: Improving Customer Satisfaction, Engagement, Relationship, and Experience (October 13, 2023)*. http://dx.doi.org/10.2139/ssrn.4616051

Rizvi, S., Zwerling, T., Thompson, B., Faiola, S., Campbell, S., Fisanick, S., & Hutnick, C. (2023). A modular framework for auditing IoT devices and networks. *Computers & Security, 132*, 103327. https://doi.org/10.1016/j.cose.2023.103327

RTInsights. (2016). *How Rolls-Royce maintains Jet Engines with the IoT*. https://www.rtinsights.com/rolls-royce-jet-engine-maintenance-iot/

Soori, M., Arezoo, B., & Dastres, R. (2023). Internet of things for smart factories in industry 4.0, a review. *Internet of Things and Cyber-Physical Systems, 3*, 192–204. https://doi.org/10.1016/j.iotcps.2023.04.006

Thilakarathne, N. N., Kagita, M. K., & Priyashan, W. M. (2022). Green internet of things: The next generation energy efficient internet of things. In *Applied Information Processing Systems: Proceedings of ICCET 2021*. https://doi.org/10.1007/978-981-16-2008-9_38

Vermesan, O., Bröring, A., Tragos, E., Serrano, M., Bacciu, D., Chessa, S., & Saffiotti, A.. (2022). Internet of robotic things–converging sensing/actuating, hyperconnectivity, artificial intelligence and IoT platforms. In *Cognitive hyperconnected digital transformation* (pp. 97–155). River Publishers. https://doi.org/10.1201/9781003337584

10 5G-enabled IoT applications in healthcare

Transforming the Industry 5.0 healthcare landscape

Mohamad Nazim Jambli[1], *Mohd Zul Haziq Mohd Fadzli*[1], *Sinarwati Mohamad Suhaili*[2], *and Nur Haryani Zakaria*[3]

[1] *Faculty of Computer Science and Information Technology, Universiti Malaysia Sarawak, Sarawak, Malaysia*

[2] *Pre-University, Universiti Malaysia Sarawak, Sarawak, Malaysia*

[3] *School of Computing, Universiti Utara Malaysia, Kedah, Malaysia*

10.1 The synergy of 5G and IoT in revolutionising healthcare services

In our age of Industry 5.0 and its merging of digital, biological, and physical dimensions, healthcare is an emerging industry experiencing revolutionary transformation. Due to rising healthcare system burdens and an international need to ensure efficient patient care delivery, Remote Patient Monitoring (RPM) has taken centre stage among medical innovations. Its capabilities and potential are being driven forward by 5G technologies and the Internet of Things (IoT). Emerging technology, particularly the proliferation of 5G-enabled IoT applications for RPM, promises to revolutionise our health and wellness management approach. The foundation of this chapter lies in exploring recent advancements of these technologies as applied to chronic disease management; ailments like diabetes, cardiovascular ailments, and respiratory conditions take an immense toll on global health metrics, so their efficient management becomes paramount.

There are numerous advantages of integrating 5G and IoT for healthcare applications, from real-time monitoring of patients, increased engagement, cost reductions, and potential new revenue sources to artificial intelligence (AI)/machine learning techniques that may make healthcare strategies less reactive but become proactive over time. 5G should support intelligent healthcare applications by meeting key benchmarks such as high bandwidth consumption and energy efficiency. However, creating an integrated 5G IoT healthcare ecosystem can sometimes be treacherous. Issues related to energy conservation, data privacy, system security, and regulatory

DOI: 10.1201/9781003479727-10

framework are prevalent, yet their potential advantages provide plenty of insights, debates, and considerations that this chapter seeks to dissect further.

The recent research methodologies used in RPM to make sense of processes and algorithms set new standards in this area of medicine. For instance, its three-layered methodology of data acquisition, preprocessing, and disease prediction reveals some of the subtle complexities involved with collecting patient data to achieve optimal results while emphasising the use of machine learning algorithms for predictive accuracy when monitoring diabetic patients. As we embark on this analytical journey through this chapter, readers will gain a holistic overview of 5G-enabled IoT applications in RPM today. This chapter seeks to pave the way for future research in this exciting space by drawing attention to any gaps or inconsistencies found within existing literature.

5G IoT technology's revolutionary effect in healthcare can only be witnessed today through RPM; hospitals especially can attest to this revolutionary phenomenon as its application provides unparalleled improvements for patient treatment. A combination of cloud computing and 5G offers unprecedented advances in treatment outcomes. As evidenced during the COVID-19 pandemic, RPM became even more evident as traditional patient management methods proved insufficient against direct contact transmission virus challenges.

According to Li (2019), 5G outshines its predecessor, 4G, by accommodating more simultaneous users simultaneously and boasts dramatic latency reduction—from 20 milliseconds seen with 4G LTE down to as little as one millisecond with 5G, which makes for quicker responses for applications like Telemedicine or Virtual Reality applications. Impact during COVID-19: During COVID-19, RPM proved its value. Vedaei et al. (2020) highlighted its usefulness when an IoT platform was put in place to track key vital signs connected with edge devices connected with 5G infrastructure.

Hospitals are creating sophisticated telehealth infrastructures, employing skilled technicians for seamless electronic health record (EHR) transmission and expert knowledge of medical data standards (Gupta et al., 2021). With 5G, doctors can quickly offer medical advice via video calls, while medical imaging requiring high-speed transmission becomes seamless. 5G not only offers hospital patient monitoring benefits but can also elevate wearable smart medical device monitoring for individuals, as Li (2019) stated. It facilitates real-time remote monitoring necessary for making complex decisions while simultaneously supporting multiple sensors or video cameras. Mobile health (mHealth), called mobile informatics (MI), encompasses mobile phones, sensors, wearables, implants, and more that provide personalised health informatics. According to Kyriacou and Sherratt (2019), its scope extends far beyond smartphones; instead, its goal is to bring health assistance directly into rural areas via technology solutions aimed at broadening assistance beyond smartphones—potentially changing healthcare in developing nations with limited infrastructure by meeting unique healthcare requirements more efficiently than before.

5G offers limitless opportunities yet also presents daunting obstacles—data privacy issues, security threats, infrastructure deployment, and regulatory concerns concerning healthcare data can all present issues for consideration. However, its potential advantages, such as mitigating infection risks and increasing hospital intelligence services, should not be forgotten. 5G has already proven its worth in healthcare by being successfully deployed in China's Sichuan province, where improved video quality for CT imaging of COVID-19 patients led to more efficient diagnoses that helped cut fatality ratios by 25% (Hong et al., 2020). Keerthi et al. (2020) highlighted the rising need for integrated systems specifically to support elderly care needs, with applications offering health status views, medication reminders, and medical appointment scheduling with connected remote monitoring devices. These developments are being explored.

10.2   Exploring innovative 5G-enabled IoT applications in the healthcare industry

5G integration with IoT has created significant change within healthcare, especially RPM. Understanding the depth and potential of these advancements is vital. Cloud computing and 5G technologies have revolutionised hospital patient care, surpassing traditional methodologies. When combined with global challenges such as the COVID-19 pandemic outbreak, their significance becomes even more apparent, such as decreasing direct transmission while managing patients effectively. 5G promises an impressive leap over its predecessor, 4G. Boasting lower latency (from 20 ms in 4G down to as little as 1 ms with 5G) and supporting more users simultaneously than previous wireless technologies, 5G stands as an invaluable solution for healthcare telemedicine, virtual reality applications, seamless data transmission between systems, seamless patient monitoring capabilities, and seamless telehealth support services (Li, 2019).

Real-time RPM with wearable smart medical devices (Li, 2019); enhanced telemedicine capabilities to ensure equitable distribution of healthcare resources—particularly in areas lacking medical personnel; Advanced applications that display vital statistics through smartphone apps and provide predictive insight on infection risks (Vedaei et al., 2020) offer potential solutions. RPM technologies hold great potential to ease hospital overcrowding and manage anticipated data surges more effectively, providing medical practitioners with information to make more informed decisions, thus improving patient outcomes and streamlining hospital operations.

The recent pandemic has underlined the value of RPM as an essential strategy in combating infectious disease outbreaks. Kyriacou and Sherratt (2019) highlighted the rapidly developing field of mHealth encompassing devices like mobile phones, medical sensors, and wearables, as well as wearable trackers with location-tracking features; this field could soon revolutionise health services by providing customised treatments with limited health infrastructure in regions like Afghanistan. Rghioui et al. (2020) designed AI algorithms for diabetic patients using 5G technology and big data analysis for real-time decision-making, improving quality of life while decreasing healthcare system costs. These systems enhance healthcare costs overall while simultaneously monitoring patients on an ongoing basis and offering continuous monitoring systems to monitor progression over time.

While 5G and IoT bring numerous advantages, they also present unique difficulties. Data privacy concerns, security threats, network deployment limitations, regulatory proposals, and network deployment limitations require an unbiased approach to adopting them in healthcare environments. Integration of 5G into healthcare demands robust telecom infrastructures. Due to real-time transmission requirements for medical images, patient records, and telehealth consultations, telecom operators could play an integral role in this transformational effort, potentially unlocking new revenue streams (Gupta et al., 2021).

10.3   Addressing challenges and ensuring security in 5G-enabled IoT healthcare systems

Wearable sensors have quickly emerged as pivotal technologies in RPM, providing healthcare professionals with access to vital physiological data such as vital statistics and essential health markers in real-time, which they transmit back through real-time data transmission to both local and distant servers for analysis by healthcare professionals to effectively evaluate each patient and make necessary medical interventions. Zaabar et al. (2021) identified blockchain technology as an essential way of guaranteeing transactional security within RPM systems. For their study, Hyperledger Fabric, a permissioned blockchain platform, was chosen due to its modular structure, which can adapt its configurations according to individual stakeholder needs in RPM—such as different encryption techniques, consensus algorithms, or service ordering mechanisms.

Su et al. (2021) proposed an innovative cloud-based platform to manage chronic diseases using edge computing and cloud computing. Their dual computing approach improves patient monitoring through edge imaging and time series modules integrating edge computing, thus providing essential data to healthcare teams. Ianculescu et al. (2020) stressed the significance of multilayered security measures within RO-Smart Ageing system to combat cyber threats, with continuous monitoring and adherence to robust security protocols proving crucial as technology rapidly develops. Heydari et al. (2020) offer additional strategies for device security by emphasising selective jammers for safeguarding Bluetooth low energy (BLE) devices as well as moving target defence (MTD) tactics. By employing lightweight virtual machines (VMs) on smartphones and desktop computers, sensitive software or data can be isolated more effectively, protecting medical device integrity.

Braeken and Liyanage (2021) highlighted the many advantages of integrating 5G mobile edge computing (MEC) IoT, including high scalability, enhanced security, and greater privacy. Furthermore, using symmetric keys ensures efficiency against cybersecurity breaches, while Akram et al. (2022) highlighted AES encryption as a key to safeguarding patient records while only permitting authorised access. Multiple research studies have validated blockchain's utility in protecting data privacy and secure communication in RPM (Basnolli & Cana, 2020).

Lin et al. (2021) presented an SC-UCSSO strategy explicitly designed for 5G-IoT telemedicine systems and demonstrated its security through various tools and methodologies. This strategy is protected from potential threats while creating an ideal operating environment for telemedicine activities. As 5G and IoT continue their revolution in healthcare, it remains crucial that any challenges relating to their deployment be met head-on with robust security. Multiple layers of protection, from blockchain to encryption standards, must remain in place to preserve integrity and trustworthiness within these advanced healthcare systems.

10.4   Implementation of 5G-enabled IoT applications in remote patient monitoring

5G's disruptive impact in healthcare, specifically IoT applications for RPM, has been widely covered in academic scholarship. Its speed, reliability, and bandwidth capabilities offer unique possibilities to enhance patient care while making healthcare more accessible and efficient for everyone. Zhang et al. (2020) were pioneering researchers who recognised the transformative potential of MEC. Their groundbreaking telemedicine system relied heavily on MEC coupled with AI. Their work highlighted how this combination could change patient treatment methods while becoming more cost-efficient and effective; when healthcare costs continue to skyrocket, such innovations provide hope for more cost-efficient medical care options.

Lakshmi et al. (2018) also pioneered innovative ideas with their proposed cloud-centric IoT healthcare sensor mechanism. Their system would monitor various health parameters remotely, from heart rate and stress levels to advanced metrics such as eye colour, enabling timely intervention if required. 5G healthcare applications go well beyond speed and efficiency; their main benefit is improving care quality as a whole. Peralta-Ochoa et al. (2023) provided an in-depth exploration of this concept with their systematic review, highlighting 5G networks' profound ramifications combined with the Internet of Medical Things (IoMT) tools. Together, these collaborations could create entirely new standards of personalised and responsive medical treatments—potentially setting new benchmarks in quality standards of medical care delivery and making treatments even more personalised and responsive over time.

Thayananthan's (2019) research adds an intriguing layer to this discussion. By employing ICT together with IoT on 5G platforms, he introduced an innovative healthcare management strategy. His work showed how efficient management protocols could be harmonised with eHealth applications for optimal care of seniors and those needing continuous monitoring. Ahad et al. (2023) foresaw that 5G networks will play an instrumental role in healthcare's future, showing their ultra-low latency, significant bandwidth, and energy-saving capacities as indispensable tools in smart healthcare applications. They illustrated these characteristics by exploring its various uses, such as ultra-low latency applications with ultra-low latency network elucidation techniques, to demonstrate what 5G offers smart healthcare applications.

Braeken and Liyanage (2021) introduced an ingenious protocol designed to increase security and efficiency within 5G networks by emphasising mutual authentication and unlinkability. Their work focused on IoT devices, MEC centres, and registration centres, which come together, thus emphasising how seamless collaborations could occur within these environments while remaining secure.

Rismawaty Arunglabi et al. (2022) demonstrated how 5G can bring real-time advantages, particularly when used alongside deep learning techniques, making immediate patient monitoring, disease diagnosis, and timely treatments possible. Their work demonstrated this reality beautifully.

Kumar et al. (2020) shed light on how 5G can significantly advance smart healthcare practices by developing an adaptive multi-faceted detection approach designed to optimise network latency, spectrum, and throughput attributes. Lloret et al. (2017) conducted an exhaustive comparative analysis of 5G's particular advantages. They noted how it outshone previous generations by offering higher bandwidth and reduced delays—two benefits of 5G, an ideal candidate for persistent patient monitoring, particularly chronic cases. Nasri and Mtibaa's (2017) contribution concluded our exploration by adding a mobile dimension. Their proposal of an IoT health solution using 5G technology that uses a smartphone interface offers timely detection of health anomalies while alerting medical personnel at an earlier point than before.

Overall, 5G technology combined with IoT applications promises revolutionising RPM. Each research breakthrough brings us one step closer towards an ideal healthcare model aimed at being efficient and patient-centric. Oleshchuk and Fensli (2010) stated that healthcare's transition towards adopting advanced remote monitoring techniques depends upon having access to an established mobile communication infrastructure with systems boasting high bandwidth and superior service quality—the vision may seem promising, but overcoming its many hurdles presents unique challenges that must be understood thoroughly for success. Boikanyo et al. (2023) assert that geographical placement and its implications are critical, not simply as logistical matters but rather to determine their effectiveness and efficiency. Urban areas might appear suitable for implementation; however, with their limited connectivity, rural areas present additional obstacles that must be navigated carefully to succeed. Urban environments, though better connected, present their own set of unique challenges. Mobile nodes experience inconsistent network speeds and connectivity due to being transient devices; data delivery in densely trafficked areas often takes much longer compared to its counterparts stationed elsewhere.

Mishra et al. (2021) explored the challenges associated with data storage and dissemination, specifically offline patient storage, which presents many logistical obstacles when fast information retrieval and sharing are key priorities. EHRs provide an invaluable digital repository of patient data, acting not only as a practical storage solution but also as a hub, encouraging interoperability and creating unhindered exchange between caregivers and patients in transactions and interpersonal communications—not simply transactional exchange. Healthcare practitioners can now better tailor personalised medication regimens that ensure timely medical interventions utilising digital data. But even with all this digital progress, a strong communication backbone must remain. A heterogeneous technological framework designed for high-data-rate transmission across diverse frequency bands becomes the need of the hour.

5G integration into the existing technological landscape is not seamless; Pons et al. (2023) identified potential issues like interference issues and network optimisation that require fine-tuning by network managers to maintain optimal service provision for IoT applications, therefore requiring meticulous tuning of architecture to meet demanding scenarios efficiently. Li (2019) explored connectivity from various angles and highlighted its central role in industrial Internet environments. Here, diverse devices ranging from sensors to computers must operate seamlessly, while data transmission lines must be fast and completely reliable to guarantee uninterrupted functionality of all machinery connected via the industrial Internet.

Siriwardhana et al. (2020) highlighted 5G's current commercial deployment as incipient, noting its benefits are contingent upon consistent, wide-scale connectivity, something still unrealised. Georgiou et al. (2021) described how volumetric data analysis becomes tedious as volumes grow; further, their system could quickly become overwhelmed due to such an immense influx of images. Li (2019) noted the 4G era's bandwidth limitations as one of its defining traits, even among more advanced variants like 4G LTE-advanced, which provided download speeds that barely scratched the surface of potential healthcare demands. Ahad et al. (2019) focused on the challenges of expansive IoT device connectivity and how one can ensure consistent connection across many devices when mobility comes into the mix.

Additionally, prolonging battery lifespan becomes paramount to sustainable healthcare deployments internationally. Hayajneh et al. (2020) highlighted the urgency healthcare applications pose to society. For example, by monitoring glucose levels with a Wireless Body Area Network (WBAN), prompt response mechanisms can save lives regarding swift insulin dosage adjustments—emphasising the necessity of fast and secure authentication protocols. While 5G holds tremendous promise for revolutionising RPM, many challenges must be navigated carefully to unlock its full potential.

10.5   Future development of remote monitoring on 5G

The emergence of 5G networks heralds an important chapter in wireless communications history, opening doors for unprecedented advancements in real-time operational control, remote functionalities, and seamless data gathering. Existing infrastructure, most notably Long-Term Evolution (LTE), has served its purpose well and played an essential part in wireless evolution; yet, as Szalay et al. (2020) findings indicate, when combined with an optimised edge computing framework, 5G's potential becomes evident—providing enhancements like delay/jitter reduction of unprecedented proportions previously unimaginable enhancements formerly unattainable before.

History shows that the evolution of Internet networking is both predictable and revolutionary. Today's global populace enjoys 4G wireless network technology as the fourth rendition of macrocell-based mobile connectivity, yet as Abdalla et al. (2019) highlighted, 5G promises more excellent wide area coverage—an expansion to connectivity beyond ever imagined. 5G New Radio (NR) represents more than just another step in network evolution; it promises to transform how data transmission occurs and is experienced. Wang et al. (2021) explore network delays through clock-synchronised devices, specifically measuring parameters such as air interface delay and end-to-end delay in laboratory settings. However, these attempts also shed light on existing challenges, including those associated with synchronising clocks of two Automated Guided Vehicles (AGVs) within industrial wireless networks.

Security, an essential feature of digital development, plays an essential part in 5G considerations. Braeken and Liyanage (2021) dug deep into this topic by proposing an intricacy symmetric key-based protocol for 5G devices. This exercise is not academic; the intent here is to enhance performance while building an impregnable fortress against cyber threats. Basnolli and Cana (2020) and Daraghmi et al. (2019) have produced groundbreaking studies exploring the explosive growth of digital healthcare. The studies provide insight into its future trajectory. Their studies advocate combining 5G low-latency capabilities and blockchain's immutability features, thus creating enhanced data protection, reduced fraud risks, and an unbreakable framework to support its continued advancement into future healthcare spheres.

Kumar et al. (2021) examined 5G's potential in-depth, emphasising its edge computing integration as key in mitigating latency and jitter levels and surpassing current LTE configurations. Jia et al. (2020) added further depth by proposing an innovative wireless input/output (I/O) system designed specifically to transmit signals between I/O nodes in 5G-centric local area network (LAN) environments, taking full advantage of the Open Platform Communications United Architecture (OPC UA) protocol capabilities to do so. As Kecskés et al. (2021) highlighted, 5G does not come without challenges. While serving as an epicentre of modern communications technology, its security implications pose unique security issues in its dynamic ecosystem—thus necessitating rigorous network traffic analysis for 5G networks.

Giannopoulos et al. (2021) introduced another element into this tale by discussing network slicing. This practice allows multiple virtual networks on a single infrastructure to offer tailored services across diverse fields with increasing popularity through models like Network Slice as a Service (NSaaS) model. By broadening their view, Wu and Zhu (2020) showcased all the diverse applications of 5G, from pinpointing distribution network anomalies to improving video transmission fidelity. Its features stem from 5G's generous bandwidth and rapid transmission rates. 5G promises more than mere ripples in telecommunications waters; instead, it has immense promise to transform remote monitoring by adding efficiency, security, and expansivity. Once established in various sectors across society, its imprint will linger long into its future, inexorably shaping digital interactions and operations.

Industry 5.0 marks an exciting chapter in industrial history where human-machine collaboration reaches new heights. This chapter highlighted the complex relationships involved with this partnership, specifically within RPM enabled by 5G networks. Human intuition, judgement, empathy, and 5G's computational speed and efficiency represent a paradigm shift in healthcare delivery. At its heart, data management goes far beyond simple transmission speed; instead, it must serve people directly. As 5G continues its early stage and network discrepancies appear across various terrains, the principles behind Industry 5.0 provide guidance. Its potential is immense, emphasising co-creating value through human/machine collaboration. Dream of Industry 5.0 does not simply refer to an automated world that serves humans; instead, it emphasises an environment in which machines work alongside us as partners in understanding and fulfilling human needs and desires.

Innovation, empathy, and the relentless pursuit of an improved human experience through technology are its paths towards realisation.

Acknowledgement

This work was supported by the Ministry of Education Malaysia under Prototype Development Research Grant Scheme 2023 (PRGS/1/2023/ICT02/UNIMAS/02/2).

References

Abdalla, A. M., Rodriguez, J., Elfergani, I., & Teixeira, A. (Eds.). (2019). *Optical and wireless convergence for 5G networks*. John Wiley & Sons.

Ahad, A., Ali, Z., Mateen, A., Tahir, M., Hannan, A., Garcia, N. M., & Pires, I. M. (2023). A comprehensive review on 5G-based smart healthcare network security: Taxonomy, issues, solutions and future research directions. *Array, 18*, 100290. https://doi.org/10.1016/j.array.2023.100290

Ahad, A., Tahir, M., & Yau, K.-L. A. (2019). 5G-based smart healthcare network: Architecture, taxonomy, challenges and future research directions. *IEEE Access, 7*, 100747–100762. https://doi.org/10.1109/access.2019.2930628

Akram, M., Iqbal, M. W., Ali, S. A., Ashraf, M. U., Alsubhi, K., & Aljahdali, H. M. (2022). Triple key security algorithm against single key attack on multiple rounds. *Computers, Materials & Continua, 72*(3), 6061–6077.

Basnolli, A., & Cana, H. (2020, August). A novel sensor-based architecture using 5G and blockchain for remote and continuous health monitoring. In *International Symposium on Health Information Management Research*. https://open.lnu.se/index.php/ishimr/article/view/2519

Boikanyo, K., Zungeru, A. M., Sigweni, B., Yahya, A., & Lebekwe, C. (2023). Remote patient monitoring systems: Applications, architecture, and challenges. *Scientific African, 20*, e01638. https://doi.org/10.1016/j.sciaf.2023.e01638

Braeken, A., & Liyanage, M. (2021). Highly efficient key agreement for remote patient monitoring in MEC-enabled 5G networks. *The Journal of Supercomputing, 77*, 5562–5585. https://doi.org/10.1007/s11227-020-03472-y

Daraghmi, E. Y., Daraghmi, Y. A., & Yuan, S. M. (2019). MedChain: A design of blockchain-based system for medical records access and permissions management. *IEEE Access, 7*, 164595–164613.

Georgiou, K. E., Georgiou, E., & Satava, R. M. (2021). 5G use in healthcare: The future is present. *Journal of the Society of Laparoscopic & Robotic Surgeons, 25*(4), e2021.00064. https://doi.org/10.4293/jsls.2021.00064

Giannopoulos, D., Papaioannou, P., Tranoris, C., & Denazis, S. (2021). Monitoring as a service over a 5G network slice. In *2021 joint European conference on networks and communications & 6G summit (EuCNC/6G summit)* (pp. 329–334). IEEE. https://doi.org/10.1109/EuCNC/6GSummit51104.2021.9482534

Gupta, N., Juneja, P. K., Sharma, S., & Garg, U. (2021). Future aspect of 5G-IoT architecture in smart healthcare system. In *2021 5th International Conference on Intelligent Computing and Control Systems (ICICCS)* (pp. 406–411). IEEE. https://doi.org/10.1109/ICICCS51141.2021.9432082

Hayajneh, A. A., Alam Bhuiyan, M. Z., & McAndrew, I. (2020). Security of broadcast authentication for cloud-enabled wireless medical sensor devices in 5G networks. *Computer and Information Science, 13*(2), 13. https://doi.org/10.5539/cis.v13n2p13

Heydari, M., Mylonas, A., Heydari, V. F. T., Benkhelifa, E., & Singh, S. (2020). Known unknowns: Indeterminacy in authentication in IoT. *Future Generation Computer Systems*, *111*, 278–287, ISSN 0167-739X. https://doi.org/10.1016/j.future.2020.03.005

Hong, Z., Li, N., Li, D., Li, J., Li, B., Xiong, W., & Zhou, D. (2020). Telemedicine during the COVID-19 pandemic: Experiences from Western China. *Journal of Medical Internet Research*, *22*(5), e19577. https://doi.org/10.2196/19577

Ianculescu, M., Coardoş, D., Bica, O., & Vevera, V. (2020, October). Security and privacy risks for remote healthcare monitoring systems. In *2020 International Conference on e-Health and Bioengineering (EHB)* (pp. 1–4). IEEE. https://doi.org/10.1109/EHB50910.2020.9280103

Jia, Z., Xia, W., Li, D., & Zhang, W. (2020). 5G remote I/O system design and implement in industry. In *2020 IEEE Conference on Telecommunications, Optics and Computer Science (TOCS)* (pp. 243–246). IEEE. https://doi.org/10.1109/TOCS50858.2020.9339619

Kecskés, M. V., Orsós, M., Kail, E., & Bánáti, A. (2021, November). Monitoring 5G networks in security operation center. In *2021 IEEE 21st International Symposium on Computational Intelligence and Informatics (CINTI)* (pp. 000223–000228). IEEE. https://doi.org/10.1109/CINTI53070.2021.9668469

Keerthi, A. M., Raksha, R., & Rakesh, N. (2020, November). A novel remote monitoring smart system for the elderly using Internet of Things. In *2020 4th International Conference on Electronics, Communication and Aerospace Technology (ICECA)* (pp. 596–602). IEEE. https://doi.org/10.1109/ICECA49313.2020.9297403

Kumar, A., Albreem, M. A., Gupta, M., Alsharif, M. H., & Kim, S. (2020). Future 5G network based smart hospitals: Hybrid detection technique for latency improvement. *IEEE Access*, *8*, 153240–153249. https://doi.org/10.1109/access.2020.3017625

Kumar, N. S., Kaur, U., Anuradha, T., Majji, S., Karanam, S. R., & Deshmukh, R. G. (2021, December). 5G network virtualisation for the remote driving enhancement. In *2021 4th International Conference on Computing and Communications Technologies (ICCCT)* (pp. 458–463). IEEE. https://doi.org/10.1109/ICCCT53315.2021.9711894

Kyriacou, A., & Sherratt, C. (2019). Online health information–seeking behavior by endocrinology patients. *Hormones*, *18*, 495–505. https://doi.org/10.1007/s42000-019-00159-9

Lakshmi, G., Ghonge, M., & Obaid, A. (2018). Cloud based IoT smart healthcare system for remote patient monitoring. *EAI En-Dorsed Transactions on Pervasive Health and Technology*, 170296. https://doi.org/10.4108/eai.15-7-2021.170296

Li, D. (2019). 5G and intelligence medicine—How the next generation of wireless technology will reconstruct healthcare? *Precision Clinical Medicine*, *2*(4), 205–208. https://doi.org/10.1093/pcmedi/pbz020

Lin, T.-W., Hsu, C.-L., Le, T.-V., Lu, C.-F., & Huang, B.-Y. (2021). A smartcard-based user-controlled single sign-on for privacy preservation in 5G-IoT telemedicine systems. *Sensors*, *21*(8), 2880. https://doi.org/10.3390/s21082880

Lloret, J., Parra, L., Taha, M., & Tomás, J. (2017). An architecture and protocol for smart continuous eHealth monitoring using 5G. *Computer Networks*, *129*, 340–351. https://doi.org/10.1016/j.comnet.2017.05.018

Mishra, L., Vikash, & Varma, S. (2021). Seamless health monitoring using 5G NR for internet of medical things. *Wireless Personal Communications*, *120*(3), 2259–2289. https://doi.org/10.1007/s11277-021-08730-7

Nasri, F., & Mtibaa, A. (2017). Smart mobile healthcare system based on WBSN and 5G. *International Journal of Advanced Computer Science and Applications*, *8*(10), 147–156. https://doi.org/10.14569/ijacsa.2017.081020

Oleshchuk, V., & Fensli, R. (2010). Remote patient monitoring within a future 5G infrastructure. *Wireless Personal Communications*, *57*(3), 431–439. https://doi.org/10.1007/s11277-010-0078-5

Peralta-Ochoa, A. M., Chaca-Asmal, P. A., Guerrero-Vásquez, L. F., Ordoñez-Ordoñez, J. O., & Coronel-González, E. J. (2023). Smart healthcare applications over 5G networks: A systematic review. *Applied Sciences*, *13*(3), 1469. https://doi.org/10.3390/app13031469

Pons, M., Valenzuela, E., Rodríguez, B., Nolazco-Flores, J. A., & Del-Valle-Soto, C. (2023). Utilisation of 5G technologies in IoT applications: Current limitations by interference and network optimisation difficulties - a review. *Sensors*, *23*(8), 3876. https://doi.org/10.3390/s23083876

Rghioui, A., Lloret, J., Sendra, S., & Oumnad, A. (2020). A smart architecture for diabetic patient monitoring using machine learning algorithms. *Healthcare*, *8*(3), 348. https://doi.org/10.3390/healthcare8030348

Rismawaty Arunglabi, A. T., Charnia, & Askar Taliang, M. R. (2022). 5G technology in smart healthcare and smart city development integration with deep learning architectures. *International Journal of Communication Networks and Information Security*, *14*(3), 99–109. https://doi.org/10.17762/ijcnis.v14i3.5575

Siriwardhana, Y., De Alwis, C., Gur, G., Ylianttila, M., & Liyanage, M. (2020). The fight against the COVID-19 pandemic with 5G technologies. *IEEE Engineering Management Review*, *48*(3), 72–84. https://doi.org/10.1109/EMR.2020.3017451

Su, H., Yao, L., Hou, D., Sun, M., Hou, J., Ying, J., Feng, H. Y., Chen, P. Y., & Hou, R. (2021). Cloud computing management architecture for digital health remote patient monitoring. In *Proceedings—2021 IEEE International Conference on Smart Computing, SMARTCOMP 2021* (pp. 209–214). IEEE. https://doi.org/10.1109/SMARTCOMP52413.2021.00049

Szalay, Z., Ficzere, D., Tihanyi, V., Magyar, F., Soós, G., & Varga, P. (2020). 5G-enabled autonomous driving demonstration with a V2X scenario-in-the-loop approach. *Sensors*, *20*(24), 7344. https://doi.org/10.3390/s20247344

Thayananthan, V. (2019). Healthcare management using ICT and IoT based 5G. *International Journal of Advanced Computer Science and Applications*, *10*(4), 305–312. https://doi.org/10.14569/ijacsa.2019.0100437

Vedaei, S. S., Fotovvat, A., Mohebbian, M. R., Rahman, G. M., Wahid, K. A., Babyn, P., & Sami, R. (2020). COVID-SAFE: An IoT-based system for automated health monitoring and surveillance in post-pandemic life. *IEEE Access*, *8*, 188538–188551. https://doi.org/10.1109/ACCESS.2020.3030194

Wang, L., Liu, Q., Zang, C., Zhu, S., Gan, C., & Liu, Y. (2021). Formation control of dual auto guided vehicles based on compensation method in 5G networks. *Machines*, *9*(12), 318. https://doi.org/10.3390/machines9120318

Wu, W., & Zhu, Y. (2020). Intelligent terminal monitoring system of distribution network for 5G network. In *2020, 4th International Conference on Power and Energy Engineering (ICPEE)* (pp. 43–47). https://doi.org/10.1109/ICPEE51316.2020.9311059

Zaabar, B., Cheikhrouhou, O., Ammi, M., Awad, A. I., & Abid, M. (2021). Secure and privacy-aware blockchain-based remote patient monitoring system for internet of healthcare things. In *2021 17th International Conference on Wireless and Mobile Computing, Networking and Communications (WiMob)* (pp. 200–205). IEEE.

Zhang, Y., Chen, G., Du, H., Yuan, X., Kadoch, M., & Cheriet, M. (2020). Real-time remote health monitoring system driven by 5G MEC-IOT. *Electronics*, *9*(11), 1753. https://doi.org/10.3390/electronics9111753

11 Enhancing data capacity of a QR code

Empowering Industry 5.0 applications

Puteri Nurul'Ain Adil Md Sabri, Azizi Abas, and Fazli Azzali

School of Computing, Universiti Utara Malaysia, Sintok, Kedah, Malaysia

11.1 QR code technology: Fundamental and applications

Initially conceived for inventory management in the automotive sector, quick response (QR) code technology has transformed into a versatile tool with broad applications. Beyond its roots, QR codes are now pivotal in contactless payments, ticketing, and seamless information retrieval through smartphones. As we delve into Industry 5.0, QR codes become even more integral, facilitating enhanced connectivity and data exchange between humans, machines, and smartphones. This synergy not only streamlines real-time monitoring and improves efficiency in industrial processes but also underscores the technology's role in fostering the integration of digital advancements across various sectors. The advancement in smartphone technology also plays a significant role in the daily usage of QR codes. Digital media and communications technology are rapidly growing along with the use of smartphones. Consequently, wireless and mobile communication technology seamlessly allows various activities, including social networking and online shopping, creating object recognition and payment methods through QR codes. It has led to a larger storage capacity needed to store data information in industry settings, for example, packaging or storing product information, passenger control on the ticketing system, and prescriptions, to name a few.

The inception of two-dimensional barcodes dates back to 1990, significantly influencing privacy and copyright fields due to their ability to store more information than 1D barcodes. Denso, a prominent company within the Toyota group, pioneered QR code technology in September 1994, earning international recognition as a standard by the International Standard Organisation (ISO), specifically ISO/IEC18004, in June 2000 (Ebner, 2008). As a matrix barcode readable by smartphones and mobile devices, QR codes, commonly recognised as white squares with black geometric shapes, efficiently encode text, URLs, or other data. The global adoption of QR codes, particularly in Japan and Korea, is rising as they prove increasingly popular and practical for real-life applications, given their swift decoding capability.

QR codes serve as data visualisation, facilitating rapid content scanning through QR code scanners. They have gained popularity for their ability to store substantial amounts of data in a compact space. The QR code system comprises two key components: a QR code encoder and a QR code decoder

DOI: 10.1201/9781003479727-11

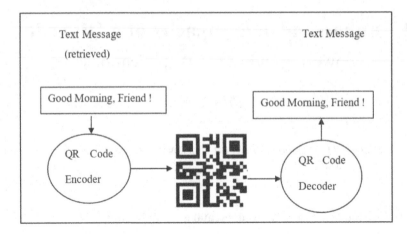

Figure 11.1 Overview of QR code encoding and decoding.

(Tiwari, 2017). The encoder is responsible for encoding data and generating the QR code, while the decoder focuses on extracting and decoding the data from the QR code. Figure 11.1 illustrates the process of encoding and decoding text into a QR code.

The QR code system comprises 40 versions, each capable of encoding varying data sizes. However, it is crucial to note that higher data capacity increases paper space consumption (Clover et al., 2016). The size of a colour QR code is influenced by three key factors, detailed in Table 11.1, which outlines QR code specifications. Firstly, the data type, whether numeric, alphanumeric, or binary, impacts the size as data needs to be converted to bits for transmission. Secondly, the error correction level (ECL), categorised into four levels, inversely affects the data capacity within the QR code—the higher the ECL, the less data can be encoded. Lastly, the number of layers in the colour QR code contributes to expanding data size, with additional layers facilitating increased information storage.

The flexibility of a QR code's symbol size is determined by the amount of data to be stored and the chosen reading method, with sizes ranging from 21 × 21 cells

Table 11.1 QR code specifications

Symbol size	Minimum Version 20 - Maximum Version 40 (with 4-cells interval)	
Information type and Volume	Numeric	7089
	Alphanumeric	4296
	Binary	2953
	Kanji	1817
Error Correction Level (ECL)	Level L	Up to 7% restoration
	Level M	Up to 15% restoration
	Level Q	Up to 25% restoration
	Level H	Up to 30% restoration

to the largest size of 177 × 177 cells, increased by four cells in both vertical and horizontal directions. Regarding information type and volume, the QR code accommodates a diverse range of data, including numerical characters, alphabets, signs, Kanji characters, Hiragana, Katakana, control signs, and images, adhering to ISO/IEC 646 and ISO/IEC 10646 standards. These data types can coexist simultaneously, as detailed in Table 11.1. Additionally, the QR code integrates four ECLs to aid in data restoration, allowing users to choose the level that suits their specific usage requirements.

The QR code is a two-dimensional matrix symbol with a square cell structure. It contains functional designs for facilitating effortless reading and managing the stored data area and various elements, including discovered designs, alignment designs, timing designs, and a designated quiet zone (Singh et al., 2017; Smith, 2016; Taveerad & Vongpradhip, 2016). Each QR code symbol comprises square modules arrayed in a regular square array, function patterns, and an encoding region. Furthermore, the entire symbol shall be surrounded by a calm zone border on all four sides (Thonky, 2020). Figure 11.2 illustrates the QR code's architecture. The description of the components is explained in Table 11.2.

QR codes simplify numerous tasks at home and in the workplace, finding applications across various business sectors such as manufacturing, distribution, retail, pharmaceuticals, and services. This versatile method conserves paper space and extends its utility to essential documents like identity cards, passports, and driving licenses. A primary challenge associated with the existing QR codes lies in their size limitation, as highlighted by many previous studies (Badawi et al., 2019a, 2019b; Yang et al., 2018). Addressing this constraint, researchers have proposed data compression techniques, explicitly employing the Huffman algorithm and Lempel-Ziv-Welch (LZW) (Welch, 1984), to extend the QR code's capacity

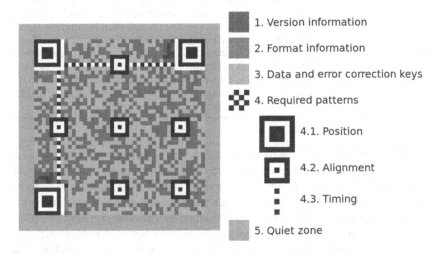

Figure 11.2 QR code architecture.

Source: International Standard Organisation (2006). Adapted with permission.

Table 11.2 QR code components

QR code components	Description
Version information	Available in two rectangle boxes near the right upper corner and left bottom corner position patterns. The exact version can be determined by scanning the QR codes of these two boxes, such as Version 1 or Version 2. The total number of modules present in the QR code can be known in version information.
Format information	QR code is placed near all three position patterns. During the decoding process, format information is the first part to be decoded. This section of QR codes obtains data error correction and mask codes. It is used to determine which ECL mask pattern is used to create QR codes. There are 28 possible format information strings and seven possible mask patterns in general.
Data and error-correction area	The grey cells in the QR code represent the data and error correction. It contains actual data stored in QR code and error correction words based on the Reed-Solomon algorithm. Data is first placed in grey cells during the QR code's encoding process, and then error correction code words are stored.
Position pattern	The position pattern is located at the left upper corner, right upper corner, and left bottom corner. It makes a QR code that can be scanned in all directions.
Alignment pattern	A model for adjusting the QR code's distortion. It is extraordinarily effective at adjusting nonlinear distortions. In order to rectify the symbol's distortion, the central coordinate of the alignment pattern will be identified. In order to facilitate the detection of the alignment pattern's central coordinate, an isolated black cell is aligned in a conjunction pattern for this purpose.
Timing pattern	A model for discovering the central coordinate of each cell in a QR code that alternates between black and white designs. It is utilised to rectify the central coordinate of the information cell when the symbol is distorted or the cell pitch is incorrect. Both the vertical and horizontal orientations are supported.
Quiet zone	The presence of a margin area is crucial for the effective scanning of a QR code. A quiet zone facilitates the recognition of symbols within an image captured by the charge-coupled device (CCD) sensor or barcode scanner. A minimum of four cells is necessary to establish a quiet area.

effectively. The storage capacity of these codes is influenced by factors such as version size and the nature of the encoded data. Compression methods, essential for optimising data storage, involve removing redundant information to enhance overall capacity. The importance of compression becomes evident when transmitting large files through networks, as highlighted by Arora et al. (2018). Furthermore, Abas et al. (2020) emphasise that compression not only reduces file sizes but their innovative approach, converting text data into binary form and creating a hash map from this binary data, results in a QR code capable of accommodating over four megabytes of data—a substantial improvement from the conventional

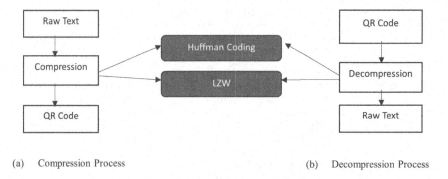

(a)   Compression Process   (b)   Decompression Process

Figure 11.3 (a) Compression process; (b) Decompression process.

four kilobytes. It underscores the seamless integration of QR code technology with advanced compression methods, enhancing its utility in diverse settings.

Figure 11.3(a) illustrates the model for analysing the input data stream to identify various forms such as text, bits, bytes, numeric, and data meta-alphanumeric to be encoded, while Figure 11.3(b) shows the opposite operation. Umaria and Jethava (2015), the compression process is started by converting the data information into American Standard Code for Information Interchange (ASCII), which provides characters with a unique number that can easily be converted into their equivalent binary values so faster data computation can be done. Then, the binary data can be faded into the ZIP compression algorithm to obtain compressed binary data. Compression helps to store data more efficiently, reducing transmission costs and faster transmission time. Then, the compressed binary data for encoding is divided into smaller parts. Finally, all generated QR codes are multiplexed with a 2n combination; here, n = 5, so five are multiplexed. Therefore, it can increase the amount of data capacity compared to the original data capacity of the QR codes and keep secret information.

As illustrated in Figure 11.3, hardware compressors effectively eliminate numerous redundant bits in the original text. This compression process significantly reduces the required storage space for the compressed text. Subsequently, during the decompression stage, the original text is seamlessly recovered. Kasumov (2010) emphasises the efficiency of compressing data before storage and decompressing it upon retrieval to expand device storage capacity. Considering the constant data transfer rate on the Internet, there is a substantial opportunity for significant improvements in data speed through effective data compression whenever feasible.

As extensively discussed by Sharma (2020), various data compression techniques fall into two main categories: lossy data compression, commonly applied to image data files, and lossless data compression, employed for transmitting or storing binary files. Lossless compression finds widespread use in applications like text files, database tables, and medical images, primarily driven by regulatory requirements (Ramya & Pushpa, 2016). This technique encompasses well-known methods such as Run Length Encoding, Arithmetic Encoding, Shannon-Fano, LZW, and Huffman. In contrast, lossy compression algorithms, frequently used

Table 11.3 The techniques in lossless compression algorithms

Factors	Lossless compression techniques	
	LZW	Huffman
Advantages	• The compression technique employed is both straightforward and effective. • A dynamic code word table is constructed for each file. • The decompression process involves the creation of a code word table, eliminating the requirement for its transmission.	• The implementation process is straightforward. • This task involves generating lossless compression for photos.
Speed	Fast compression	Fast to execute
Applications	TIFF, GIF, PDF	ZIP, ARG, JPEG, MPEG
Drawbacks	• The management of string tables poses challenges. This method applies solely to English language material. • Every individual requires a dictionary.	• The speed is relatively modest. • The outcome is contingent upon the statistical model employed to analyse the data. The process of decoding poses challenges because of variations in coding durations. • The overhead resulting from the use of Huffman.

when the original data is not crucial post-decompression, involve techniques like transform coding, discrete cosine transform, discrete wavelet transform, and fractal compression. Table 11.3 provides comparisons between techniques in the lossless compression algorithm.

Huffman is a complicated and lossless compression with an entropy encoding algorithm commonly .employed in computer science and information theory to achieve lossless data compression (Kumar, 2015). The term "variable-length code table" refers to a coding system that assigns varying lengths to different source symbols, such as characters in a file. This code table is constructed in a particular manner, considering the estimated likelihood of each potential value for the source symbol. The characters in a data file are converted to binary code, with the most frequently occurring characters having the shortest codes. No information loss occurs after decoding (Langdon, 1984). Huffman coding is still popular because of its simpler implementation, faster compression, and lack of patent coverage (Jayasankar et al., 2021). A text file must be compressed with the following character frequencies to observe the Huffman function.

When Huffman coding and LZW are combined to compress QR codes, the resulting codes can hold substantially more information than uncompressed codes. Combining the two compression techniques permits a more efficient representation of the data, reducing the number of bits necessary to store it. The compressed data can form a QR code, which any QR code reader can scan and read. Several studies have shown that using Huffman and LZW together can significantly enhance the data storage capacity of QR codes. For instance, a study by Marlapalli et al. (2021) found that using the two compression algorithms together can increase the capacity of a QR code by up to 80%. Another study by Gupta and Jain (2016) found that using Huffman and LZW together can increase the capacity of a QR code by up to 78%.

LZW coding is a lossless data compression algorithm developed by Abraham Lempel, Jacob Ziv, and Terry Welch in 1977 (Robert et al., 2011). It involves two steps: (1) parsing and (2) coding. During the parsing phase, strings of symbols were divided into variable-length substrings based on a set of rules (Kasumov, 2010). Each substring was encoded sequentially into a fixed-length code during the coding phase (Blanco & Barreiro, 2010). It is a dictionary-based compression algorithm that replaces repeated occurrences of data patterns, such as strings of characters with shorter codes. LZW is a commonly used compression technique utilised in GIF, TIFF, and PDF. LZW is an essential data compression technique due to its adaptability and simplicity. It facilitates increasing the hard drive's storage capacity. The LZW algorithm works as follows:

1　Initialise a dictionary with all possible single-character strings.
2　Read input data and find the longest string already in the dictionary.
3　Replace that string with a code, and add the new string to the dictionary with the following available code.
4　Repeat steps 1-3 until all input data has been processed.
5　Output the codes generated by the algorithm.
6　When decoding, initialise the dictionary with all possible single-character strings and use the codes to look up the corresponding strings.
7　Reconstruct the original data by concatenating the decoded strings.

Table 11.4 provides insights into the performance of LZW and Huffman based on various parameters. The researcher notes that LZW exhibits a notably higher compression ratio than Huffman for smaller file sizes. Regarding compression time, the study observes that both algorithms demonstrate similar compression times for small file sizes, but as the file size increases, Huffman compression surpasses that

Table 11.4 Comparison of Huffman and LZW

File size	Huffman			LZW		
	Compression ratio (%)	*Compression time (ms)*	*Decompression time (ms)*	*Compression ratio (%)*	*Compression time (ms)*	*Decompression time (ms)*
2.2 KB	54.20	0.0	0.0156	105.56	0.0	0.0
15.5 MB	54.203	123.664	115.858	3.604	8.560	29.734
33.2 KB	54.205	0.015	0.231	49.94	0.0156	0.0156
62.1 MB	54.203	1945.389	470.933	1.827	53.198	469.634

Source: Sharma (2020).

of LZW. Regarding decompression time in smaller file sizes, the decompression time for both algorithms is almost identical. However, LZW performs relatively better for larger files, yielding slightly different results.

11.2   Advancement for increasing data capacity in QR codes

Advancements in QR code technology have focused on increasing data capacity, enabling them to store more information in a smaller space. These advancements have significantly expanded their potential applications. From logistics and inventory management to multimedia content distribution, the increased data capacity has opened up new possibilities for leveraging QR codes in various industries and contexts, supporting and accelerating Industry 5.0. A QR code of version 40 contains 177 rows and columns of modules and can store up to 7,089 numeric or 4,296 alphabetic characters. A version 40 QR code is approximately 1,734 modules in size. Table 11.5 shows the size of data text before and after compression using Huffman and LZW with their parameters like compression rate, compression time, and decompression time. The first row shows the size of the data text before compression in bits, followed by the size after compression in bits. Researchers use four sizes of data text as raw data or input, which are 800, 1200, 1600, and 2000 bits. The Huffman performs good compression for 800 and 2000 bits of data text. The 1200 and 1600 data text go to LZW.

The average time to compress for Huffman is less than for the LZW. The Huffman is less complex than the LZW, so it takes less time to compress the data text. Meanwhile, the average time for the decompression section for LZW is less than for the Huffman. It is because the LZW only needs to scan the LZW code through the library, whereas the Huffman needs to read the input bit-by-bit, which is slower. Therefore, QR codes can hold more data using these two techniques due to much space-saving size after compression. In addition, Huffman and LZW are two widely used compression techniques that are crucial in reducing data size for efficient storage and transmission. Compressing data using Huffman before encoding it into a QR code allows more efficient use of its capacity. It can be critical for storing large amounts of information in a limited space. In Industry 5.0, this can be used to encode textual information related to products, instructions, or any other

Table 11.5 Size of bits of data text before and after Huffman and LZW

Data type	Size before compression (bits)		Size after compression (bits)		Compression ratio		Compression time (sec)		Decompression time (sec)	
			Huffman	*LZW*	*Huffman*	*LZW*	*Huffman*	*LZW*	*Huffman*	*LZW*
Text	800		367	504	0.46	0.63	0.178	0.697	0.053	0.055
	1200		567	696	0.47	0.58	0.222	1.730	0.135	0.075
	1600		753	840	0.47	0.53	0.447	1.984	0.106	0.107
	2000		936	960	0.47	0.48	0.446	2.046	0.136	0.171

Source: Jambek and Khairi (2014).

relevant data. Meanwhile, LZW is excellent for compressing various data types, including text, images, and other structured information. Using LZW compression prior to encoding data into a QR code can significantly improve the efficiency of the code. More information can be stored in a single QR code, providing detailed instructions, specifications, or other relevant data.

11.3   Leveraging QR codes for Industry 5.0 integration

The data compression techniques such as Huffman and LZW can significantly increase the storage capacity of QR codes. By compressing the data stored in QR codes, it is possible to store more data in a smaller space, making QR codes even more versatile for sharing information. In Industry 5.0, where humans and advanced technologies collaborate closely, the efficient handling of information becomes crucial. QR codes can be used as a powerful tool for text and data compression, allowing for streamlined communication and storage of information. Companies can maximise the information stored in each code by applying Huffman or LZW compression techniques to the data before encoding it into QR codes.

Compressed data within QR codes allows for more efficient communication between humans and machines. It is crucial in Industry 5.0, where real-time access to accurate information is essential for seamless collaboration. Compression is a significant technique in multimedia. The data capacity can be decreased, making transmitting and storing the data cheaper and quicker. Several image and video compression formats are implemented, including JPEG, JPEG 2000, MPEG-2, and MPEG-4. Huffman is superior to LZW. Meanwhile, LZW allows for a higher compression ratio than the Huffman. On the other hand, Huffman requires more time to execute than LZW. In certain instances, Huffman can be used to achieve a high-compression ratio without regard to time. In comparison, time is significant for real-time applications and LZW. Integrating Huffman and LZW compression techniques with QR codes in Industry 5.0 could allow companies to enhance data storage, communication, and collaboration efficiency. It leads to more streamlined operations and improved productivity in the manufacturing environment.

11.4   Security consideration of QR code in Industry 5.0

Security considerations are crucial in implementing QR code technology within Industry 5.0. As Industry 5.0 emphasises the integration of advanced technologies, the reliance on QR codes for data exchange and process optimisation grows significantly. However, this increased connectivity also introduces potential security vulnerabilities that must be carefully addressed. One primary concern in the security landscape of QR codes is the risk of unauthorised access and data manipulation (Tekawade et al., 2018). Given that QR codes often contain sensitive information, such as product details, manufacturing specifications, or employee credentials, unauthorised access can lead to data breaches with severe consequences. Implementing robust encryption measures, secure data transmission protocols, and access controls is imperative to mitigate these risks (Chen, 2017).

Moreover, the potential for QR code spoofing (Alnuaimi et al., 2023) or manipulation threatens the integrity of information within Industry 5.0. Malicious actors may attempt to replace legitimate QR codes with fraudulent ones, leading to inaccurate data capture and potentially disrupting the manufacturing or logistics processes. Ensuring the authenticity of QR codes through digital signatures or cryptographic techniques becomes essential in maintaining the integrity of the information flow (Pangan et al., 2022). In Industry 5.0, where the convergence of physical and digital systems is prominent, the security of QR code-enabled communication networks is vital. Protecting against man-in-the-middle attacks, eavesdropping, and other cyber threats requires the implementation of secure communication protocols and regular security audits.

Furthermore, as QR codes become integral to supply chain processes in Industry 5.0, ensuring the security of the entire supply chain becomes crucial. It involves securing QR code generation, distribution, and scanning points to prevent tampering or inserting malicious codes at any stage of the supply chain (Muzafar et al., 2023). While QR codes offer tremendous efficiency gains in Industry 5.0, addressing security considerations is paramount. Implementing robust encryption, authentication measures, and secure communication protocols is essential in safeguarding the integrity and confidentiality of data exchanged through QR codes in the industrial landscape. Regular security assessments and updates should be integrated into the Industry 5.0 framework to adapt to evolving cyber threats and ensure a resilient and secure environment.

As a step forward, several proactive measures can be taken to enhance the security of QR codes in the context of Industry 5.0. First, developing and adopting industry-wide standards for secure QR code generation and scanning are essential. These standards should encompass encryption protocols, digital signatures, and authentication mechanisms to ensure the authenticity and integrity of QR code data. Education and awareness programmes are crucial to improving QR code security (Kumar et al., 2022). Training employees and stakeholders on best practices for handling QR codes, recognising potential security threats, and understanding the importance of secure data transmission can contribute significantly to overall cybersecurity.

Integrating blockchain technology is another promising avenue for enhancing the security of QR codes (van Groesen & Pauwels, 2022) in Industry 5.0. Blockchain's decentralised and immutable nature can provide a transparent and tamper-resistant ledger for tracking the entire lifecycle of QR codes, from generation to scanning. It ensures data integrity and creates a trust layer within the supply chain. Regular security audits and vulnerability assessments should be conducted to identify and address potential weaknesses in the QR code infrastructure. This proactive approach helps stay ahead of emerging cyber threats and adapt security measures accordingly. Continuous monitoring of QR code-related activities can also enable the swift detection of anomalies and potential security breaches.

Collaboration between industry stakeholders, cybersecurity experts, and regulatory bodies is vital for establishing comprehensive security frameworks for QR code usage in Industry 5.0. This collaboration can lead to the formulation of guidelines, regulations, and best practices that promote a secure environment for QR code implementation. Another approach is investing in research and development to innovate new security features for QR codes, which can contribute to staying one step ahead of cyber threats. Technologies such as dynamic QR codes (Zhou et al., 2021), which change their content over time, or biometric authentication integrated into QR code systems can add an extra layer of security. Securing QR codes in the era of Industry 5.0 requires a multifaceted approach that combines technological advancements, industry collaboration, and a commitment to ongoing education and improvement. By implementing these measures, businesses can harness the benefits of QR code technology while mitigating the associated security risks in the dynamic landscape of the Industry.

Acknowledgements

The authors thank the reviewers for their valuable comments. This work was funded by the School of Computing, Universiti Utara Malaysia, Sintok, Kedah, Malaysia.

References

Abas, A., Yusof, Y., Din, R., Azali, F., & Osman, B. (2020). Increasing data storage of coloured QR code using compress, multiplexing and multilayered technique. *Bulletin of Electrical Engineering and Informatics, 9*(6), 2555–2561. https://doi.org/10.11591/eei. v9i6.2481

Alnuaimi, A., Hawashin, D., Jayaraman, R., Salah, K., & Omar, M. (2023). Trustworthy healthcare professional credential verification using blockchain technology. *IEEE Access.* https://doi.org/10.1109/ACCESS.2023.3322359

Arora, M., Kumar, C., & Verma, A. K. (2018). Increase capacity of QR code using compression technique. In *Proceedings of 3rd International Conference and Workshops on Recent Advances and Innovations in Engineering (ICRAIE), 2018*(November), (pp. 1–5). https:// doi.org/10.1109/ICRAIE.2018.8710429

Badawi, B., Aris, T. N. M., Mustapha, N., & Manshor, N. (2019a). A smart fuzzy auto suggestion system for a multilayer QR code generator. *Journal of Theoretical and Applied Information Technology, 97*(13), 3585–3603.

Badawi, B., Aris, T. N. M., Mustapha, N., & Manshor, N. (2019b). Fuzzy encoder framework for four layers color QR code. *Malaysian Journal of Computer Science, 2019*(Special Issue 3), 118–130. https://doi.org/10.22452/mjcs.sp2019no3.8

Blanco, R., & Barreiro, A. (2010). Probabilistic static pruning of inverted files. *ACM Transactions on Information Systems, 28*(1), 1–33. https://doi.org/10.1145/1658377.1658378

Chen, C. (2017). QR code authentication with embedded message authentication code. *Mobile Networks and Applications, 22*(3), 383–394. https://doi.org/10.1007/s11036-016-0772-y

Clover, D. E., Sanford, K., Bell, L., & Johnson, K. (2016). *Adult education, museums and art galleries: Animating social, cultural and institutional change* (Vol. 20). Sense Publishers. https://doi.org/10.1007/978-94-6300-687-3

Ebner, M. (2008). QR Code—The business card of tomorrow. In *FH science day* (pp. 431–435). Shaker-Verlag GmbH.

Gupta, S., & Jain, R. (2016). An innovative method of text steganography. In *Proceedings of 2015 IEEE 3rd International Conference on Image Information Processing (ICIIP)* (pp. 60–64). https://doi.org/10.1109/ICIIP.2015.7414741

International Standard Organisation (2006). ISO/IEC 18004:2006 - Information technology—Automatic identification and data capture techniques—QR Code 2005 bar code symbology specification. https://www.iso.org/obp/ui/#iso:std:iso-iec:18004:ed-2:v1:en

Jambek, A. B., & Khairi, N. A. (2014). Performance comparison of Huffman and Lempel-Ziv-Welch data compression for wireless sensor node application. *American Journal of Applied Sciences*, *11*(1), 119–126. https://doi.org/10.3844/ajassp.2014.119.126

Jayasankar, U., Thirumal, V., & Ponnurangam, D. (2021). A survey on data compression techniques: From the perspective of data quality, coding schemes, data type and applications. *Journal of King Saud University-Computer and Information Sciences*, *33*(2), 119–140. https://doi.org/10.1016/j.jksuci.2018.05.006

Kasumov, N. K. (2010). The universal coding method in the data compression algorithm. *Automatic Control and Computer Sciences*, *44*(5), 279–286. https://doi.org/10.3103/S0146411610050056

Kumar, N., Jain, S., Shukla, M., & Lodha, S. (2022, June). Investigating Users' perception, security awareness and cyber-hygiene behaviour concerning QR code as an attack vector. In *International conference on human-computer interaction* (pp. 506–513). Springer International Publishing. https://doi.org/10.1007/978-3-031-06394-7_64

Kumar, V. (2015). Compression techniques vs Huffman coding. *International Journal of Informatics and Communication Technology (IJ-ICT)*, *4*(1), 29. https://doi.org/10.11591/ijict.v4i1.pp29-37

Langdon, G. G. (1984). Introduction to arithmetic coding. *IBM Journal of Research and Development*, *28*(2), 135–149. https://doi.org/10.1147/rd.282.0135

Marlapalli, K., Bandlamudi, R. S., Busi, R., Pranav, V., & Madhavrao, B. (2021). A review on image compression techniques. *Lecture Notes in Networks and Systems*, *134*, 271–279. https://doi.org/10.1007/978-981-15-5397-4_29

Muzafar, M. A., Bhargava, A., Jha, A., & Nand, P. (2023). Securing the supply chain: A comprehensive solution with blockchain technology and QR-based anti-counterfeit mechanism. *International Journal of Performability Engineering*, *19*(5), 312–323. https://doi.org/10.23940/ijpe.23.05.p3.312323

Pangan, A. M. S., Lacuesta, I. L., Mabborang, R. C., & Ferrer, F. P. (2022). Authenticating data transfer using RSA-generated QR codes. *European Journal of Information Technologies and Computer Science*, *2*(4), 18–30. https://doi.org/10.24018/compute.2022.2.4.73

Ramya, K. A., & Pushpa, M. (2016). A survey on lossless and lossy data compression methods. *International Journal of Computer Science and Engineering Communications*, *4*(1), 1277–1280.

Robert, L., Shanmugasundaram, S., & Lourdusamy, R. (2011). A comparative study of text compression algorithms biological DNA sequence compression view project a comparative study of text compression algorithms. *Article in ICTACT Journal on Communication Technology*, *1*(3), 68. https://doi.org/10.21917/ijct.2011.0062

Sharma, G. (2020). Analysis of Huffman coding and Lempel–Ziv–Welch (LZW) coding as data compression techniques. *International Journal of Scientific Research in Computer Science and Engineering*, *8*(1), 37–44.

Singh, A., Verma, V., & Raj, G. (2017). A novel approach for encoding and decoding of high storage capacity color QR code. In *Proceedings of 2017 7th International Conference Confluence on Cloud Computing, Data Science and Engineering* (pp. 425–430). https://doi.org/10.1109/CONFLUENCE.2017.7943188

Taveerad, N., & Vongpradhip, S. (2016). Development of color QR code for increasing capacity. In *Proceedings of 11th International Conference on Signal-Image Technology and Internet-Based Systems (SITIS)* (pp. 645–648). https://doi.org/10.1109/SITIS.2015.42

Tekawade, N., Kshirsagar, S., Sukate, S., Raut, L., & Vairagar, S. (2018). Social engineering solutions for document generation using key-logger security mechanism and QR code. In *2018 Fourth International Conference on Computing Communication Control and Automation (ICCUBEA)* (pp. 1–5). IEEE. https://doi.org/10.1109/ICCUBEA.2018.8697420

Thonky (2020). QR Code Tutorial: Introduction—QR Code Tutorial. (n.d.). Retrieved 25 July 2023, from https://www.thonky.com/qr-code-tutorial/introduction

Tiwari, S. (2017). An introduction to QR code technology. In *Proceedings of 15th International Conference on Information Technology (ICIT)* (pp. 39–44). https://doi.org/10.1109/ICIT.2016.021

Umaria, M. M., & Jethava, G. B. (2015). Enhancing the data storage capacity in QR code using compression algorithm and achieving security and further data storage capacity improvement using multiplexing. In *Proceedings of International Conference on Computational Intelligence and Communication Networks (CICN)* (pp. 1094–1096). https://doi.org/10.1109/CICN.2015.215

van Groesen, W., & Pauwels, P. (2022). Tracking prefabricated assets and compliance using quick response (QR) codes, blockchain and smart contract technology. *Automation in Construction, 141*, 104420. https://doi.org/10.1016/j.autcon.2022.104420

Welch, T. A. (1984). A technique for high-performance data compression. *Computer, 17*(6), 8–19. https://doi.org/10.1109/MC.1984.1659158

Yang, Z., Xu, H., Deng, J., Loy, C. C., & Lau, W. C. (2018). Robust and fast decoding of high-capacity color QR codes for mobile applications. *IEEE Transactions on Image Processing, 27*(12), 6093–6108. https://doi.org/10.1109/TIP.2018.2855419

Zhou, Y., Hu, B., Zhang, Y., & Cai, W. (2021). Implementation of cryptographic algorithm in dynamic QR code payment system and its performance. *IEEE Access, 9*, 122362–122372. https://doi.org/10.1109/ACCESS.2021.3108189

12 Augmented reality meets artificial intelligence towards personalised user experience in cultural heritage sites

Juliana Aida Abu Bakar[1], Eidlan Hadi
Mazlan Hanafi[1], Rimaniza Zainal Abidin[2],
Ulka Chandini Pendit[3], and Haslina Arshad[2]

[1]*Institute of Creative Industry Management and Sustainable Culture,*
School of Creative Industry Management & Performing Arts,
Universiti Utara Malaysia, Kedah, Malaysia

[2]*Institute of IR4.0, Faculty of Information Science & Technology,*
Universiti Kebangsaan Malaysia, Selangor, Malaysia

[3]*Department of Computing, Faculty of Business, Technology and*
Engineering, Sheffield Hallam University, United Kingdom

12.1 Overview of augmented reality and artificial intelligence

Augmented reality (AR) refers to a concept typically registered in three dimensions (3D), combining actual and virtual experiences with interactivity in real time (Azuma, 1997). AR technology allows users to experience both virtual and real worlds by simultaneously overlaying the virtual object in the real world (Pendit et al., 2014). To superimpose the virtual object on the real environment, AR must be run on a mobile device's sensor with a camera, accelerometer, gyroscope, and magnetometer (Blut & Blankenbach, 2021). It categorises AR into two types: marker-based AR and markerless AR. Marker-based AR uses printed markers to superimpose the virtual content, while markerless AR directly superimposes the virtual content in a real environment using only surface ground without the printed marker (Pooja et al., 2020). Within the framework of Industry 5.0, AR and Artificial Intelligence (AI) play pivotal roles in preserving and enriching cultural heritage (CH). AR facilitates immersive experiences by superimposing historical information onto physical artefacts, while AI empowers data analysis and preservation efforts, contributing to a harmonious blend of technology and CH conservation.

AR can be used to create virtual tours of historical sites, allowing visitors to explore the site more engagingly and interactively. Incorporating AR tools and applications can enhance the physical interaction with historic sites through a quality interpretation of the values associated with cultural sites. Mobile AR guide systems can also be used as an auxiliary tool for user experience in CH sites. The systems integrate location-based navigation and puzzle games to enhance user experience. On the other hand, AI can personalise these experiences by analysing visitor data

DOI: 10.1201/9781003479727-12

and providing recommendations based on their interests and preferences. AI has been used in various CH applications, including element or mineral identification, virtual museums, historical document analysis, natural language processing, semantics and knowledge extraction, automated processes in digitisation, recommenders, storytelling, and personalisation. AI can help preserve cultural and creative resources in digital form to amass the data needed to put AI at the service of CH and museums. AI can also benefit archaeological and historical research, helping to deepen knowledge and localise sites.

Microsoft has launched an AI for CH initiative that leverages AI's power to empower people and organisations dedicated to preserving and enriching CH. The program supports specific individuals and organisations through collaboration, partnership, and investment in AI technology and resources. Microsoft has committed $10 million over five years to expand access to Microsoft Azure and AI resources (Microsoft, 2023). The program focuses on four core areas: people, places, languages, and historical artefacts. AI is a powerful tool to help us better understand, preserve, and share our CH. By using AI algorithms to analyse historical artefacts, reconstruct lost or damaged CH, or simulate historical events, we can gain new insights into our cultural legacy and make it more accessible to people around the world.

12.2   Personalised user experience in cultural heritage sites

CH sites include a place, locality, natural landscape, settlement area, architectural complex, archaeological site, or standing structure recognised and often legally protected as a place of historical and cultural significance (International Council on Monuments and Sites, 2008). Many CH sites have been eroded and ruined; hence, restoration work is being done to prevent further damage. However, due to huge expenditures, most CH sites suffer, and the best that the authorities could do is restrict tourists to a few segments of these sites (Champion, 2011). Moreover, these CH sites typically cover a significantly large area where several mini-sites or points of interest (POI) are bounded inside the compound, and other amenities such as restrooms, food stalls, and gift shops for tourists are within reach.

Personalisation may vary with different types, such as age groups, learning styles, disabilities, level of learning attention, and available time for visits (Damala, 2007). Personalisation is a feature that enables tourists to modify, construct, and adjust the system (Damala et al., 2007, 2008). It also includes the system's customisation, configuration, and adaptivity, which tourists can do. In terms of technical, the preferences to choose a terminal and the available bandwidth may also be included. Therefore, it is not a surprise to witness abundant research work in the attempt to provide a pleasant user experience for these heritage sites. For example, a personalised and content-adaptive CH path recommendation system may model location using mean-shift clustering trained with actual user movement patterns (Alexandridis et al., 2019). It provides an overall architecture applied to data collected from actual visits to the CH sites, and an extensive analysis of visitor movement patterns was subsequently conducted, especially in comparison to the curated paths made initially by tourists.

Personalisation adapts the content based on user context and enables users to personalise the content. It invokes experiences of meaningfulness, surprise, inspiration, motivation, and privacy. Personalisation is also necessary, allowing visitors to learn at their own pace (Ardissono et al., 2012; Damala et al., 2008). Tourists can choose from a set of options to display the right content to fulfil their needs. According to Pendit et al. (2018), these components must be included as a set of options for tourists: a historical period where tourists may select the era of their interests and can read or visualise the information; site preferences where one may opt for experiencing natural heritage rather than visiting built heritage; radius range within the site as they can plan their mode of transportation; and language to communicate. Using state-of-the-art technology, we attempted to gather samples on personalised user experience at CH sites.

12.2.1   *Personalised tour guide services*

Several CH sites, especially prestigious museums which house culturally significant artefacts worldwide, have implemented personalised user experiences to enhance tourists' experiences. The museum curator may provide a typical personalised tour guide service to provide tourists with customised tours based on their interests. The Louvre Museum, for example, offers such services over group tourist booking. Tourists can choose from several themes, such as art history, ancient civilisations, or Islamic art.

The British Museum offers a personalised tour guide app that provides tourists with customised tours based on their interests. The app uses beacon technology to track tourists' locations and provide them with relevant information about the exhibits they are viewing. On the other hand, the Smithsonian National Museum of Natural History offers a personalised tour guide app using AR technology to enhance tourists' experiences by providing them with interactive exhibits and actively promoting it on its website.

Prestigious museums have begun offering personalised tour guide services using mobile apps to provide personalised user experiences to their tourists. In most cases, only smartphones are used—as they are personal and handy and widely accepted—to provide specific, if not all, user experience. These services are promoted on their websites, as depicted in Figure 12.1.

Indoor museums are suitable to utilise the audio apps as personalised tour guide services due to the closed surrounding area whereby they can filter loud noise and control the sound volume. Such luxury may not be available outdoors; hence, CH sites may opt for AR technology to assist their tourists.

12.2.2   *Personalised points of interest*

The advent of smartphone technology and services encouraged more integrated features to provide a better-personalised user experience, as in visualising specific point locations that tourists may find useful or interesting, which is called point of interest (POI). These POIs can be tourist attractions or sites of cultural,

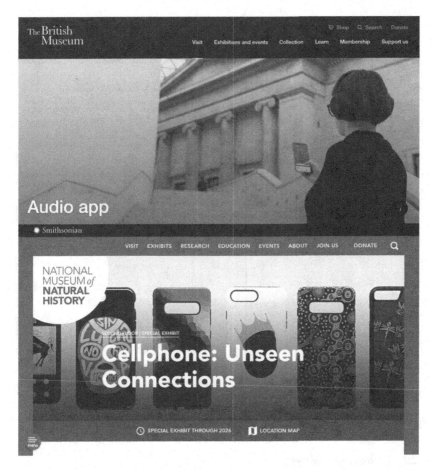

Figure 12.1 Applications at the British Museum (top) and the Smithsonian National Museum of Natural History (bottom).

architectural, historical, and archaeological interest. Abidin et al. (2018) proposed a Location-based AR (LBAR) application known as TourismGo that leveraged an innovative technology to enhance tourist experience by integrating Multimodal Interaction (MMI) and Adaptive Interfaces as depicted in Figure 12.2. The visualisation of the POI based on the current user location and preferences is made possible and happens in real-time as tourists move around the area. This integration is expected to reduce occlusion problems, which prevent users from seeing cluttered screens due to massive number of POIs appearing, and eventually be able to personalise the POIs based on user preferences.

With the ability to capture user preferences, TourismGo provides only information tailored to the user's needs and interests. Apart from removing non-POIs not to declutter the user screen, it minimises error-tapping the wrong ones while showing only personalised POIs.

Figure 12.2 TourismGO application allows users to input preferences.

12.2.3   Personalised content

Personalised user experience is a process of tailoring content and services to meet the specific needs of individual users. In the context of CH sites, personalised user experience involves providing tourists with customised information and services based on their interests, preferences, and needs. Based on mindfulness and multimedia learning theories, the AR@Melaka application provides POIs visualisation, a variety of content options for tourists to select from, and a sharing option on social media, as depicted in Figure 12.3. It also provides decent user interface design components through layered information, one-tap access for frequent menus, clues for scenes with augmented content, a quick button to go to the main menu, a big font, enough contrast between text and background, and appropriate size of content.

Personalised user experience has several benefits for tourists to CH sites. It helps them navigate the site more efficiently, find information relevant to their interests, learn more about its history and significance, connect with other tourists who share similar interests, and have an enjoyable experience while visiting CH sites.

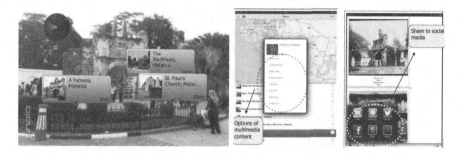

Figure 12.3 AR@Melaka provides personalised content to tourists.

12.3 Augmented reality and artificial intelligence: A synergistic approach to personalised user experience in cultural heritage sites

CH sites may utilise state-of-the-art technology such as AR and AI, whose intrinsic characteristics exude a gigantic charm while providing a personalised user experience. AR may provide enjoyable informal learning at CH sites, enabling tourists to consume information effortlessly. Pendit et al. (2014, 2018) suggest that AR should provide a variety of media to deliver CH information, activities such as games and quizzes to keep tourists occupied while resting, and POI to proceed within the area. As Orea-Giner et al. (2022) imply, dimensions of AI applications can be classified into three groups: functional, which relates to user satisfaction and usefulness, also known as usability; contact, which relates to the social presence where tourists feel connected with other tourists; and co-experience which tourists post-visits may share thoughts with other tourists and eventually create a collaborative experience.

It is anticipated that the combination of AR and AI can provide optimum personalised user experience at CH sites. Tourist information is captured and compared with the trained data using machine learning (ML) filters, where this data has been categorised into a specific set of attributes based on user preferences. New users would need to input their preferences minimally, where they will be assigned to certain personas and given a recommended path. This can be amended later according to the user's real-time data input.

12.3.1 The proposed framework

The emergence of AR and AI has allowed tourism sectors to move ahead from the traditional sources of tourist information providers such as tourist websites, tourist guides, and mobile applications to enhance a tourist's experience further. Travellers face different challenges before, during, and after travel. These are more about how to adapt to new situations and how to get personalised information. To solve the problems, technologies and techniques that can be considered in developing personalised location-based AR tourism applications that leverage deep learning methods are proposed.

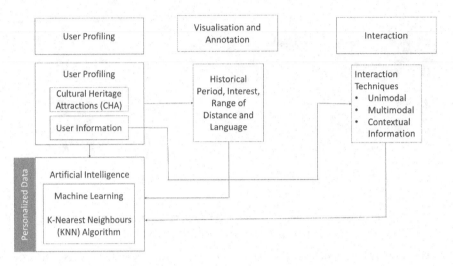

Figure 12.4 Proposed personalised user experience using AR and AI for CH sites framework.

Personalised recommendation services aim to suggest products and services that meet users' preferences and needs, while location-based services focus on providing information based on users' current positions. Due to the fast-growing user needs in the mobile tourism domain, how to provide personalised location-based tour recommendation services become a critical research and practical issue. More than 200 CH attraction (CHA) data were extracted based on the map of Malacca, Malaysia. Malacca is one of the historical states in Malaysia based on the United Nations Educational, Scientific and Cultural Organization (UNESCO), which comprises a core zone and buffer zone area.

The CHA data was divided into four types of heritage: built, natural, personal, and living. In AR, CHA information was visualised as virtual annotation overlaid with the real world. However, with a large amount of CHA data, it is found that there is difficulty visualising all CHA data at once. Therefore, personalised information such as user profiling, user interaction and visualisation are anticipated to provide a personalised user experience. With AI algorithms, in this case, ML and K-Nearest Neighbours (KNN) algorithms, the AR apps could train the CHA and user input data. Figure 12.4 shows the proposed Personalised User Experience using AR and AI for CH Sites Framework.

12.3.2 User profiling

User Profiling in this framework includes two main elements: CHA and User Information. CHA data may include the type of CHA and CHA category, while user information includes meal preferences, travel type, travel companion, and travel period.

12.3.3   Machine learning—KNN algorithm

The K-Nearest Neighbours (KNN) algorithm is a simple and popular supervised ML algorithm used for classification, regression tasks, estimation, and prediction (Guo et al., 2003; Larose & Larose, 2014). It is a non-parametric and instance-based learning algorithm which does not make any assumptions about the underlying data distribution. KNN algorithm works based on two phases (Peterson, 2009). First, the training phase involves the algorithm storing the entire training dataset in memory. Each data point in the training dataset is associated with a class label (for classification) or a numerical value (for regression). Second, in the prediction phase, given a new, unseen data point (the one you want to classify or predict), the algorithm calculates the distance between this data point and all other data points in the training set. Typical distance metrics include Euclidean distance, Manhattan distance, or others, depending on the problem. The algorithm then identifies the k-nearest data points (the data points with the smallest distances to the new data point). These nearest neighbours serve as a neighbourhood around the new data point. For classification, KNN counts the occurrences of each class among the k-nearest neighbours and assigns the class with the highest count to the new data point. For regression, KNN calculates the average (or weighted average) of the target values of the k-nearest neighbours and assigns this value as the prediction for the new data point.

Choosing the parameter "K" (the number of neighbours to consider) is a crucial decision in KNN. A small value of "k" can make the model sensitive to noise, while a large value can result in underfitting. KNN is a very intuitive algorithm and can be used for tasks where the decision boundaries are complex and not easily represented by mathematical equations. In this research, KNN was chosen as a versatile algorithm to train input data retrieved from the system and user preferences to recommend and personalise the list of POI to be displayed in AR.

12.3.4   Visualisation and annotation

These elements typically provide personalised content to users. During their visit to CA sites, they can choose to visualise the content or annotate it. Among the content features are historical period, interest, range of distance, and language. Upon selection, for example, for historical periods, only videos related to the requested historical period would pop out and could be played. This would hinder the cluttered vision of the relatively small mobile screen.

12.3.5   Interaction modalities

Once the user profiling has been determined, AR can identify which interaction techniques work well with the users. These interactions may include unimodal interaction, referred to as providing single interaction input such as keyboards or keypads. Multimodal interaction techniques, on the other hand, may include system input and user input. Contextual information would represent the current mood and ambience, whether in broad daylight or at night.

12.4   Implementation of AR and AI in cultural heritage sites

The personalised user experience would succeed in better tourists' experiences at CH sites. By providing customised information and services, CH sites can help tourists navigate these sites more easily, learn more about their history and significance, and have a more enjoyable and memorable experience. A set of traits, goals, frustrations, personality, motivation, skills, preferred channels, and a brief biography were set and included. Each element is meant to represent a real end-user.

12.4.1   User persona: Tibor

Tibor was created with a focus group discussion with the purpose of creating a representation of a general idea of end users. There are 11 experts with academic backgrounds in AR, AI, User Interface and User Experience, or Human-Computer Interaction who contributed to the discussion and helped define and create the persona, as shown in Figure 12.5.

TIBOR

Age: 35
Work: Computer Scientist
Family: Married
Nationality: Dutch

PERSONALITY
- Adventurous
- Likes to plan ahead
- Open to opinions
- Straightforward
- Wrong is wrong

TRAITS   Clever   Friendly   Organised   Adventurous
Tech Oriented

GOALS
- Getting to know local cultures and heritage
- Be friends with the locals
- Enjoy local delicacies
- Experience nature

FRUSTRATIONS
- Confusing UI in apps and devices
- Inaccurate and misleading information
- Too many paid features in an app

BIO
Tibor is someone who likes to plan ahead. He is open to meeting new people and experiencing new lifestyles and cultures such as local delicacies and heritage buildings. He likes activities that involves nature. He is multilingual and has advanced digital literacy.

MOTIVATION
Incentive
Growth
Social
Convenience

SKILLS
- Scientific Communicatior
- Computer Programmer
- DIY person
- Multilingual - French, Italian, Dutch, English
- Maps reader

PREFERRED CHANNELS
Google
Social media
Tourism Website
Advertisement

Figure 12.5 The proposed personalised User Experience using AR and AI for CH sites framework.

12.4.2 Use case

A use case is a written description or documentation of how users will perform tasks on the application. Each use case is portrayed as a series of simple steps that start with a user's goal and end when that goal is achieved. From the persona created earlier, a use case was set up to emphasise the context and determine the possible system input and modalities to be assigned to him. Use case for Tibor is formulated as follows:

> On a Monday afternoon, a non-Muslim foreigner arrived in the Malacca heritage site buffer zone. He opens the application. He fills in travel preferences. (Foreigner, Married, Living Heritage, Moderate). The POI pop up based on his location and travel preferences. He wants to find restaurants that serve local food. He searched by typing "living heritage". New set of POI appear.

From the statement, it is suggested that the system input involved is a gyroscope and the Global Positioning System (GPS). The interaction modalities are by touching the appropriate keypads and the need for device input such as time and date, also known as explicit and implicit interaction input modalities. Figure 12.6 depicts the user flow for Tibor during his quest to search for a specific CH site.

The developed application has demonstrated the abovementioned user flow. The AI algorithms would determine user preferences as soon as users logged in to the app. The personalised user experience has been thoroughly adapted prior to, during, and after their encounter with the application. The implementation of the application

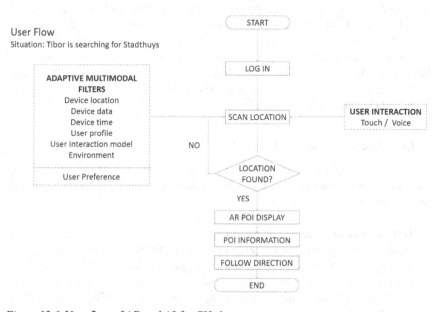

Figure 12.6 User flow of AR and AI for CH sites.

Figure 12.7 Usability testing for AR and AI apps during the day (right) and night at CH
sites (left).

has been tested on tourists in terms of its usability, as shown in Figure 12.7, to which
their responses are generally satisfactory. Although the implementation is still in
progress, it is anticipated that the integration of AI would assist in determining user
profiles according to their preferences as accurately as possible. It would be an input
to AR to display only personalised content to tourists.

12.5   Challenges and future directions

AR and AI are two emerging technologies that can potentially enhance the user
experience at CH sites. AR can provide immersive and interactive ways of accessing and visualising historical information (Refae et al., 2023), while AI can offer
personalised and adaptive content based on the user's preferences, context, and
behaviour (Orea-Giner et al., 2022). However, several challenges and limitations
must be addressed before these technologies can be fully integrated and exploited
in the CH domain.

12.5.1   Challenges of AR and AI for CH

Apart from the benefits that tourists may gain from AR and AI innovation, challenges remain to be addressed. The main challenges of AR and AI for CH, including but not limited to, are as follows:

1 **Technical issues:** Developing and deploying AR and AI applications for CH
   requires high-quality 3D models, accurate positioning and tracking systems,
   reliable network connectivity, robust recognition and reasoning algorithms,
   and user-friendly interfaces (Voinea et al., 2019). These technical aspects pose
   significant difficulties in terms of cost, complexity, scalability, compatibility,
   security, and privacy.

2 **Content creation and management:** Creating and managing engaging and informative content for AR and AI applications is a time-consuming and labour-intensive task that requires collaboration among different stakeholders, such as domain experts, content providers, developers, and users. The content must be accurate, relevant, up-to-date, diverse, contextualised, and adaptable to user profiles and scenarios (Meng & Liu, 2021).

3 **User acceptance and satisfaction:** Understanding and meeting the needs and expectations of the users is essential for the success of AR and AI applications for CH. The users may have different levels of familiarity, interest, motivation, learning styles, preferences, and feedback regarding the use of these technologies. Moreover, the users may encounter various usability issues, such as cognitive overload, distraction, confusion, frustration, or boredom, that may affect their experience and perception of the CH site, as partly mentioned in De Paolis et al. (2023) and Refae et al. (2023).

4 **Ethical and social implications:** The use of AR and AI for CH raises some ethical and social questions that need to be carefully considered and addressed. For example, how can we ensure the authenticity, integrity, and preservation of the CH site and its values? How do we balance enhancing the user experience with respecting the local culture and community? How do we deal with the potential biases, inaccuracies, or misinterpretations of historical information? How do we evaluate the impact of these technologies on the user's learning outcomes, attitudes, and behaviours?

These challenges must be addressed to ensure stakeholders' and tourists' buy-ins. Successful case studies have proven that rigorous research and development must occur, and long-lasting sustainability must consider user evaluation and feedback.

12.5.2   *Future directions*

With the abovementioned evidence and argument, it is anticipated that the future of AR and AI will benefit tourists by helping them better personalise their user experience. However, the growing interests of various authorities and parties must be governed to meet specific guidelines to ensure the sustainable development of CH sites. Future directions of AR and AI for CH are:

1 **Interdisciplinary collaboration:** Fostering interdisciplinary collaboration among researchers, practitioners, policymakers, and stakeholders from different fields, such as computer science, engineering, design, psychology, education, history, archaeology, art, tourism, and communication, is crucial for advancing the state-of-the-art of AR and AI for CH. Such collaboration can facilitate the exchange of knowledge, skills, resources, and best practices, as well as the identification of common goals, challenges, and opportunities.

2 **User-centred design:** Adopting a user-centred design approach is essential for developing AR and AI applications tailored to the users' specific needs and

preferences. This approach involves involving the users in all stages of the design process, from defining the requirements to evaluating the prototypes. User-centred design can help to ensure the usability, accessibility, acceptability, and effectiveness of these applications.

3 **Evaluation methods:** Developing appropriate evaluation methods is necessary for assessing the quality and impact of AR and AI applications for CH. These methods should consider both quantitative and qualitative measures that capture various aspects of the user experience, such as usability, engagement, enjoyment, learning outcomes, emotional responses, attitudes, and behaviours. Moreover, these methods should consider the context of use (e.g., location, time) and individual differences among users (e.g., age, gender, culture).

4 **Ethical guidelines:** Ethical guidelines are important for ensuring CH's responsible use of AR and AI. These guidelines should address the ethical principles and values that guide these technologies' design, development, and deployment, including respect for human dignity, autonomy, privacy, diversity, inclusion, transparency, accountability, and sustainability. These guidelines should also provide recommendations and best practices for dealing with potential ethical dilemmas or conflicts that may arise in relation to these technologies.

In summary, this chapter has examined the synergistic integration of AR and AI within the context of Industry 5.0, focusing on their collective potential to craft personalised and immersive user experiences within CH sites. The discourse encompasses assessing the cutting-edge technologies in AR and AI for CH and outlining the challenges and opportunities inherent in their fusion and evaluation. A conceptual model has also been introduced, delineating key elements and use cases that constitute these enriched experiences. Proposals for future directions aim to address existing gaps, overcome limitations, and explore the profound impact of AR and AI on users' learning outcomes, emotions, attitudes, and behaviours within the evolving landscape of Industry 5.0. This contribution serves as a valuable guide for researchers and practitioners, offering insights to design and develop innovative AR and AI solutions that amplify the accessibility, inclusiveness, and engagement of CH sites for a diverse audience.

Acknowledgement

This work was funded by the Ministry of Higher Education Malaysia, under the Research Excellence Cluster Grant (KPT-KKP) Extended Reality and Human Interaction Centre of Excellence, JPT(BKPI)1000/016/018/25(48) SO14978.

References

Abidin, R. Z., Arshad, H., Shukri, S. A. I. A., & Ling, M. F. (2018). Leveraging multimodal interaction and adaptive interfaces for location-based augmented reality Islamic tourism application. *International Journal on Advanced Science, Engineering and Information Technology*, 8(4-2), 1784–1791. http://dx.doi.org/10.18517/ijaseit.8.4-2.6822

Alexandridis, G., Chrysanthi, A., Tsekouras, G. E., & Caridakis, G. (2019). Personalised and content adaptive cultural heritage path recommendation: An application to the Gournia and Çatalhöyük archaeological sites. *User Modeling and User-Adapted Interaction*, *29*(1), 201–238. https://doi.org/10.1007/s11257-019-09227-6

Ardissono, L., Kuflik, T., & Petrelli, D. (2012). Personalisation in cultural heritage: The road travelled and the one ahead. *User Modeling and User-Adapted Interaction*, *22*, 73–99, https://doi.org/10.1007/s11257-011-9104-x

Azuma, R. T. (1997). A survey of augmented reality. *Presence: Teleoperators & Virtual Environments*, *6*(4), 355–385. https://doi.org/10.1162/pres.1997.6.4.355

Blut, C., & Blankenbach, J. (2021). Three-dimensional CityGML building models in mobile augmented reality: A smartphone-based pose tracking system. *International Journal of Digital Earth*, *14*(1), 32–51. https://doi.org/10.1080/17538947.2020.1733680

Champion, E. (2011). *Playing with the past*. Springer-Verlag.

Damala, A. (2007). Design principles for mobile museum guides using visitor studies and museum learning theories. In *Proceedings of the 2007 IADIS M-Learn Conference (Mobile Learning), Lisbon, Portugal* (pp. 277–281).

Damala, A., Cubaud, P., Bationo, A., Houlier, P., & Marchal, I. (2008). Bridging the gap between the digital and the physical: Design and evaluation of a mobile augmented reality guide for the museum visit. In Proceedings of the 3rd International Conference on Digital Interactive Media in Entertainment and Arts (pp. 120–127). Athens, Greece: ACM. https://doi.org/10.1145/1413634.1413660

Damala, A., Marchal, I., & Houlier, P. (2007). Merging augmented reality based features in mobile multimedia museum guides. In Anticipating the Future of the Cultural Past, CIPA Conference 2007, 1-6 October 2007 (pp. 259–264).

De Paolis, L. T., Gatto, C., Corchia, L., & De Luca, V. (2023). Usability, user experience and mental workload in a mobile augmented reality application for digital storytelling in cultural heritage. *Virtual Reality*, *27*(2), 1117–1143. https://doi.org/10.1007/s10055-022-00712-9

Guo, G., Wang, H., Bell, D., Bi, Y., & Greer, K. (2003). KNN model-based approach in classification. In *On the move to meaningful internet systems 2003: CoopIS, DOA, and ODBASE: OTM Confederated International Conferences, CoopIS, DOA, and ODBASE 2003, Catania, Sicily, Italy, November 3-7, 2003. Proceedings* (pp. 986–996). Springer. https://doi.org/10.1007/978-3-540-39964-3_62

International Council on Monuments and Sites. (2008). ICOMOS charter for the interpretation and presentation of cultural heritage sites. https://www.icomos.org/images/DOCUMENTS/Charters/interpretation_e.pdf

Larose, D. T., & Larose, C. D. (2014). *Discovering knowledge in data: An introduction to data mining* (Vol. 4). John Wiley & Sons. https://doi.org/10.1002/9781118874059.ch7.

Meng, L., & Liu, Y. (2021). A meaning-aware cultural tourism intelligent navigation system based on anticipatory calculation. *Frontiers in Psychology*, *11*, 611383. https://doi.org/10.3389/fpsyg.2020.611383

Microsoft (2023). AI for Cultural Heritage. https://www.microsoft.com/en-us/ai/ai-for-cultural-heritage

Orea-Giner, A., Muñoz-Mazón, A., Villacé-Molinero, T., & Fuentes-Moraleda, L. (2022). Cultural tourist and user experience with artificial intelligence: A holistic perspective from the industry 5.0 approach. *Journal of Tourism Futures*. https://doi.org/10.1108/JTF-04-2022-0115

Pendit, U. C., Zaibon, S. B., & Abu Bakar, J. A. (2014). Mobile augmented reality for enjoyable informal learning in cultural heritage site. *International Journal of Computer*

Applications, *92*(14), 19–26. Retrieved from https://citeseerx.ist.psu.edu/document?repid =rep1&type=pdf&doi=bed3c44f1bdd4eab023cf93f40c59c1a24908a18

Pendit, U. C., Zaibon, S. B., & Abu Bakar, J. A. (2018). Conceptual model of mobile augmented reality for cultural heritage. In: N. Lee (Ed.), *Encyclopedia of computer graphics and games*. Springer. https://doi.org/10.1007/978-3-319-08234-9_79-1

Peterson, L. E. (2009). K-nearest neighbor. *Scholarpedia*, *4*(2), 1883. https://doi.org/10.4249/ scholarpedia.1883

Pooja, J., Vinay, M., Pai, V. G., & Anuradha, M. (2020). Comparative analysis of marker and marker-less augmented reality in education. In 2020 IEEE International Conference for Innovation in Technology (INOCON) (pp. 1–4). IEEE.

Refae, S., Ragab, T., & Samir, H. (2023). Augmented reality (AR) for urban cultural heritage interpretation: A user experience evaluation. In: A. Visvizi, O. Troisi, & M. Grimaldi (Eds.), *Research and innovation forum 2022. RIIFORUM 2022*. Springer Proceedings in Complexity. Springer. https://doi.org/10.1007/978-3-031-19560-0_23

Voinea, G. D., Girbacia, F., Postelnicu, C. C., & Marto, A. (2019). Exploring cultural heritage using augmented reality through Google's Project Tango and ARCore. In: M. Duguleană, M. Carrozzino, M. Gams, & I. Tanea (Eds.), *VR technologies in cultural heritage. VRTCH 2018. Communications in computer and information science*, vol. 904. Springer. https:// doi.org/10.1007/978-3-030-05819-7_8

Index

Note: Page numbers in *italics* and **bold** refer to figures and tables, respectively.

Printed in the United States
by Baker & Taylor Publisher Services